PREPARING
COUNSELORS
AND
THERAPISTS

Creating
Constructivist
and
Developmental
Programs

THE
DONNING COMPANY
PUBLISHERS

Written and Compiled by:

Garrett McAuliffe
gmcaulif@odu.edu
(757) 683-5075
College of Education
Old Dominion University
Norfolk, VA 23529

Karen Eriksen
keriksen@waldenu.edu
(540) 831-5629
Counselor Education Program
Radford and Walden Universities
Radford, VA 24142

FOR INFORMATION, WRITE:
The Donning Company/Publishers
184 Business Park Drive, Suite 106
Virginia Beach, VA 23462

STEVE MULL, General Manager
BERNIE WALTON, Project Director
DAWN V. KOFROTH, Assistant General Manager
RICHARD HORWEGE Senior Editor
RICK VIGENSKI, Graphic Designer

Library of Congress Cataloging-in-Publication Data

Available on Request

Printed in the United States of America

Table of Contents

Preface
Garrett McAuliffe

Old Dominion University

••

Part One
Constructivist Teaching and Learning Principles

Part One outlines the general constructivist worldview upon which the book is based and offers background on what we know about the psychology of learning. Guidelines for constructivist teaching are explicated from these principles.

Part Two
Designing Constructivist Programs

Part Two suggests the application of constructivist principles to the overall design of counselor education programs. The extensive use of democratic groups, cohorts, and narrative-generating activities are considered. Specific attention is given to reconstructing the admissions and evaluation processes in a more dialogical, multicultural direction.

Part Three

Applying Constructivism to Teaching: Exemplars of Best Practices

Part Three offers illustrations of counselor education course designs that use constructivist principles.

Part Four

Conclusions

Preface
Garrett McAuliffe, Old Dominion University

True teachers defend their pupils against the teacher's own influence. Such teachers inspire self-trust. They guide their pupils' eyes from the teacher him or herself to their own spirit that quickens them. The true teacher will have no disciple. (Adapted from Bronson Alcott, 1840)

Through dialogue, the teacher-of-the-students and the students-of-the-teacher cease to exist and a new term emerges: teacher-student with students-teachers. (Paolo Friere, 1994)

This is a book for those who would prepare counselors for their work. It is aimed at both those students who are training to be counselor educators and those who are already preparers of counselors. Anyone who has the responsibility to supervise counselors is also invited to walk through the constructivist door with us. But you must be warned: it will be difficult to return to business as usual in counselor training and supervision.

We believe that this is the first book of its kind. And that it is sorely needed, for despite their position in "higher" education, college professors are the least prepared to teach of all educators. Preparers of mental health professionals are no exception. Their heavy responsibility to protect future clients by producing ethical and intelligent counselors stands in ironic contrast with their light preparation in the means for doing so. The litany of professors' lack of formal teaching training is well-known: they study no methods, they are never, or rarely, observed, and their knowledge of educational psychology is minimal or nonexistent. And yet, each year thousands of professors in the mental health fields enter classrooms to propound, pronounce, plead, cajole, demonstrate, evoke, stimulate, and act up in any ways which supposedly will produce intellectually and emotionally sophisticated counselors and therapists.

Despite the short shrift given to teacher training, many counselor educators struggle mightily to teach energetically and innovatively, hoping for felicitous results. Some go so far as to stretch inherited pedagogical boundaries, challenging the "cult of expertise" that has made professors into high knowledge priests and students into lay supplicants in so many universities. The pedagogical boundary stretchers instead create egalitarian atmospheres, participatory activities, opportunities for reflection, and experiential exercises in order to trigger development in future mental health professionals. It is those efforts that we wish to extend in this volume.

Much has already been crafted well in counselor education. Instruction in interviewing skills has been raised to a high art. Training in group therapy is, in its best moments, intensely experiential and self-reflective. And, more recently, developmental instruction has emerged as a frontier of teaching practice. The "guide on the side," as opposed to the "sage on the stage," is the current clever metaphor for engaging students to be partners in their own learning.

Despite these successes, the teacher as "talking head" seems still to be alive and well, as a walk down a college corridor will testify. Whether behind or in front of the lectern, or even informally sitting on the desk, we can hear teachers pronouncing, "Here is the most effective counseling approach" or "Listen to my accurate diagnosis." Perhaps it is easier to "tell" than to "evoke." Sometimes abstraction dominates the discourse to the exclusion of concrete case analysis or demonstration. At its worst, the "banking deposit" model of teaching, to use Friere's (1994) metaphor for instructor-centered teaching, communicates that knowledge is the domain of the few, who pass it on to the many. And such teaching tends to replicate itself by communicating to future mental health professionals that clients can also change through passive reception of insight and supposed wisdom. For whatever reasons, the expert who delivers "finished" knowledge to the "audience" of students still dominates college teaching.

This teacher-as-expert and student-as-receiver model has been increasingly challenged as ineffective, particularly in our field which is ostensibly dedicated to bringing forth professionals who themselves might create knowledge through interior conversation and open public discourse. So-called postmodernist educators (so-called because of their interest in bringing many voices, disciplines, and ways of knowing into the academy), like bell hooks (1994) and Henry Giroux (1992) have opened up the conversation about who learns from whom and how power and privilege are used, toward what ends, in the classroom. They invite teachers to "not-know," to "deconstruct" cherished notions of how knowledge is created, and to encourage tolerance for ambiguity and self-disclosure in the classroom. Such notions are enough to make most college teachers tremble.

This effort to kick-start a re-examination of how we know and teach in the helping professions offers some thoughts that are new and border-crossing, to use Henry Giroux's (1992) phrase for a postmodern education. But these thoughts also reiterate much that educators of mental health practitioners already struggle mightily to do: to risk "losing control" over subject matter, to hear student voices, to pose dilemmas, to challenge their own assumptions in the presence of their students. In that regard, many counselor educators are already among the minority of educators who attempt to be "midwife" teachers, to use Belenky, Clinchy, Goldberger, and Tarule's (1986) vivid metaphor; that is, teachers who assist students in giving birth to their own ideas. We believe that this "midwife" role is one that the practicing mental health professional can also apply to her- or himself, that of coaching clients to bring forth more adaptive stories in their lives and relationships.

However, we believe that among the disciplines counselor training is well-poised for this type of conversation. Our work has always been touched by an experiential, participatory teaching brush. Counselor educators have traditionally incorporated both "head" and "heart" into the learning environment. Equality, genuineness, and respect have been watchwords for our professions. Awareness of people as socially constructed, cultural beings is slowly infusing our curricula. This book attempts to build on these practices and to transform others so that an impactful, progressive mental health education can be implemented.

Thus we join the national conversation about the purposes and methods of higher education in a postmodern era. In so doing, we hope, perhaps with hubris, to trigger a broad self-examination by counselor educators—a dialogue on the nature of knowing, the political implications of teaching, and the content of mental health training.

In addition to being a response to the swirling discussions about higher education, this book is also a product of its authors' personal struggles to teach well. We have all experienced the palpable tension of entering a classroom filled with expectant and diverse adults. In that setting our consciences prick us—we all know well the time, money, and, yes, the energy that most students pour into their educations. We ask ourselves, "Are we up to the task of meeting our students' hopes and expectations, aspirations that are so well voiced at our orientations and in beginning classes?"

A final incentive for this work is the very pragmatic concern that we share about accountability for teaching, which is being increasingly demanded of college faculty. Student evaluations and peer reviews of teaching are now central in the maintenance and progress of our careers. Citizens view our primary job to be teaching. Teaching is the major arena in which we meet the public, no matter how much we know that writing, research, and professional presentations are part of our broad educational charge.

We ask you, as readers of this volume, to face the task of reflexively examining, or "deconstructing," your common assumptions and methods in all areas of counselor education. Ask yourself, "What are the intended and unintended educational outcomes of students' experiences in the classroom, the library, the lab, and the advising office?" In that learner-centered or "constructivist" vein, we challenge the notion that we can ever "provide" knowledge to another. Certainly the works of Piaget, Dewey, Friere, and many other so-called "constructivist" thinkers offer a severe challenge to the common "banking deposit" model of teaching. Instead, we might consider teaching to "merely" be the setting up of conditions for the learner to know, through a cycling and recycling of experience, reflection, and abstract conceptualization.

Our biases are these: We favor the "constructivist" and "developmental" educational theories. These theories ask us to pay attention to the learner's experience and to let the learner make sense for herself by struggling with ambiguities which are just beyond the level she can tolerate. We also favor the notion of the social construction of knowledge, as we might practice it through classroom discourse. We think that a fine metaphor for teaching is Robert Kegan's (1994) notion of "over the shoulder" inquiry, in which students together puzzle over problems which emerge during the many discourses of their education, discourses which are often instigated by the educator. We also favor an inclusive, dialogical program practice, from admissions through portfolio evaluation, one in which we as faculty are learners-among-learners.

The inspiration for this book comes from a series of moments during the 1996 national meeting of the Association for Counselor Education and Supervision (ACES). Tom Sexton of the University of Nevada set up a number of "reflective discussions" during the three days of that conference. I was asked to guide the five-session discussion on "Teaching Methodology." In fact, the sessions needed little guidance. The combined energy of the assembled counselor educators crackled the air of our conference room, as we returned five times to frankly share our successes, doubts, frustrations, and innovations in trying to prepare counselors and therapists. The overall conference theme of "transformation" became our watchword. We shared our personal transformations as former graduate students and our transformative teaching moments as instructors. The spirit moved us from day to day. Early on, Chris Lovell of Old Dominion University, in his prescient way, suggested the idea for this volume and, even as the conference continued, Karen Eriksen of Radford and Walden Universities pounded out an outline.

This work is no final product, of course. We hope that the project continues to evolve through the ensuing discourse in university hallways and at future conferences in psychology, human services, counseling, and social work. Many of us will continue to do empirical research to test these teaching ideas. And yet we can also take comfort in what we seem to already know. We stand on the shoulders of "giants" who have offered us much to ponder about the purposes and methods of teaching, from Dewey's (1963) experiential education, to Freire's (1994) liberatory education, to Knefelkamp's (1984) developmental instruction, to hooks' (1994) "teaching to transgress," to Kolb's (1984) experiential learning, to name only a few prominent innovators in the fields of teaching and learning.

Our work here is a beginning—we know of no other such volume on mental health education. We offer this "socially constructed" project with humility, recognizing the boundedness of our vision by the historical, political, and temperamental contexts of our time. It is up to the reader to try out these ideas, to expand them, and possibly to reject them in favor of even more developed ones.

Who, specifically, is this book for? First, and most grandly, our audience is all who are involved in adult education. Let not constructed disciplinary boundaries keep us from exchanging ideas. More specifically, we expect it to be useful to all those who prepare mental health practitioners—from counselors to psychologists to human service workers to clinical social workers to psychiatrists. We hope that it might be a text in counselor education courses and a companion for practicing counselor educators.

The book is divided into four segments, as follows. Part One opens the discussion of constructivist and developmental teaching with principles and research. McAuliffe and Lovell establish guidelines for a constructivist-developmental education in Chapter One, while, separately, McAuliffe and then McNamara, Scott, and Bess map out the cognitive foundations for learning in Chapters Two and Three.

Part Two consists of bold proposals for transforming counselor education programs. In Chapter Four, Paisley and Hayes describe a social construction-oriented curriculum and the use of cohorts to promote student development. They also raise the ever-present and controversial issue of setting "standards." Winslade, Crocket, Monk, and Drewery introduce the use of the narrative metaphor for counselor training in Chapter Five. In Chapter Six, Disque, Robertson, and Mitchell delineate a plan for a postmodern reconstruction of the admissions process. In Chapter Seven, Cobia, Carney, and Shannon offer a guide for using portfolios in constructing the evaluation process.

Offering constructivist exemplars of how to transform specific courses is the aim of Part Three. In Chapter Eight, Montgomery, Marbley, Contreras, and Kurtines plumb the power and the limits of a Multicultural Awareness course as an entry for students into a socially constructed world. In Chapter Nine, Peterson helps students to discover human development in an inductive fashion.

In Part Four, we conclude by trying to discover why such supposedly inspiring programmatic and teaching ideas haven't been implemented more frequently, and what it might take to persuade counselor educators to integrate constructivist and developmental thought into their programs.

No preface which paradoxically purports to "promote" a constructivist frame for teaching should end on so certain a note. Doubt and humility are central themes in postmodern and constructivist thinking. Thus, our words are offered in the spirit of dialogue. We hope the conversation continues through you, the readers, writing to us and you joining (or starting!) the next discussion of teaching at your local or national conference. We hope that this is the first major foray in an evolving, ongoing engagement of the construction of the counselor in our postmodern environment. Woe to us who take it lightly and who pass on no more than a received world of how-to's and fixed practices. Somehow I suspect that we do less of that in counselor education than in other disciplines. Instead, many of us try to set the conditions for "evolutions in knowing" to occur in students. Let this volume be a warning, nevertheless, that we, as educators and as therapists, must live within the ambiguity of emergent understanding, of partial "truths" that must be rolled around on the tongues of dialogue. And let us be consistently reflective on our practices and our most cherished notions.

We hope that more than a few ideas from this book will encourage risk-taking and trigger experiments in teaching. Good. That is what we set out to do.

Our thanks for innocently beginning this project go to the aforementioned Tom Sexton of the University of Nevada, who set up the "Reflective Discussions" at the national ACES convention. What he hath wrought! For the ACES discussions themselves modeled social construction of knowledge as a practice. We hope that every professional meeting offers opportunities for such multisession exchanges. We also thank the thirty or so participants who gave of their time, their ideas, and their "secrets," for so many of you shared your fears, thrills, successes, and doubts during those five sessions. This book is a product of the felt need among those who care passionately about what they do. I can still remember Ann Vernon of the University of North Iowa waxing poetic about her own transformation and her enthusiasm as a graduate student. Her proclamation was one of many that started us on this road. The hard work that followed was shep-

herded, above all, by Karen Eriksen, who persistently and collaboratively prodded, reminded, and reconstructed this work along the way.
And, most recently, we thank the ACES leaders who were, we believe,
suitably inspired by this endeavor, and moved to sponsor this book.
Special thanks for diligent indexing, vigilant proofreading, graphic
suggestions, and overall nurturance go to Stephanie Stone, Steve
Eriksen, and Ann McAulliffe. Let us now begin.

References

Belenky, M. F., Clinchy, B. M., Goldberger, N. R., and Tarule, J. M.
(1986). *Women's ways of knowing.* New York: Basic Books.

Dewey, J. (1963). *Experience and education.* New York: Collier.
Originally published in 1938.

Friere, P. (1994). *Pedagogy of the oppressed.* New York: Continuum.

Giroux, H. (1992). *Border crossings: Cultural workers and the politics
of education.* New York: Routledge.

hooks, b. (1994). *Teaching to transgress.* New York: Routledge.

Kegan, R. (1994). *In over our heads.* Cambridge, MA: Harvard.

Knefelkamp, L. (1984). Developmental instruction. In L.
Knefelkamp and R. R. Golec (Eds.). *A workbook for using the
Practice-to-Theory-to-Practice Model.* University of Maryland
at College Park.

Kolb, D. (1984). *Experiential learning.* Englewood Cliffs, NJ:
Prentice-Hall.

Lovell, C. W., and McAuliffe, G. J. (1997). Principles of constructivist training and education. In T. L. Sexton and B. L.
Griffin (Eds.), *Constructivist thinking in counseling practice,
research, and training.* New York: Teacher's College.

McAuliffe, G. J., and Lovell, C. W. (1996). *The making of the con-
structivist counselor.* Paper presented at the meeting of the
Association for Counselor Education and Supervision,
Portland, OR.

Piaget, J. (1971). *Psychology and epistemology.* Harmondsworth,
England: Penguin.

Part One

CONSTRUCTIVIST TEACHING AND LEARNING PRINCIPLES

Part One outlines the constructivist worldview upon which the book is based and offers background on what we know about the psychology of learning. Guidelines for constructivist teaching are explicated from these principles.

Chapter One
Encouraging Transformation
Guidelines for Constructivist and Developmental Instruction

Garrett McAuliffe and Christopher Lovell, Old Dominion University

"I don't teach 'the material,' I teach students." Some time ago, you may have heard this from a college teacher, and you may have—as we did the first time we heard it—thrilled to the inherent epistemological challenge. Imagine someone abandoning the usual objectivist stance which holds that knowledge is about "information!" Think of it: a teacher moving toward the notion that the knower is at least as important as the known! A vision of learning that is student-centered rather than focused on content! As a teacher with a special interest in psychotherapy and counselor education, you may also have seen the parallels between such a teaching emphasis and Rogers' (1951) client-centered orientation.

We propose that the turn away from "content" or "problem," and toward increased interest in the person—student or client—who is making meaning heralds a revolution in both teachers' and counselors' world views; it constitutes a fundamental epistemological shift from "objectivism" to "constructivism." The turn is away from the "subject matter" of the course or the "diagnosed problem" of the client, and it is toward a concern for the student's or client's subjective understanding. We believe the shift is crucial to good teaching and to good counseling, and we suspect that you, as a counselor or psychotherapist as well as a teacher, may well have made this shift.

If you have made the turn toward a learner-centered frame, you are already, in a sense, a "constructivist" educator; you have some convictions that, in teaching, the "action" lies in your students' processes of making meaning of the ostensible "subject matter," not in anything you "do" to them. Of course, you have not abandoned that "subject matter"; you understand, simply, that a teacher "is a mediator between the knower and the known" (Palmer, 1983, p. 29). It is likely, further, that you subscribe to a theory of knowing that "does not divorce the knower from the known, but understands knowledge to be a result of their dynamic interaction" (p. 27).

The first purpose of this book is to share with you instructional tools which may be useful in your work as a constructivist educator, that is, as that mediator between the knower (in this case, the counselor or therapist-to-be) and the known (practices that help clients). In many of the coming chapters, counselor educators will open their "bags of tricks," giving you some concrete advice about how to proceed in the constructivist environment. The second purpose is much more personal: it is to challenge you, the educator, to consider how constructivist your teaching is, to ask you to let go, somewhat, of "content" in favor of attending to the learner, and to encourage you to consider what it takes to influence students themselves to take a constructivist stance toward their lives and work.

Many of the constructivist teaching tools presented in the book are designed either directly or indirectly to promote the development of a new epistemology in your students. Without creating too confusing a hall of mirrors here, let us just assert that we view a teacher's modeling of constructivist attitudes and employment of constructivist methods in the classroom to be itself conducive to students' epistemological development. The isomorphism between constructivist teaching and the work of counseling makes the counseling field a prime candidate for this reflexive pedagogy. Close, ongoing, empathic attention to each person's meaning-making, in the large class group or in the individual encounter, is the common ground between constructivist education and constructivist counseling. Kegan (1994) quotes Kierkegaard on the matter: "Instruction begins when you put yourself in [the learner's] place so that you may understand what he understands and the way he understands it" (p. 278). The aim of the present chapter is to elaborate on the notion that a path to the student's "way of understanding" lies through the ground of constructivism.

"Constructivism" refers to both the social constructionist and the developmental (psychological) constructivist traditions. Each is founded on the assumptions that (a) humans are active creators of meaning, and (b) the individual comes to phenomena with pre-understandings that shape the meaning that gets created. Constructivism might be broadly defined as a group of theories of learning which posit that, on the basis of social or cognitive influences, an individual 'constructs' concepts as [he or she interacts] with the world. We would elaborate this dual definition ("social" or "developmental") in this way:

1. The social constructionist suggests that all knowing is embedded in social contexts, and all knowing is rooted in time, place, and history. Consequently, there are no "eternal verities." Further, "objectivity," at least as it is conventionally construed, is not possible. Such social identities as gender, age, race, religion, ethnicity, ability, class, and sexual orientation constrain each social actor from knowing beyond the bounds set by identity. As teachers, it is our task to be aware of the social constructions that inform our propositions and those of our students.

2. The developmental constructivist perspective similarly attends to the primacy of meaning-making. Of interest are the "pre-understandings" through which a person creates experience. Adults, in this neo-Piagetian tradition, evolve through several general mental frameworks for knowing (sometimes called "stages" or "knowledge structures"). Because they evolve at differing rates, and because they reach different developmental "end points," persons may differ in "constructive capacity." We as teachers account for that capacity, or readiness to learn, in order that we not be "under" or "over" the heads of students, but rather poised to adjust our teaching to the students' levels of development.

Both of these theories ask educators to be watchful about the nature of their own knowing and that of their students. The two constructivist paradigms can complement each other thus: (a) while social construction is pervasive, the sand of "truth" shifts depending on the social context, but (b) the meanings which a person makes depend on his or her developmental constructive capacity. We will explore these notions below.

Social Constructionism

The social constructionist perspective respects the primacy of the human being as a "subject," as opposed to his or her being an "object" to whom things are done (such as being taught). Social constructionism challenges any assumptions that (a) knowledge is the province of the few, and (b), in any social science field, perfection of methods will lead to objective truth. (The reader may hear strains of postmodernism in what we are saying, and that is for good reason: many assumptions, both epistemological and political, are shared by postmodernist philosophy and social constructionism.) The following three tenets are central to a social constructionist education (Burbules and Rice, 1991):

1. A rejection of absolutes. There are no "metanarratives," such as a grand counseling scheme or a best procedure for gaining knowledge, that are not expressions of particular points of view, choices of questions, and preferences for certain methods of inquiry. Social constructionism is, ironically, a meta-narrative that rejects the possibility of meta-narratives, as the search for universals is seen as resulting in a restriction of human possibilities. "Reflexivity" thus becomes a central notion in social constructionist practice. Since knowledge is developed in community rather than being an absolute, social constructionist educators ask themselves to be consistently self-reflective, to be open to the limits of their current positions and methods, and to seek feedback about teaching content and process from other learners. The social constructionist educator is aware of "standpoint," or the current (and decidedly tentative) perspective that he or she may take on phenomena. The teacher is asked to shed any "totalizing" narratives.

2. The saturation of all social discourse with power or dominance. Any assumed scheme of what is "good," "right," or "true" is synonymous with the hegemony of a particular social and political order. From this perspective, it is a task of teachers to "deconstruct" any such schemes; that is, to examine critically how ideological, economic, physical, and institutional power play into their practices and to consider the political consequences of their own vocabulary, arguments, and conclusions. In the classroom, teachers can unthinkingly perpetuate broader patterns of dominance, especially in their use of authority. Power relationships can be subtly reinforced or challenged through how or whether we as teachers ask for students' voices in the classroom, through whether we use titles and names, through our openness to being questioned on our own teaching practices, and through the way we set up the physical classroom itself. A postmodern perspective asks the teacher to choose such practices "reflexively," that is, with awareness of their implications for power.

3. The celebration of "difference." Social constructionism assumes that the constitutive quality of existence is plurality. In contrast, the objectivist or positivist stance proclaims that the diversity of ideas is a temporary state on the way to perfect knowing. From the social constructionist framework, any singular, unified discourse is to be treated skeptically, since it is likely that such discourse is in the language of the dominant group. For most teachers this assumption is a call to particularly attend to the perspectives and experiences of so-called "marginalized" groups. "Participation," therefore, becomes a watchword, and active invitations to voices which might otherwise be excluded become critical. The social constructionist "curriculum" thus sets a demanding, often seemingly impossible, agenda for the traditional educator in all of us; that is, the part of us that either believes in the sanctity of our own authority, or that believes that we have perfected the best methods for knowing and subsequently for counseling. In contrast, we ask ourselves as educators to embrace the concept of learner as knower and of ourselves as learners, as does Paolo Friere: "Through dialogue, the teacher-of-the-students and the students-of-the-teacher cease to exist and a new term emerges: teacher-student with students-teachers" (1994, p. 62).

Constructive Development

And how does the learner know? It is here that the second theme, that of constructive development, enters. According to constructive developmental thinkers, it is the task of the educator to trigger transformations in how students construct knowledge, not merely to teach skills or to pass on information. The constructive-developmental "meta-theory" guides counselor educators in their efforts to increase students' capacities to accommodate difference and newness and to engage complexity. Evidence exists (Benack, 1988; Neukrug and McAuliffe, 1994) that increased "constructive capacity" is prerequisite for such essential counselor or therapist characteristics as empathy, ethical sense, multicultural awareness, and coherent multi-theoretical applications. To practice developmentally, constructivist educators are likely to first account for student readiness, or current capacity. Then, they provide optimal supports and challenges in the learning environment. "Support" might be described as "matching" learners' current ways of knowing, while "challenge" consists of "mismatching" their current capacities by stretching them beyond their current level of complexity, much like a pacer does in a race. Constructive development occurs through the experience of being "shaken up," of experiencing conflict and doubt over the efficacy of an old way of knowing. Such epistemological dissonance is called, in the Piagetian tradition, "disequilibration."

A simplified version of the major constructive transition in adulthood can be described as the shift from tendencies toward unquestioning conformity toward more autonomy in knowing. Beyond this move from externality to greater internality is a horizon rarely reached, a way of consistently living in dialogue within oneself and with the environment. These changes have been plotted and given somewhat different labels. Terms for the first stage, which we call conformist knowing, include "dualism" (Perry, 1970), "received knowing" (Belenky, Clinchy, Goldberger, and Tarule, 1986), and "the interpersonal balance" (Kegan, 1982). The second adult stage, or autonomous knowing has been called "procedural knowing" (Belenky et al., 1986), and "the institutional balance" (Kegan, 1982). Finally, the dialectical tendency has been called "relativism" (Perry, 1981), "constructed knowing" (Belenky et al., 1986), and "interindividual balance" (Kegan, 1982).

Becoming a Social Constructionist— A Developmental Achievement

It has been proposed (Kegan, 1994; Lovell and McAuliffe, 1996) that social constructionist thinking is itself a constructive developmental achievement. If this is tenable, it might then behoove teachers and students to consider the desirability of any or all of the following constructivist characteristics as goals for themselves. Belenky et al. (1986) suggest, first, that the "constructivist knower" recognizes that she or he, as teacher, and all students, in fact all human beings, are engaged in the construction of knowledge. Thus, with the constructivist position is born humility about one's beliefs. This recognition of the universality of human constructing can lead to a deepened commitment to attend to others and to feel related to them in spite of what may be great differences. Similarly, according to Belenky et al., constructivist knowers notice what is going on with others and care about the lives of people around them. They accept responsibility for continually evaluating their assumptions about knowledge, since knowing is ultimately a social construction. Such knowers can take a position outside of a particular frame of reference, whether that frame be logic, culture, family, or any other context. They are intensely "self-conscious;" that is, aware of their own thoughts, judgments, moods, and desires. They have a high tolerance for internal contradiction and ambiguity. They recognize the inevitability of conflict and of learning to live with it. Their discourse is characterized by "real talk," which includes sharing ideas, listening carefully, and encouraging emergent ideas to grow; this is in contrast to "didactic talk," in which the speaker's intention is to hold forth.

Finally, those who consistently live in this constructivist mode exhibit a larger community commitment by wanting their voices and actions to make a difference in the world. All of this may pose a tall order for a counselor educator, let alone students of counseling (Kegan, 1994). Ask yourself, "Can I as a teacher appreciate the socially constructed nature of my knowledge?" "Can I engage in dialectical give-and-take with students and colleagues?" "Can I 'give up' the finality of hard-won 'positions'?" "Can I abandon hope of a positivist science in favor of multiple ways of knowing?" "Can I deconstruct some of my favorite counseling theories and teaching methods?" "Can I reach into the learner's experience for knowledge, for her understandings, and can I learn from the student—about both counseling itself and about my teaching?" "Can I stimulate students to consider 'how' to know as well as 'what' to know?" "Can I decenter from my cultural assumptions and actively seek marginalized voices?" "Can I spur 'personal revolutions' in my students, as well as skill development and theoretical understanding?" It is likely that most of us are over-challenged by some of these expectations and yet, as we will discuss in Chapter Ten, those capacities are desirable for implementing constructivist education.

The importance of "reflective uncertainty" in constructivist education is central. It makes our advocacy of teaching which is aimed at producing constructivist thinking ironic. The very notion of advocating a "constructivist method" contradicts the very reflexivity and openness to emerging explanations we seek. However, in this chapter we will nevertheless tentatively offer guidelines and methods which follow constructivist principles. To be sure, the instructional methods themselves must be consistently deconstructed for their own "situatedness" in the social context for how it might be done otherwise—for example, for gender, age, race, religion, ethnicity, ability, class, or sexual orientation bias. And the instructional goals must be consistently reconstructed in a community—students, faculty, practitioners, the public, supervisors, and researchers. Constructivist teaching principles are guided by a call for reflexivity; that is, the active search for alternative explanations and the limits of autonomous knowing. Despite these provisos, we make a clear commitment here to "constructivist methods." Such methods are infused with the themes of valuing experience, promoting active learning, engaging in reflective practice, expecting learners to participate in their own education, offering and receiving feedback, promoting egalitarianism, and inviting dialogue. In the following pages, five guidelines for constructivist-developmental counselor education are proposed.

Guidelines for a Constructivist Counselor Education

By now, we hope that you understand that we make no pretense to having the final word on "constructivist education." Indeed, our early idea was that this volume would be an "open-ended," three-ring binder of intriguing ideas and methods drawn from and directed toward fellow teachers. The notion was to collect constructivist "things to do" for teachers who intend to help shape constructivist counselors and therapists, along with some ideas to jog those teachers' thinking about their own constructivist efforts. The binder would leave room for inclusion of more methods, materials, and ideas which might be created by educators and users in the course of continued exploration. We thought that this way of reaching our audience was more "constructivist" than the usual packaging. We have succumbed, obviously, to the blandishments of the marketplace and, yes, to convention. But, we are hopeful that the original "loose-leaf binder" spirit persists in the pages of this book: that you will not only be able to reap useful "stuff" from these pages, but will also find ways to collect your own "stuff." What follow are guidelines which have been constructed by the authors out of the literature on progressive teaching, feminist pedagogy, developmental instruction, social learning theory, and educational psychology in general.

Guideline One—Personalize Your Teaching

"This class really rocked, and the instructor was so in tune with the students that she knew all forty names by the end of the second class." So reads part of one student's evaluation of a counselor educator of our acquaintance. Through no particular legerdemain, this teacher is quickly able to commit to memory her student's names. As we write this, we are aware of at least two possible strains of queasiness in our readers. The objectivist will say something like, "And, yes, I'll bet that teacher gets lots of positive evaluations from her students. But, are they learning anything?" The other reaction, from someone with a humanist bent, "Remembering names is only the beginning. What really is needed for the good classroom is more than names; it's personhood. Is the teacher building authentic relationships with her students? Is she promoting a learning community?"

Living in the tension between the supposed learning "content" and the learning relationship is the constructivist response to the objectivist complaint, "But are they learning anything?" We propose that the two are inextricable. In one of his last writings, Carl Rogers (1983), commenting on the constructivist revolution, offered that all knowledge is at the core a personal matter, not a disembodied entity that is somehow "found" by learners through purely abstract and objective procedures.

As it is described here, "personalizing instruction" means promoting interactions among all participants in the learning environment, as well as making connections between subject matter and personal issues. Brown, Collins, and Duguid (1989) have shown that a local school (in the present case, classroom, program, or college) culture which emphasizes authentic, personal relationships provides a superior ground for learning. Dryden and Feltham (1994) argue that authenticity and genuineness, involving the "use of trainees' own material," in the counseling classroom leads to development-enhancing creative introspection" (pp. 92-93). Sanford (1966) suggests that a development-enhancing environment requires at least a moderate amount of "personalism," especially for concrete, dualistic knowers. Some central elements in such a personalized teaching environment follow.

Creating a Community

The superordinate idea of "community" might guide the personalization of mental health education. From making simple seating arrangements in the classroom to encouraging dialogue, the instructor can intentionally encourage community building. At least seven elements contribute to creating community: encouraging disclosure, engaging differences, emphasis on dialogue, instructor presence, enthusiasm, sharing methods, and being available.

Individuals might discover their "knowing voices" through the instructor's *encouraging disclosure* and allowing all participants to struggle together to create knowledge *in a challenging but nonpunitive environment.* Such an atmosphere is one in which all are allowed to voice uncertainty without the fear of ridicule. It is enhanced by instructors who themselves can show doubt and who can verbally reflect student contributions in an affirming manner. Belenky and her colleagues (1986) describe this "connected classroom" as a place in which everyone contributes and everyone's presence is valued. All participants in the connected classroom are asked to take responsibility for the experience. To do this, an instructor encourages participation, perhaps sometimes intentionally asking each student for an idea or for a process comment.

Differences can be engaged and encouraged as necessary elements for building community. As Yalom (1985) has described it, the emergence of a "true" community requires that inevitable conflict be expressed in a dialectical fashion, so that the greater goal of participants' being able to learn from new perspectives is served. In contrast, a "pseudo community" is one in which everyone conspires to be alike. It behooves the instructor to therefore model open-minded challenge to students' ideas and to even "push" an incipient difference of views into the open for group consideration.

An *emphasis on dialogue and interaction* have replaced the unidirectional model of college-teaching-as-lecturing, which remains the single most common method of instruction in most fields. In the connected, personalized classroom, participants are encouraged to listen to each other and to build on each other's ideas. The instructor helps to create an atmosphere in which participants can, in Noddings' words (cited in Belenky et al., 1986, p.221), "nurture each other's thoughts to maturity." Noddings asks instructors to respond to student questions and offerings on the student's own terms, not in a point-counterpoint fashion of debate and competition. This "struggling together" notion is especially important for dualistic, authority-centered knowers. Confidence in themselves as knowledge creators is a desirable, and likely, consequence of participating in the social construction of knowledge in the classroom. In a similar vein, Freire (1994) calls teachers to help students "put their words on the world," as opposed to treating knowledge as being outside of themselves. As students move toward relativism, separate and debate-oriented classroom discourse might complement the connected manner of discussion.

The instructor's *personal presence in the classroom* further promotes student empowerment as knowledge creators. The traditional model of knowing as a dispassionate exploration of objective truth is replaced by the notion of the teacher as a "subject" (Shotter and Gergen, 1993) among other subjects. In contrast, the common "objectification of the teacher" (hooks, 1994, p. 16) requires that teachers' selves be "emptied out" so that the "untidy" personal contents of their lives and thinking don't intrude on their objectivity. Hooks proposes instead that teachers bring their biases and uncertainties into the learning space.

Such a personal presence can be extended to the aforementioned encouragement of self-disclosure and of emotional expression in the classroom. Hooks (1994) asks teachers to be vulnerable in the classroom in order that learners might gain confidence through experiencing the teacher's thinking and feeling in-the-moment. In this way the "above-the-shoulders" truncation of the rationalist teacher who models the "purity" of intellect and reason is transformed into the "whole body" presence of the constructivist instructor who shares uncertainty and emotion.

Fifth, *enthusiasm* can contribute to the personalized classroom. In many academic circles, showing excitement for ideas and for each other is considered, in bell hooks' (1994) words, to be a "transgression of boundaries." Excitement in the traditional objectivist classroom is viewed with suspicion, seen as disruptive to the serious atmosphere that is assumed to be necessary for learning. However, learning has been shown to be more potent (Bandura, 1986) in emotionally charged situations. Such enthusiasm might extend not only to ideas, but, in hooks (1994) words, to "our interest in one another, in hearing one another's voices, in recognizing one another's presence" (p. 8). Generating and maintaining enthusiasm is therefore a collective effort in the personalized social constructionist classroom.

Instructors might also extend their personal presence through the transparency of *sharing* with the class *the teaching methods* and the decision processes used to decide on those methods. The instructor can give up further control by asking students to choose preferred methods and content from a menu of possibilities.

A final element in personalizing teaching is simply *to be available*. In Chickering and Reisser's (1993) words, "Frequent student-faculty contact in and out of classes is the most important factor in student motivation and involvement" (p. 374). They share a few simple strategies for increasing such contact: encourage students to drop by the office just to visit, be willing to mentor students on career issues and personal concerns, share your past experiences, attitudes, and values with students, and know students by name within the first two weeks of the term.

Lest our own enthusiasm for personalizing teaching appear overzealous, a proviso is needed. Sound learning can occur through lecture, and reason is, of course, a powerful and rigorous method for problem analysis. Personalizing, if translated into a sloppy "be nice, be supportive, be unconditionally positive about all student ideas and submissions" is decidedly nondevelopmental and even crippling. If, however, the class "rocks," in the aforementioned student's words, because students are included in our world, and if they thus join the learning community, we will have encouraged the creation of confident, engaged, constructivist professionals.

Guideline Two—Vary the Structure

A source of continuing delight for one of us who teaches the occasional course in educational psychology is the "aha" moment which arises when student teachers, puzzling over the educational implications of wide student variation in learning style, cognitive stage, and the like, finally see how—painlessly—to reach diverse learners without individualizing the whole enterprise. Often, young student teachers hear, "Vary instruction based on student cognitive level and learning style," and they respond, "How can you ever assess all the different stages and styles, let alone come up with lessons which adequately support and then challenge each individual?" Soon it starts to dawn on them: cycling through a variety of methods of instruction—many of which are presented in this book—will both meet some learners where they are and challenge others to "stretch" toward less congenial or familiar ideas.

The notion of "varying the structure" is a relief. The hard way to meet individual learners' needs is to try to explicitly pair instruction with assessment of students' styles and stages, assessment done either at the outset of a semester or at the beginning of the student's program (and we have done both; see Kolb, 1984; Moore, 1987 for examples of style and stage assessment). However, finely pairing instruction with the results of such assessment is not usually necessary. Simply varying instruction—giving your class the rich pedagogical clutter which Chickering (1972) calls the "junkyard curriculum"—will, we believe, ensure sufficient periodicity of "confirmation" and "contradiction" (Kegan, 1994) of the learner's current inclinations.

Our advice for the aspiring instructor would therefore be, "Go vary, young educator." Brookfield, an adult education theorist, elaborates the variation notion thus in his book *The Skillful Teacher*:

Given the bewildering complexity of teaching and learning, a good rule of thumb is to *use a diversity of materials and methods in your practice* (italics ours). This is important for two reasons. First, if you try out a range of materials and methods, there is a good chance that at some point in the activity the majority of students will find that their preferred learning style is being addressed. They will experience this as reassuring and reaffirming. Second, by introducing students to styles with which they are unfamiliar, you will be broadening their repertoires and helping them to flourish in a greater range of situations than would otherwise have been the case. (1990, p. 202)

"Structure" is defined here as the amount of direction and framework given to students on such things as assignments and discussions. The instructor stays on the lookout for the subtle, but inevitable fatigue of overchallenge in some students or the decline of engagement due to lack of challenge in others. More concrete "receivers" of knowledge find high structure to be supportive of their current expectations and low structure to be threatening (Baxter-Magolda, 1988; Knefelkamp, 1984), while more constructivist knowers find high structure constraining and low structure freeing and enlivening.

Ways of providing high structure, especially for those students who tend toward received knowing, have been proposed by both Knefelkamp (1984) and Chickering and Reisser (1993). High structure is most supportive for more concrete, authority-centered students. Three examples of providing higher degrees of structure include: early in the process, describing the "context" of a course to students in terms of its sequence in a curriculum and its place in the philosophical debates in the field, providing vivid examples of abstract concepts, and starting simply and increasing complexity. This last guideline is illustrated by Ivey's (1997) microskills approach. The initial high structure of learning the disaggregated ("micro") skills gives way as the semester progresses. During subsequent practice interviews, fuzzier situations arise as students integrate and apply those skills. It has been our experience that the more authority-centered thinkers are initially overchallenged when asked to apply the skills in the more amorphous environment of role played counseling situations. They benefit from practice, reflection, and critique in a supportive setting. Kegan (1994) calls this process "over the shoulder teaching"—the instructor guides, poses, and asks while the student struggles to construct understandings by resolving dilemmas. The "semi-structure" of over the shoulder teaching provides a supportive challenge for more authority-centered thinkers.

In contrast, relativistic thinkers generally relish less structure; their epistemology is supported by more open-ended tasks. Thus, for example, the relativistic thinker benefits from choosing a topic of interest for a paper, analyzing a case from multiple perspectives, being offered questions rather than directives during supervised practice, and co-constructing client assessments in dialogue with peers. Relativists thrive on creating knowledge through dialectical exchanges of ideas— both within themselves and among co-learners.

A specific example of how learners might become "con-structurers" ("structurers with") of a course lies in the instructor's active inquiry about learners' experiences. We have found the following in-class inquiries to challenge all learners: "How is the course going for you?" "Which issue would you like to emphasize today?" "How would you like to learn that?" In the ensuing in-class dialogue, students can be challenged to partially construct their own education, much as we hope that they will construct the act of counseling itself someday. In this dialogical engagement with the class, the instructor is explicitly enacting social construction. A more immediate benefit lies in the instructor's receiving immediate feedback. Subsequently, the course can be more responsive to students' unfolding learning needs.

Guideline Three—Value and Promote Experience

We define "experience," simply and operationally, as sensory activity that engages the learner's attention. The power of introducing concrete and emotionally valent experience in order to maximize learning has been demonstrated by recent research on the brain, as is shown in the next chapter. Pictures, sounds, smells, and touches seem to be worth a large number of words, as the brain seems to process these sensory data more directly than it does symbols for them. Sensory experience also generates high affect, which has been shown to enhance retention. Thus "doing" begets knowing.

The less-powerful conditions, in order of potency, include vicarious learning (i.e., modeling and demonstration) and verbal persuasion (e.g., lecturing). Dale's (1969) triangle of retention also supports the need for experiential learning by pointing out the following retention rates:

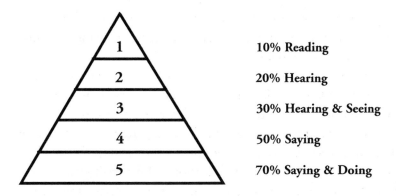

Grounding thinking in experience is particularly germane to constructivist teaching. Concrete experiences tend to trigger divergent thinking, which is oriented toward "possibilities" and "hypothesis-generating" (Chickering and Reisser, 1993).

Further evidence for this bias toward experiential teaching lies in Bandura's (1986) social learning research, in which direct experience (called "performance accomplishments") emerges as the most potent among the conditions for learning.

As might be expected, these findings have been explicitly applied to education. The call for inductive, experience-based instruction can be traced to the sensitivity training and humanistic education movements of the past thirty years, the experiential learning model of Kolb (1984), and the research on androgogy of Knowles (1970). All of these models recognize the need for a judicious mixing of the sensory, concrete, and abstract. A dialectical tension exists between concrete and abstract, involvement and detachment, passion and distance. In the counseling field, Ivey (1986) similarly has promoted the value of multiple levels of experiencing in his adaptation of Piaget to counseling practice. In his view, a mixture of sensory, concrete, and formal/abstract knowing optimizes personal change.

In contrast to the evidence for experience-based learning and the accompanying models for teaching, college education continues to be dominated by teacher-centered, abstraction-oriented information giving (Chickering and Reisser, 1993; Knefelkamp, 1984). Affect and experience have been viewed with suspicion in the Western intellectual tradition (hooks, 1994). Instead, disembodied abstraction has been raised as purer and more objective, and therefore more truthful, in the Enlightenment tradition of the academy. This mistrust of the senses has led to an overemphasis on words and talk, and an avoidance of direct, concrete instigations into the sensorium of experience.

The above evidence leads to this plea: Let us remind ourselves that research consistently shows that student learning is inversely proportional to the amount of "teacher talk." Let us create conditions for students to do, feel, discover, and ponder (Kolb, 1984), followed up by subsequent observations and reflections. The challenge for the mental health educator can be stated thus: Will you pay attention to the "process" as well as the "content" of learning by generating experiences through activity, case study, illustration, role play, interviewing, teamwork, and data collection rather than delivering the knowledge goods only through lecture and discussion?

Lest we be accused of blind advocacy and true believerhood in our strident declarations of the superiority of the experiential, we reiterate here that learners do need regular reflection on and abstraction from experience in order to generate broad, useful conceptual knowing. Experience alone is not the best teacher. Kolb's (1984) experiential learning model provides a template for the mixing of four learning modes. In his model, immediate concrete experience forms the basis for subsequent observation and reflection, from which students can, in turn, build concepts or generalizations. From there the educator's task is to encourage further "active experimentation" with those generalizations, which then brings students full circle to new concrete experience, further reflection, and reconstructed abstractions.

The amount of concrete versus vicarious experiencing can be varied by instructors. Knefelkamp (1984) proposes that dualistic thinkers require the heaviest dose of direct, concrete experience, while relativists are able to manage more vicarious learning conditions. However, every learner can benefit from at least initial contact with concrete situations, from which generalizations might be pulled. Experiential instruction thus emphasizes *inductive* teaching methods. Teacher training models have traditionally advocated such beginning-of-class activities as "providing the motivations for the lesson." Such initial illustrations as anecdotes, demonstrations, or activities serve the purposes of "set induction" or "advanced organizer" in that they ready learners to generate working hypotheses, which can then be tested by rational analysis and further reflection on experience (Chickering and Reisser, 1993). And, in the social constructionist tradition, the instructor him- or herself might also discover new knowledge in the dialectical co-construction of abstract meaning with the students.

Mental health educators are especially well-positioned to use experiential methods to teach, as most counseling practice is itself infused with metaphor, affect, and in-session experiences. Gestalt exercises, role plays, and guided imagery are common tools for helping clients to revisit experiences. The following is an illustration from the author's (McAuliffe) teaching experience. In the initial session of a counseling skills class, the instructor begins class by asking the circled students to help him with a problem. The students proceed to counsel the instructor, willy nilly. After the session, the instructor provides an accounting of what the students offered (e.g., advice, empathy, inquiries), while students identify what they think was most helpful. From there, the group pulls out beginning principles of helping from this and their own previous experiences. They compare those principles to what they actually did and then attempt to define "what is helpful." The work is organic in that it partially comes out of in vivo experiencing and experiment. The class moves through Kolb's four levels during the class period.

Such inductive, experiential instruction is not a panacea for all teaching dilemmas. Drawbacks of experiential teaching include its being more time-consuming and "messier" than didactic, abstract instruction. Teachers need to carefully monitor the mix of experience, reflection, and abstraction so that the learners don't become swallowed in a morass of unexamined experience, to the exclusion of potentially rational analysis and experimentation. The constructive-developmental instructor must live with the tension between "covering material" and teaching for discovery. However, the ultimate value of "coverage" depends on what is retained for future use.

Guideline Four—Emphasize Multiple Perspectives

Constructivist teaching serves the dual aims of helping to enlarge the learner's sense of how knowledge is socially constructed and of stimulating cognitive development. These are really two descriptions of the single process of developing greater complexity and empathy as a person. Toward those ends, students can be asked to examine issues and dilemmas from several angles as they arise within the classroom.

At least two ways of promoting such perspective-shifting are available: first, evoking and validating the multiple perspectives represented by the many students in the course; and second, turning to and exploring the diverse approaches to the material presented by a particular curricular area.

However, many seeming perspective-taking activities are not so. For example, while classroom discussion surely is an instructional staple for all counselor educators, serious ratification of all student voices, validating even those regarded as irritants by the other students and/or the instructor, is not widespread. Often, indeed, teachers are fearful and abhorrent of student "oppositional" arguments. We have heard colleagues refer to those who would challenge the instructor's perspective as "sharks in the audience." In contrast, the constructivist educator strives to value the student whom we have come to call "the man with the big cigar in the back of the classroom who, tilting back in his chair, from time to time calls out, 'that's fine, but. . . .'" Such challenges from students can yield instructional gold; the "true" constructivist will be alert for and will value dissenting views.

Some mental health education courses lend themselves quite directly to the second method for evoking multiple perspectives: exploring the different approaches to the curricular material. For example, the fairly recent emphasis on "multicultural counseling" offers students a forum for serious consideration of the issues of gender, ability, race, religion, ethnicity, class, and sexual orientation as they relate to counseling. Within this context, a mental health educator can act as a "critical pedagogue": a teacher who helps students change their "stagnant or stereotypical views" about groups other than their own (Kanpol, 1994, p. 43). And any rigid notion of multiculturism itself can be challenged, as Montgomery et al. illustrate in Chapter Eight of this volume.

The counseling theories course is another "natural" source of curricular material which aligns with the teaching of multiple perspectives. At last count over four hundred different theories existed in our field. For many students, encountering the sheer abundance of solutions to the riddle of helping carries with it considerable epistemological challenge. "If so many experts view this business of counseling in such radically different ways, surely some are at least posturing, if not dead wrong," goes the frequent complaint. If supported well by a teacher at this moment, many such students can "tip over" to the constructivist understanding that theories are only approximations, and that—in the business of becoming a therapist or a counselor—selection of and commitment to a theoretical stance (including eclecticism) is helpful but not final. Steenbarger (1996) described the analysis of theories from the ground of the larger "world views" that they represent.

Other courses and topics, of course, offer possibilities. Debates about the validity of testing and assessment methods and about diagnosis, controversies about legal matters and ethical dilemmas, the always perplexing skills quandary of giving directives while being "non-directive"; all these and more present likely opportunities for exploring multiple perspectives.

A caution is in order. The multiple perspectives approach will match the cognitive structures of many students (the so-called "multiplists" or "subjectivists"; a stage midway between nonconstructivist and constructivist thinking) so closely in form that, rather than stimulating development, the approach is likely to maintain the epistemological status quo for them. They will further drown in a sea of multiplicity if perspectives are merely offered side-by-side, without evidence or context for use. Their multiplicity will not be challenged toward relativism; that is, toward not stopping at mere acceptance of the many choices available, but moving on to find procedures for evaluating and choosing what might be most helpful in particular situations. (So far, we have not dwelt extensively on the properties of the "stages" of adult development, stages which are given similar descriptions by an array of theorists. We expect that many of our readers are familiar with these theories; others may be interested in some of the standard works on constructive development listed in the reference section of this chapter.)

By way of example, let's turn to the earlier-mentioned multicultural counseling class. In discussions in this course, students who are multiplists tend to argue that all cultural forms are equally valid with no reference to context. In our teaching, we offer students the case of the immigrant who, hailing from parts where corporal punishment is a father's prerogative, "chastised" his daughter by striking her violently for wearing lipstick against his explicit directives. He did this in the United States, on school property, in full view of pupils and teachers. We find that, while students measuring lowest on a scale of constructive development hold punitive views toward the cross-cultural actor, those in multiplicity express a measure of understanding of—even empathy toward—his culturally relative "perspective." However, it's only those few respondents who embrace a fully constructivist epistemology that tend to see that "diversity" is itself diversified. They ruminate on interaction effects ("the father must be under much stress having moved so recently"); they sense that action or inaction is always a choice ("maybe calling the police right away is not necessary"); they are alert to what has been called "all the elements on the horizon" ("I'm struck by the opportunity for learning about other cultures for the pupils in the schoolyard"). In short, they are sensitive to the relativism of "reality," the complex interconnections, the fragility of the moment and the actors, and the constructed nature of what emerges in any given situation.

By simply encouraging attention to "diversity," by only working with the "multiple" part of perspective-taking, the teacher may do a disservice to those in the stage of cognitive multiplicity. (Estimates of the numbers of counseling students, and adults in general, in multiplicity range from 40 to 70 percent [Kegan, 1994; Neukrug and McAuliffe, 1993]). By teasing out somewhat more complex, evidence-based analyses, by calling on constructivist students in the classroom, and by stressing temporary commitments, systems thinking, and contexts, the constructivist educator can stimulate multiplistic students to move toward constructivist thought. Perry comments on how this is done:

We gather from what our students have told us that the educational impact of diversity can be at its best when it is deliberate. When a teacher asks his [sic] students to read conflicting authorities and then asks them to assess the nature and meaning of the conflict, he is in a strong position to assist them to go beyond simple diversity into the disciplines of relativity of thought through which special instances of diversity can be productively exploited. He can teach the relation, the relativism, of one system of thought to another. (1970, p. 35)

This warning about reinforcing multiplicity leads us to a second caution: the promotion of "alternative perspectives" may be pursued somewhat overzealously, to the point of affirming rigidity. Brookfield (1987) hints at this excess of "whatever-goes" when he writes of how validating a learner's experience may only firm up rigid perspective, making the already slow-to-move intractable. For instance, validation of a learner's experience may lead the student to conclude, "See, I'm right, the teacher agrees with me." In Brookfield's words:

We are frequently caught within our constructed and narrowly constraining paradigms—that is, the frameworks of understanding through which we make sense of the world. We define our needs from within these paradigms, and unless confronted with alternatives we may find it extremely hard to imagine these of our own volition. Educators and trainers who plan their programs based upon felt needs as defined by learners appear to be operating democratically. They may, however, be doing a disservice to these learners by implicitly condemning them to remain within their existing paradigms of thought and action. (1987, p. 112)

Thus, according to Brookfield and others, it is helpful for a teacher to also challenge existing student ways of knowing, to put them up to a test of viability, presuming that this challenging will lead to changed outlook.

Much care is needed here, however. Instead of exploring and analyzing perspectives, all too often the proposed antidote to allowing learners to wander in the putative slough of "narrowly constraining paradigms" has indeed been "to confront with alternatives." We find the notion of confrontation at once risky and a touch arrogant. The risk, of course, is around causing a student to dig in, withdraw, regress. Further, the notion of a teacher arrogating to herself the role of judging the limitations of a student's "paradigms," and then offering superior alternatives, strikes us as somewhat too redolent of the teacher-as-philosopher-king model, and therefore emphatically non-constructivist. Fortunately, Brookfield and many other thinkers on adult learning propose many ways of inviting learners to consider alternative paradigms, ones which are not so "confrontive" and are more like "invitations." Many such invitations are presented in the following chapters.

Guideline Five—Encourage Intrapersonal Process Awareness, or "Metacognition"

Metacognition, or the "conscious monitoring of one's thought processes (Henderson, 1996, p. 21), is key for the practitioner who would become a constructivist. We remember fondly a recently natu-ralized Italian immigrant who found her way into a mental health preparation program. In a freewheeling discussion about positive experiences in higher education, this student glowingly vouched that her breakthrough occurred when a literature teacher persuaded her, in her words, to "thinka abouta the think." Thinking about thinking sig-nals the emergence of the individual intellect from non-constructivism toward constructivism.

What is so remark-worthy about metacognition? After all, being "reflective" and striving for "self-awareness" are widely promoted by counselor educators. However, ordinary student interpretations of these laudable habits of mind centers on content, not on process. Thus, the nonconstructivist trainee, in "reflecting" on a particular ses-sion, will mentally replay the content of client-counselor exchanges, or the concrete facts of what happened and "what I was trying to do." For those student counselors, appraisal of their and the client's cognitive-affective processes is missing, to say nothing of the absence of a vivid sense of how one's own cognitive-affective process interacts with that of the client. It is with the onset of the constructivist turn of mind, however, that the ability to—and the commitment to—reflect on one's own processes becomes salient. For the mental health educator him- or herself, such metacognition might take the form of the fol-lowing rumination: "I have a tendency to pronounce and perform in front of the class. I like playing the expert too. However, as I am cur-rently understanding it, such teaching might promote passivity in the learner. I must challenge myself to give up the attention in order to stimulate student experience through class discussion and simulations."

There is hope for students who are not reflexive about their thinking. With coaching, the emerging constructivist therapist or counselor can become alert to the within-session stream of events, the emotions on both sides of the dyad, and the goodness of fit between clinical moves and particular elements of theory or supervisor advice.

For the cognitive developmentalists, the stage at which metacognition begins to be possible is variously referred to as "relativistic thinking" (Perry, 1970), "the systemic order of consciousness" (Kegan, 1994), or "procedural knowing" (Belenky et al., 1986). These mean that the thinker is able to coordinate various competing, conflicting, or remote elements within the "self." We have elsewhere described the beginning awareness of intrapsychic dialectics as "early constructivist" (Lovell and McAuliffe, 1996).

For the full constructivist thinker, moreover, coordination of "within self" elements (called "several selves" by Kegan,1982) is never decoupled from pondering how the inner interacts with the external elements. The full constructivist self is porously relational; it is seen to be inexorably in concert with "the social." Thus, at this level, because intrapsychic phenomena are seen to be tied to the social, the therapist's metacognitive operations will involve a sense of the influence of the other. For instance, one student reflected, "I felt so bored with this client. I could hardly stay awake. What was it she was doing that I reacted to? What in me drew such a performance? What can I do at moments like this while still being alert to my "automatic reactions?" It is a short leap from this point to the psychodynamic notion of countertransference.

When a student is able to express such "meta" observations about a past session, it is a solid marker of a shift toward beginning constructivism. However, when the student reports an increasing ability to go "meta" in the actual course of an interaction, something Schon (1983) calls "reflection-in-action," full constructivism is probably being expressed. "Interpersonal process recall" training techniques (in which a video of a session is stopped and a trainee is asked what her cognitions/feelings were at that point in the session (Kagan, 1980) help to sharpen the trainee's sense of "self-talk" and awareness of affect during a session. This kind of work inevitably hastens onset of metacognitive abilities in mental health trainees.

Conclusion

In this introduction we have asked counselor educators to risk: first, we have called for us to "think about our thinking" as educators, which carries with it the risk of newness, the disruption of old habits. We have also proposed that we "let go" of the illusion of full control over our curricular content, instructional method, and classroom process. An analogy to a morning in the life of a parent might be apt. Many parents approach such a time with a specific agenda, a sequenced expectation of playtime, naptime, feeding time. These we hope will be good for our child. However, our best-laid plans are inevitably scattered like toys on the floor as we accede to the emerging present of demanding fellow learners. We have learned again that development comes out of dialectic, that we and the environments bump up against one another. Like the parent, we constructivist educators have both taught and learned, we have surprisingly tapped into many dimensions of ourselves, the cognitive, the emotional, and the physical. And through it all, both of us have been changed by the intersection of our mutually porous selves. We have shared crises and enthusiasms, we are learning to co-exist, and, like the parent at the end of the morning, we might exhaustedly anticipate a new day. And too we wonder, "Who is in charge here?," as we give over to the interaction.

So it is with a constructivist and developmental counselor education. Who is in charge of the unfolding that is counselor training? In this chapter, we have offered a fundamentally democratic response to that question. In that vein, we ask you to resist the temptations to march with the elites and the authorities and to try to be in full control. Instead, we ask you to remain porous in the face of the potential rigidities of single-theory bias, uniform teaching method, cultural encapsulation, political single-mindedness, or personal defendedness.

We hope that the constructivist venture will keep us off of the pedestals of title, age, and expertise and bring us into the circle of the learner-storytellers. We then might join our fellow learners in "storying" our field. We will share the roles of the West African griot or the Irish seanachie, the bards who hear and tell the story of a people. We, the educators, will be in the circle, animatedly posing and listening, remembering our elders on whose shoulders we stand, and then hearing the next generation who themselves will recreate our field. And, by our example, our student-colleagues will themselves, as practitioners, find the inspiration to continually create an inclusive, socially critical, reflexive counseling endeavor. It will be worth the risks.

References

Bandura, A. (1986). *Social cognitive theory*. Englewood-Cliffs, NJ: Prentice-Hall.

Baxter-Magolda, M., and Porterfield, W. D. (1988). *Assessing intellectual development*. Alexandria, VA: American College Personnel Association.

Belenky, M. F., Clinchy, B. M., Goldberger, N. R., and Tarule, J. M. (1986). *Women's ways of knowing*. New York: Basic Books.

Benack, S. (1988). Relativistic thought: A cognitive basis for empathy in counseling. *Counselor Education and Supervision* 27: 216-232.

Brookfield, H. (1987). *Developing critical thinkers*. San Francisco: Jossey-Bass.

_____. (1990) *The skillful teacher*. San Francisco: Jossey-Bass.

Brown, J. S., Collins, A., and Duguid, P. (1989). Situated cognition and the culture of learning. *Educational Researcher*, 18 (1): 32-42.

Burbules, N. C., and Rice, S. (1991). Dialogue across differences. *Harvard Educational Review* 61: 393-416.

Chickering, A. W. (1972). *Education and identity*. San Francisco: Jossey-Bass.

Chickering, A. W., and Reisser, L. (1993). *Education and identity* (2nd ed.). San Francisco: Jossey-Bass.

Dale, E. (1969). *Audio-visual methods in teaching*. New York: Holt, Rinehart, and Winston.

Dewey, J. (1963). *Experience and education*. New York: Collier. Originally published in 1938.

Dryden, W., and Feltham, C. (1994). *Developing counselor training.* London: Sage.

Friere, P. (1994). *Pedagogy of the oppressed.* New York: Continuum.

Giroux, H. (1992). *Border crossings: Cultural workers and the politics of education.* New York: Routledge.

Henderson, J. G. (1996). *Reflective teaching: The study of your constructivist practices* (2nd. ed.). Englewood Cliffs, NJ: Merrill.

hooks, b. (1994). *Teaching to transgress.* New York: Routledge.

Ivey, A. (1986). *Developmental therapy.* San Francisco: Jossey-Bass.

_____. (1997). *Intentional interviewing and counseling.* Pacific Grove, CA: Brooks/Cole.

Kagan, N. (1980). *Interpersonal process recall.* East Lansing, MI: self-published.

Kanpol, B. (1994). *Critical pedagogy: An introduction.* Westport, CT: Bergin and Garvey.

Kegan, R. (1982) *The evolving self.* Cambridge, MA: Harvard University Press.

_____. (1994). *In over our heads.* Cambridge, MA: Harvard.

Knefelkamp, L. (1984). Developmental instruction. In L. Knefelkamp and R. R. Golec (Eds.) *A workbook for using the Practice-to-Theory-to-Practice Model.* University of Maryland at College Park.

Knowles, M. S. (1970). *The modern practice of adult education; androgogy versus pedagogy.* New York: Association Press.

Kohlberg, L. (1981). *Essays on moral development.* San Francisco: Harper and Row.

Kolb, D. (1984). *Experiential learning.* Englewood Cliffs, NJ: Prentice-Hall.

Loevinger, J. (1976). *Ego development.* San Francisco: Jossey-Bass.

Lovell, C., and McAuliffe, G. (1996). From non-constructivist to constructivist counseling. Paper presented at the quadrennial meeting of the Association for Counselor Education and Supervision. Portland, OR, October 1996.

McLaren, P. (1989). *Life in schools: An introduction to critical pedagogy in the foundations of education.* New York: Longman.

Moore, W.S. (1987). *Learning environment preferences.* Olympia, WA: Center for the Study of Intellectual Development.

Neukrug, E. S., and McAuliffe, G. J. (1993). Cognitive development and human service education. *Human Service Education* 13: 13–26.

Palmer, P. (1983). *To know as we are known: A spirituality of education.* New York: HarperCollins.

Perry, W. (1970). *Forms of intellectual and ethical development in the college years.* New York: Holt, Rinehart, and Winston.

Piaget, J. (1971). *Psychology and epistemology.* Harmondsworth, England: Penguin.

Rogers, C. R. (1969). *Freedom to learn.* Columbus, OH: Merrill.

_____. (1951). *Client-centered therapy.* Boston: Houghton Mifflin.

_____. (1983). *Freedom to learn for the 80s.* New York: Macmillan.

Sanford, N. (1966). *Self and society: Social change and individual development.* New York: Atherton.

Schon, D. A. (1983). *The reflective practitioner.* New York: Basic Books.

Shotter, J., and Gergen, K. J. (1993). *Texts of identity.* London: Sage.

Steenbarger, B. (March 1996). *World view and constructivism in counselor education.* Paper presented at the annual convention of the American Counseling Association, Pittsburg, PA.

Yalom, I. D. (1997). *The theory and practice of group psychotherapy.* New York: Basic Books.

Chapter Two
How Counselor Education Influences Future Helpers: What Students Say*

Garrett J. McAuliffe, Old Dominion University

If we are to seriously engage in a conversation about constructivist education, we must include students' perceptions about what happens to them during their course of study. How does counselor education impact its own clients, that is, our students? How do students themselves experience such influences? This question has been asked periodically through the years, mostly through quantitative assessment of students' developmental and personality characteristics (e.g., Borders and Fong, 1989; Paisley and Hayes, this volume). In order to explore counseling students' perceptions of their own education, we (the research team named below) conducted an intensive qualitative study of how and why students might have changed during their program of study. In this research, we "went inductive" in order to discover such changes. In order that fresh data might emerge, we attempted to keep the drumbeat of our constructivist bias in the background of our inquiry and data analysis. Our questions were open-ended. The informants themselves named changes and influences that they perceived.

We found substantial parallels to the constructivist practices that we have proposed in Chapter One, and some divergence from them. In this chapter, I will first share our findings, and then will outline the parallels to constructivist teaching. For the purposes of this volume, my focus here will be on the program influences on student changes rather than on the student changes themselves, except when strong connections can be made between the two.

---

*Note: Special thanks go to the following individuals, who helped to interview participants and/or analyzed this data: Dr. Charles Keating of the Engineering Management Department of Old Dominion University, Dr. Karen Eriksen of Walden and Radford Universities, Old Dominion Ph.D. students Mark Blagen, James Poole, and Sylvia Hoffler, Master's degree students Angela DeVaun, Nicole Anderson, and Amy Cunningham, and, of course, the students who participated as interviewees.

Method

We interviewed fifteen graduates of a counselor education program via one-to-one interviews and a focus group. We asked two basic questions, followed by probes: "How have you changed, if at all, during your period of study?" and "What in the program influenced those changes?" We used a grounded theory-based qualitative research approach (Strauss and Corbin, 1990) in this pilot study. Our emphasis was on an inductive, "discovery" orientation to the data, although prior research on counselor education, on cognitive development (e.g., Perry, 1984), and on teaching in general were also considered in the coding of the data. The research followed four phases.

In *Phase One*, we interviewed fifteen graduating counselor education students in two different semi-structured formats: (1) a focus group, which consisted of the twelve students in a group techniques course, and (2) intensive one-to-one interviews with three students from the capstone internship seminar. We intentionally left the questions open-ended in order that all possible dimensions of change and influence might be probed. All students were in their final year of study: three had completed their internship; others were in the course which precedes the internship. They ranged in age from twenty to forty-three. Fourteen were women, one was a man.

In *Phase Two*, we transcribed the interview data from the audio tapes and entered it into the NUD*IST ("Non-numerical Unstructured Data Indexing, Searching, and Theorizing") software program.

Phase Three consisted of data analysis, using Strauss and Corbin's (1990) open coding procedure, as follows. The researchers first created 121 initial conceptual labels, generated directly from the raw data (i.e., the typed interview transcripts). We then used these labels to build second-order and first-order categories, which are hierarchically displayed in Table One. We developed first-order categories in four subphases: (1) private analyses by the two principal investigators and three doctoral students, (2) "public" analyses of those initial codings and consensus building among the five analyzers, (3) a re-analysis and re-coding by the two principal investigators, together, to reduce the categories using the data analysis software, and (4) triangulation by having a counselor educator from another university review the analysis.

Phase Four consists of this description and discussion of the categorizations from the data analysis. I present initial conclusions and consider implications for further research. I hope that the following narrative stimulates dialogue on how to teach future helpers and that it influences our instructional practices in useful ways. While the study can speak best to its local community, I invite you to extrapolate its always-tentative conclusions to other settings.

Students' Reports on Changes and Influences: Summary of Findings

Although 121 themes were initially extracted from the transcripts, after much re-coding the researchers reduced that number to seven first-order categories: three major student changes and four program influences. The first-order categories of changes in students were: (1) increased reflectiveness, (2) increased autonomy and interdependence, and (3) valuing dialogue. The four program influences were: (1) social construction of knowledge, (2) experiential learning, (3) opportunities for independent thinking, and (4) a supportive environment. It should be noted that none of these categories are exclusive; the labels are ultimately heuristics which temporarily capture the dominant themes for our discussion. Table One lists the influences and changes and includes the dominant themes and the related subthemes.

TABLE ONE

Themes and Subthemes: Program Influences and Student Changes

I. Program Influences on Student Changes
- A. Social Construction of Knowledge
  - 1. involving students in knowledge creation
  - 2. maximizing peer interaction
  - 3. introducing multiple perspectives
- B. Experiential Learning
  - 1. Encouraging activity
  - 2. Modeling and presenting case illustrations
  - 3. Grounding knowledge in personal experience
  - 4. Linking experience to abstract conceptualizations
- C. Opportunities for Independent Thinking

    D. Supportive Environment
        1. a positive, accepting, and enthusiastic manner
        2. faculty availability
        3. peer support
        4. specific feedback on student performance

II. How Students Changed
    A. Increased Reflectiveness
    B. Increased Autonomy and Interdependence
        1. creating boundaries between self and other
        2. reducing the need for control in counseling situations
        3. learning to cooperate
    C. Valuing Dialogue
        1. appreciating uncertainty
        2. recognizing others' contributions
        3. reducing their directiveness and judgmentalness
        4. deliberating dialogically

The Program Factors which Influenced Students

Because this volume is dedicated to educational practice, I will here emphasize the program influences on student changes, rather than the nature of the changes themselves. The discoveries of our research parallel much of what was proposed in Chapter One as "guidelines for constructivist education." The two columns in Table Two show the parallels between the empirically derived categories from this study, that is the "program influences," and the constructivist education guidelines from Chapter One. The paralleling of themes between each column is worth noting.

The seeming neatness of such a comparison is however, deceptive. No meta-formula for teaching is possible, especially if it were to be derived from one qualitative research study. For the four major themes found in our research, there might be one, or four, or more new ones which were not evoked by our questions.

I also am wary of imposing my own constructivist biases on the data. However, we attempted to correct for such bias by bracketing our own pedagogical preferences when we analyzed the data. Additionally, we triangulated by using multiple analyzers, bringing in three doctoral students who were not familiar with this literature, and inviting the input of one practicing psychotherapist/counselor educator from another university.

TABLE TWO

Parallels between Empirical Findings and Constructivist Education Guidelines

Program Influences on Student Change (from Qualitative Research Study)	Constructivist Education Guidelines (from Chapter One)
Social Construction of Knowledge •Involving students in knowledge creation. •Maximizing peer interaction. •Introducing multiple perspectives.	•Knowledge is developed in community. •Embrace the learner as knower and the teacher as learner. •Have the students co-design ("con-structure") the course. •Promote interactions among all participants. •Engage differences as necessary for building community. •Invite varying student views, present alternative views, examine "all the elements on the horizon" on case situations. •Ask students to read conflicting authorities and to assess the arguments.
Experiential Learning •Encouraging activity. •Modeling and presenting case illustrations. •Grounding knowledge in personal experience. •Linking experience to abstract conceptualizations.	•Instigate learner performance accomplishments. •Use the trainee's own life as material. •Encourage disclosure. •Provide a mix of the sensory, concrete, and abstract. •Cycle through doing, reflecting, abstracting, and experimenting.
Opportunities for Independent Thinking	•Loosen structure for more advanced learners. •Vary structure for all. •Allow students to choose topics, analyze fuzzy situations, respond to questions. •Teach inductively: require students to generate hypotheses. •"Relativize" theories by analyzing their foundational worldviews. •Encourage "metacognition" (reflection).
Supportive Environment •A positive atmosphere. •Peer support. •Specific feedback on student performance.	•Create a learning community. •Create challenging but nonpunitive environment. •Allow the voicing of uncertainty without the fear of ridicule. •Provide for frequent student-faculty contact. •Be a personal presence in the classroom. •Show excitement for ideas and for each other.

Social Construction of Knowledge

Students reported that they became more autonomous and confident as thinkers when faculty included them in the creation of knowledge. Such practices ranged from simple inductive problem-posing as a way to begin a class, to allowing students to redesign a course, mid-stream, with the instructor. We saw underneath these practices an expression of the social constructionist assumption *that human knowledge is created in and by human communities, rather than being the discovery of an objective essence or being a product of autonomous individual creations* (Gergen, 1991; Mead, 1934; Rorty, 1989). We named three sub-themes under this category: (1) involving students in knowledge creation, (2) maximizing peer interaction, and (3) introducing multiple perspectives.

The first subtheme, *involving students in knowledge* creation, was described by participants as teaching in an inclusive, dialogical manner. One student said: "These two instructors had a way of listening, giving suggestions but not telling you what to do. By them [sic] asking questions it brought out different ideas from me—they didn't give me the ideas—they just stimulated the thought process." Another told of an instructor's dialogical manner: "He always wanted to hear our experiences, and he had a story to match that, and you had a story to match that, and it works really well." And another, "They allowed anyone to speak and argue their ideas and things like that." Informants linked this involvement in knowledge creation with personal changes, especially with their recognition that all individuals, including themselves, construct knowledge. One said that the instructors who influenced her most were especially good at strategically "not knowing:" "The instructors communicated that 'This is a give and take and I do not know everything.' It contributed to my confidence that I had ideas to offer."

Students were also influenced to become more confident and autonomous thinkers through *peer interaction.* Through group research papers, class discussions, and in-class "break-out" groups, students were able to find their own "author-ity" (Kegan, 1982) for ideas. No longer were "truths" the exclusive province of "experts." Through the sturm-und-drang of negotiating tasks and developing ideas in peer groups, these students discovered the construction (in contrast to the handing-down) of knowledge. They also recognized the potential, and the pain, of engaging in dialogue as a way of knowing and doing. This theme echoes dimensions of Paisley and Hayes' socially constructed counselor education program, which is described in this volume.

Introducing multiple perspectives was the final program influence under the category "social construction of knowledge." Students noted that instructors who asked for and presented alternative explanations of phenomena opened the world of social construction to them. The introduction of multiple perspectives contrasted to instruction that was ideologically single-minded or expert-dominated. Lest our enthusiasm for relativism run rampant, however, informants also reminded us that instructors needed to maintain a balance between communicating simple concepts in a linear way, on the one hand, and introducing multiple perspectives—for example, in the form of alternate and competing theories—on the other hand. Student readiness is therefore an issue. Although one informant relished a dialectic of competing concepts, another noted that such complexity would have been "over her head" early in her education. The first student was more prepared for multiple perspectives, as she had already experienced many-sided discourse in her family: "[With my family] there's never one answer for anything; there's always a million other opportunities or avenues. And some of the professors have done that with me." In contrast, the other said, "I would have been overwhelmed if my instructors had introduced too many differing ideas at once. I was looking for simple training when I entered the program."

In the above comments, we note the variety of student readinesses in our programs. Dewey (1938) warned against "atomism" in education, in which students are treated as identical. Student readiness for relativism must therefore be accounted for so that overchallenge and frustration might be avoided. It seems that, instead, the layering-in of new ideas and solidifying of concepts before introducing others might be necessary when introducing new material.

Despite this promise, the message is worth heeding: an insistent invitation for students to think in multiple ways would seem to be important if future helpers are to achieve a rich "technical eclecticism" (Lazarus, 199). Informants in this study told us that they must be asked to choose practices for themselves from among a mix of theoretical options and situational variables. The case study method represents such an invitation to multiple perspective-taking.

Experiential Learning

Mental activity, or "doing," as a condition for learning (Dewey, 1938; McNamara, in this volume) has been trumpeted in both ancient and contemporary literature, from the Chinese proverb, "I hear and I forget; I see and I remember; I do and I understand. In the doing is the learning," to Dale's (1969) "pyramid" of learning conditions, to Kolb's (1984) experiential learning model. As counselors and therapists, we also assert the power of activity to instigate personal change. Counselors stimulate emotion and other vivid experiencing through imagery, role play, and gestalt activities. Our informants reminded us of how parallel the process is in counselor education.

Social cognitive research supports the primacy of experience. Bandura (1986) has consistently found activity ("performance accomplishments") to be superior to more passive modes of learning in improving self-efficacy. But sensory activity cannot stand alone as a path to professional preparation. Our informants also reminded us, as has Kolb (1984), that they need to link concrete experiences to abstract concepts, through reflection on experience and through making generalizations across situations.

In this study, experiential learning was defined from the data as *grounding concepts in personal life experience, illustrations, and experiments.* We named four subcategories of instructor actions which encouraged experiential learning: (1) encouraging activity, (2) modeling and presenting case illustrations, (3) helping students ground knowledge in personal experience, and (4) linking student experience to abstract conceptualizations.

Encouraging activity took the form of involving students in discussions, role plays, field experiences, and design of class presentations. Here are some illustrative quotes from informants: "We would read the material and then put it into play in the classroom." "All those exercises for counseling [e.g., role plays] helped. I mean, let me do it more so I can be given specific feedback." Another activity-oriented instructional method noted by informants was having students experience simulations. For example: "We had to design an assertiveness training class and we each had to lead it for a week. [It was good because] I could see the differing results in action."

A more vicarious method of active learning was modeling and presenting case illustrations. Informants emphasized the value of instructors "presenting little situations and scenarios," "modeling in class, little role-plays. And the instructor was the client . . . ," and "sharing cases, using different names" including "the instructor sharing her own feelings about her real clients." The modeling theme evokes Bandura's (1986) findings that "vicarious learning" is second only "performance accomplishments" as the most powerful method of increasing self-efficacy.

Helping students ground knowledge in personal experience was the third subcategory under "experiential learning." Informants specified the following methods of having students make personal linkages to concepts:

• *writing about personal experience:* "Our first paper . . . made me examine myself about my blind side and to see the difference between the self I show others and the self that is really true."

• *making personal connections in class:* "I can remember many times in class, going, 'That's me!' (laughing) and thinking, 'Ok, and I know that that's something that I can recognize in myself. I need to decide whether this is a closed issue for me or not because I want to be an effective counselor.'"

• *seeing one's own family patterns in the concepts:* "I could see different patterns that were in my family that I actually, in taking information from the classes, had broken out of doing."

• *linking personal development with theory:* "The instructor asked, 'At what time in your life did your own development stop, or change, what caused that?' and it's usually a pretty significant trauma. (She then gave an example of her development-triggering experience). So this program makes you learn about yourself."

• *journaling about personal connections:* "She made us write constantly. She worked you to death. But I did a lot of self-growing because a lot of papers were about our own inner workings. They were self-exploratory kinds of things. We were writing all the time about personal experiences. For example, 'Describe your greatest crisis and how it taught you to grow.'"

One student linked personal knowledge to effective counseling: "I believe that as I personally grow and become self-aware, I become more nonjudgmental and able to hear others. If I am able to hear myself then I can hear you. But if there are parts of me that are still closed off and I am in denial, then I will also react that way (e.g., defensively) when you present. Especially if it is a similar problem, and . . . if it pushes one of my buttons."

These three vivid teaching methods, that is, encouraging activity, using modeling and illustration, and personalizing—were necessary but not sufficient, however. Our informants told us that they further needed to *link experience to abstract conceptualizations.* This was the last subcategory in the overall experiential learning category. Students wanted instructors to help them make links between concrete instances and abstract concepts. One informant suggested that instructors "Put ideas into play in the classroom. Not just [ask], 'What are the stages of Erikson?' I think that anyone can memorize that. But understanding it and being able to apply it to the client you may have is important." Our informants remind us to enact Kolb's (1984) learning cycle in courses and in the program, that is, to move from concrete experience, to reflective observation, to abstract conceptualization, and to active experimentation, which then brings on further concrete experience. That cycle can be generated in any course.

Opportunities for Independent Thinking

Informants found opportunities for independent thinking to be central to the personal changes that resulted from their studies. We found no sub-categories under this theme. We defined independent thinking as *identifying one's own perspectives through deliberative activity, evidence gathering, and drawing tentative conclusions.* Opportunities for such independent thinking contrast sharply with authority-centered methods, such as overly directive academic advising, unnecessarily didactic instruction, and clinical case supervision characterized by the "pronouncing" of case conceptualizations and treatment plans *for* supervisees. Students identified the following specific independence-promoting methods.

• *Inquiry methods of teaching.* Instructors challenged students to give evidence for their ideas. Example: "I do not need to be spoon fed as much facts and figures. Dr. _____ always asks us to give reasons for our answers. He asked us 'Why?' He posed questions, rather than only delivering information."

• *Projects.* Example: "It has to be being independent, the projects they make us do, the hours and hours and hours of research."

• *Requiring "production tasks"* (Creamer, 199) in course examinations and assignments. Example: "[What were most helpful were] writing, descriptive kind of things, and arguments. Objective tests don't help you explore ideas."

Our informants seemed to be saying, "Make us generate our own possibilities. Have us take positions. Have us show evidence for those positions. This is how we will have to perform as thinking professionals. Don't only tell. Ask. Don't only show. Have us do, and then let us make sense by reflecting on and discussing our experiences."

There is irony in the notion of "independent thinking," for it seems to be a foil to the dialogical world of "social constructionist thinking." How can a mental health practitioner live in dialogue with the world and within her or himself if a "sealed-up" independence is promoted in her or his training?

A dialectical understanding of auto- and social-construction, as they live in tension, seems helpful here. We might look to the constructive developmental paradigm for one way out of this seeming conundrum. Kegan (1982), Loevinger (1976), and others (e.g., Belenky et al., 1986) have described the route to full social constructionist, or dialogical, thinking as going through a hard-earned mental autonomy. Three "orders of consciousness" seem to describe such epistemological development: (1) socially dependent conformism, (2) overly autonomous independence, and (3) dialogical interdependence. Students in each of these stages require different degrees of structure in the classroom. For example, the student who makes sense from the first, conformist, position can be encouraged to move toward greater epistemological autonomy by the instructor's instigation of "opportunities for independent thinking." Previous research on counseling student meaning-making (e.g., Borders and Fong, 1989; Neukrug and McAuliffe, 1993) reveals that most counseling trainees seem to be partially reliant on received knowledge but poised on the precipice of greater autonomy. Educators' challenge for students to generate their own ideas and show evidence for them might stimulate them to try their wings in order to leave behind the ground of conformist thinking.

Supportive Environment

A final condition contributing to positive change in future helpers is having a supportive environment. We defined this last theme, based on the data, as *creating affirming conditions and giving students useful feedback so that learners might gain confidence and be inclined to engage in further learning activity.* As we will explain later, the "supportive environment" notion seems to parallel the Chapter One idea of creating a "learning community" that is, an environment in which all participants create knowledge within a positive, respectful atmosphere. Students connected such a supportive learning environment with their increased willingness to take risks with their own ideas—that is, to begin to construct their own professional stances. Such a "holding environment" (Kegan, 1982) is the developmental ground from which the learner might try risky emotional and intellectual explorations. Thus the positive environment seems to be a foundation for utilizing the challenge of the other three program influences.

We further divided this final category of program influence into three subcategories: (A) a positive atmosphere, (B) peer support, and (C) specific feedback on student performance.

A *positive atmosphere* was captured in the following informant statements:

• *praise:* "I got a lot of praise from all of my instructors. I can think of two examples specifically. One instructor made a comment to me, 'You are going to be good at this.' And then he said that to me one or two times outside of class. And then, in her career development class, [another instructor] made some comments about what she felt my abilities were."

• *nonjudgmental manner:* "[This instructor] is the embodiment of empathy because she reacted without judgment and she taught us by her modeling being non-judgmental."

• *interest in students' ideas:* "I do not think that there was ever a time when I felt like, 'They are being way too pushy and trying to get me to buy into their way of thinking or not allowing me a voice.' Every,

every professor I had allowed anyone to speak and argue their ideas and things like that."

• *enthusiasm:* "That instructor is so focused, so intelligent, but she has so much fun. She laughs in class. And there are many professors like that. So we can be completely relaxed. Dr. G is another [enthusiastic instructor]. I love his sense of humor. Research is a dry class, just like Statistics or Testing. They're both very dry classes and both of them I was really dreading. But they were probably the most energetic classes I've taken. Dr. G has taught me that I can really enjoy research."

• *faculty availability:* "Many instructors in other disciplines are just not available. You can't reach them. They don't even offer to be available. You guys offer your home phone, your work phone, your e-mail. I mean we have every way to get a hold of somebody. Every single professor gives us more than two ways to get a hold of them."

Peer support was mentioned as a second component of a supportive environment. This theme surprised us. We had previously underestimated student community-building as a source of influence. One informant emphasized the emotional support she had experienced from her peers: "I enjoyed the peer interaction because I felt we were all in the same boat. I needed to hear that somebody else was having a tough day. I wanted to hear that." Another graduate reiterated that theme: "A lot of the professors had us do many of the projects together, which got us to know each other better. I could probably list most of the classes where we had to do things that got us to know each other, and from there we developed something else. I didn't realize until after the summer how much I missed the fellow students. The learning experience is partly due to conversations and socializing with them."

A third way faculty expressed positive attention and affirmation was providing specific feedback on student performance. Four particular occasions for feedback were mentioned:

• *practicum and internship seminars:* "The internship seminar was very helpful because I got feedback on my work in the field work there."

• *journals:* "The comments by professors on the journaling. . . . I appreciate the time the teachers took to read it and make comments that show that they had read it. . . . Because if it is something that is a struggle in your life, and the teacher is saying, 'Good insight,' then you feel validated and encouraged."

• *research papers:* "I can't even tell you how many times I called him [the instructor]. Because research is one of those things I never wanted to do. I never wanted to write, never wanted to do any of those things. He was very patient. Every time I showed him the same sheet of paper he'd find different things to look at. So I'd change it again and change it again, you know and it's taught me to be critical of my own work."

• *behavioral tryouts:* "She [the instructor] pulled me aside many times and showed me not what I was doing wrong, but how to make what I was doing better."

In each case, the student was respected as a knowledge creator. Such a congregation of faculty and students is characterized by Chapter One's ideas of "a challenging but non-punitive environment," "allowing the voice of uncertainty without the fear of ridicule," and "show[ing] excitement for ideas and for each other." The parallels to feminist pedagogy (cf. Schneidewind, 1987) are striking. Such complementarity, connection, and emotion contrast with a disembodied intellectualism that privileges argument, separateness, and desiccated reason.

The Future Constructivist Helper

Students "evolved" in important ways during their program of study. They became more reflexive, autonomous, and dialogical. These changes were consistent with cognitive developmental models of how adults can shift from more automatic, external ways of knowing toward evidence-based, "self-authoring" of ideas (e.g., Belenky et al., 1986; Kegan, 1982, 1994; Perry, 1984). The literature on the effects of college attendance on students (e.g., Chickering and Reisser, 1993; Pascarella and Terenzini, 1991) confirms such increases in tolerance, independence, reflective judgment, intellectual disposition, and non-authoritarianism. These are epistemological shifts, from an initial belief in gaining knowledge through external authorities (so-called "silent" or "received" ways of knowing; Belenky et al., 1986) to ruminative consideration of evidence (i.e., in Belenky et al.'s, 1986, parlance, "procedural knowing"). These traits seem to be critical attributes for effective professional work. They must be "cultured" (Kegan, 1982) in development-enhancing environments (Knefelkamp, 1984; Kohlberg and Mayer, 1972). A counselor training program can provide such an environment and maximize future helpers' developmental potentials.

We have called this apparent developmental shift in many of our counseling students "the movement toward constructivism" (Lovell and McAuliffe, 1997). A constructivist inclination might be an epistemological requirement for effective professional work (Kegan, 1994). In fact, I have proposed (McAuliffe and Lovell, 1996) that counselor education might be conceptualized as "the making of the constructivist helper" (1996). Empirical evidence is needed in this area, but logic would hold that mental health workers who can be reflexive, relatively autonomous, interdependent, and capable of dialogue would be more ethical, effective professionals.

My colleagues and I (Lovell and McAuliffe, 1997; McAuliffe and Lovell, 1996; Neukrug and McAuliffe, 1993) have found similar trends in our previous research on counseling student development. The so-called "non-constructivist" helper looks to experts to provide concrete direction and is epistemologically located in a convention-derived world view. Such convention-reliant thinking tends to lead to glib, judgmental labeling of clients. For example, Carroll and Furr (1998) found that authority-reliant students tended to judge addicted clients as merely "weak-willed" and "irresponsible." By contrast, the "constructivist" counselor would create complex and evolving conceptualizations of clients. She or he would emphasize context—the cultural and family environments; individual phase, stage, and style issues; and client inclinations—in developing such case formulations. Constructivist helpers would be they who can think divergently (Dewey, 1938; Schon, 1983), stand outside of culture, take multiple perspectives, and hear others' views; that is, recognize the ultimacy of subjectivity in human meaning-making. She or he would exercise reflective judgment (Kitchener and King, 1994; Steier, (1991), rather than merely applying rules to problems.

We thus believe that the constructivist helper would demonstrate the three characteristics named in this study: reflexivity (e.g. considering the limits of one's own perspective, gathering evidence before

concluding), autonomy (e.g., weighing current evidence before deciding, independent of authorities), and dialogical capacity (e.g.,
consulting with others in framing explanations of a person with an
addiction). For example, a beginning constructivist helper might say,
when confronted with the client who is addicted to alcohol:

On the one hand, I understand that the disease model as an explanation of alcoholism is helpful in promoting a non-judgmental attitude
toward people with such an addiction, and it allows for   physiologi-
cal treatment interventions. Complementarily, I also think that we
need to help the alcoholic explore her possible family roots in alcoholism, that is, use a family systems approach. I also add a behavioral
approach: teaching the alcohol-addicted person some life skills that
she may have missed out on during her years of drinking. No one
approach can capture the whole story of a person's addiction, nor can
any one approach, or combination of approaches, work with all alco-
holics during all periods of treatment. I know I feel most comfortable
with teaching life skills. I worry about my bias toward the behavioral
approach, however. I need to consult with a family therapist and a
detox specialist to gain additional perspectives and resources for my
work with this and future clients (Eriksen, 1999, personal communication).

This "constructivist" counselor recognizes that treatment approaches
are "stories" we tell about the stories we hear from clients. Such a
stance in a beginning therapist is an achievement indeed.

Conclusion: Toward Constructivist Mental Health Education

These findings point toward an isomorphic relationship between
the act of counseling and the act of preparing counselors. This is not
a new idea: Humanistic counselor education prided itself on promoting affect, congruence, experience, and disclosure in training and in
therapy. Similarly, psychoanalytic training complemented didactic
instruction with personal psychoanalysis as a training model.

What might these findings and the constructivist paradigm add?
Simply, they express a more socially constructed, reflexive, experien-

tial, inter- and independence-promoting helper training. Constructivist education puts the learner at the center of the epistemological action.

I would propose that such is not yet common in our training practices. As we have mentioned here and in Chapter One, the halls still ring with the drone of the expert-cum-lecturer, the pronouncing clinical supervisor, and the expert diagnostician. We only have to walk the halls of the academy and compare teacher-to-student talk time with student-to-teacher or student-to-student talk time in the classrooms.

If it is desirable for helpers to be reflective, self-authoring, and capable of dialogue with clients and peers, we as educators must make the same epistemological moves. This is a tall order. In Chapter Ten we address the obstacles and possibilities for such faculty development. Learner-centered, constructivist teaching requires instructor humility and demands an epistemological complexity that will be taxing for most of us. No longer can I, as an educator, rely on the confident expert stance, as in "This is just how I grade. Period." or "Just take my word, the core conditions work." or "We only consider objective criteria, that is, standardized scores and GPAs, in admissions." or "Here is my syllabus, take it or leave it." or "I only take feedback (reluctantly) at the end-of-course evaluation." or "I just won't do experiential activities; they take too much time away from covering the content." or "I only use multiple choice exams; student-generated writing is too subjective to grade."

We often speak such words from an overly autonomous epistemological place. Such a "modernist" epistemology is not adequate for the constructivist endeavor. If we hear ourselves saying those phrases, we as counselor educators may be "in over our heads" (Kegan, 1994), epistemologically speaking, for the dialogical requirements of constructivist teaching. Dialogical teaching and living require an epistemological leap for most adults. They require, in the poet Walt Whitman's words, continually "questioning everything you have been taught in school, in church, or at home." They require exquisite attention to the social and cultural surround, as in the questions "Where in my socially constructed universe did that preference/ bias/interest/value/inclination come from?" and "What in the world of my gender, ethnicity, religion, ability, class, or sexual orientation spoke just now?" Such reflexive vigilance is a hard-won epistemological achievement in a world, and an academy, which values single-minded pursuits of "truth."

Instead, constructivist education asks us to stand restless and alert in the face of any ultimate certainties about classroom method (including any overly zealous adherence to participatory and experiential education itself!), about permanent hierarchies among faculty and students, and about any canonized curriculum. For constructivism is, ultimately, a never-ending, recursive cycle, a simultaneous turning in upon oneself and outward to the world for temporary consensus on what is good and right. This is the demand we make of ourselves if we enter a constructivist universe: constant vigilance, humility, and a gerund-loving being-in-process over a noun-preferring fixity.

Consider the words of the authors who follow here, in this volume. They have engaged in the struggle to not-know so that we might instead know better. If we, in a great balancing act, heed the voices of our students, as well as our so-called "inner" voice, and the voices of our many colleagues, we will offer our future clients a more flexible, inclusive, and humane therapy. That is what I take from our students' reports in this study.

References

Bandura, A. (1986). *Social cognitive theory.* Englewood-Cliffs, N.J.: Prentice-Hall.

Belenky, M. F., Clinchy, B. M., Goldberger, N. R., and Tarule, J. M. (1986). *Women's ways of knowing.* New York: Basic Books.

Borders, L. D., and Fong, M. L. (1989). Ego development and counseling ability during training. *Counselor Education and Supervision* 29: 71-83.

Carroll, J., and Furr, S. R. (1998). *Critical incidents in the training of counselors.* Paper presented at the meeting of the American Counseling Association, Indianapolis, IN.

Chickering, A. W., and Reisser, L. (1993). *Education and identity* (2nd ed.). San Francisco: Jossey-Bass.

Creamer, D. G., (1990). *College student development.* Alexandria, VA: American College Personnel Association.

Dale, E. (1969). *Audio-visual methods in teaching.* New York: Holt, Rinehart, :and Winston.

Dewey, J. (1938). *Experience and education.* New York: Collier.

Gergen, K. (1991). *The saturated self.* New York: Basic Books.

Kegan, R. (1982). *The evolving self.* Cambridge, MA: Harvard University Press.

_____. (1994). *In over our heads.* Cambridge, Mass: Harvard.

Kitchener, K. S., and King, P. M. (1994). *Developing reflective judgment.* San Francisco: Jossey-Bass.

Knefelkamp, L. (1984). Developmental instruction. In L. Knefelkamp and R. R. Golec (Eds.) *A workbook for using the Practice-to-Theory-to-Practice Model,* (pp. 29-46). University of Maryland at College Park.

Kohlberg, L. and Mayer, R. (1972). Development as the aim of education. *Harvard Educational Review* 42: 449-496.

Kolb, D. (1984). *Experiential learning.* Englewood Cliffs, NJ: Prentice-Hall.

Lazarus, A. A. (1992). Multimodal therapy: Technical eclecticism with minimal integration. In J. C. Norcross and M. R. Goldfried (Eds.), *Handbook of psychotherapy integration* (pp. 231-263). New York: Basic Books.

Loevinger, J. (1976). *Ego development: Conceptions and theories.* San Francisco: Jossey-Bass.

Lovell, C. W., and McAuliffe, G. J. (1997). Principles of constructivist training and education. In T. L. Sexton and B. L. Griffin (Eds.), *Constructivist thinking in counseling practice, research, and training* (pp. 211-227). New York: Teacher's College.

McAuliffe, G. J., and Lovell, C. W. (1996). *The making of the constructivist counselor.* Paper presented at the meeting of the Association for Counselor Education and Supervision, Portland, OR.

Mead, G. H. (1934). *Mind, self, and society.* Chicago: University of Chicago.

Neukrug, E. S., and McAuliffe, G. J. (1993). Cognitive development and human service education. *Human Service Education* 13: 13–26.

Pascarella, E. T., and Terenzini, P. T. (1991). *How college affects students.* San Francisco: Jossey-Bass.

Perry, W. (1984). *Forms of intellectual and ethical development in the college years.* New York: Holt, Rinehart, and Winston.

Rorty, R. (1989). *Contingency, irony, and solidarity.* New York: Cambridge.

Schneidewind, N. (1987). Feminist values: Guidelines for teaching methodology in Women's Studies. In Shor, I (Ed.), *Friere for the classroom* (pp. 170-179). New York: Boynton/Cook.

Schon, D. A. (1983). *The reflective practitioner.* New York: Basic Books.

Steier, F. (1991). *Research and reflexivity.* New York: Sage.

Strauss, A., and Corbin, J. (1990). *Basics of qualitative research: Grounded theory procedures and techniques.* Newbury Park, CA: Sage.

Chapter Three

Building Blocks Of Knowledge: Cognitive Foundations for Constructivist Counselor Education

Danielle S. McNamara, Jennifer Scott, and Tammy Bess,
Old Dominion University

Constructivist instruction is characterized by its focus on both the student and the teacher. Constructivism posits that the student, rather than acquiring knowledge from the instructor, constructs knowledge in an environment created by the instructor (e.g., Pressley and McCormick, 1995). The heart of constructivism (at least from the constructive developmental perspective) grounds learning in what the student brings into the learning situation. Students' widely varying prior experiences, knowledge, learning strategies, and personalities heavily influence the learning process and constructivist teaching.

This chapter offers a cognitive psychological perspective on constructivism. Cognitive psychology is the study of the thought processes involved in performing a task, and includes the study of human attention, memory, learning, thought, language, decision making, and problem solving. Cognitive psychology studies how humans encode, store, transform, elaborate, retrieve, convey, and otherwise use information. Learning can be maximized by accounting for these mental processes. Hence, knowledge of cognitive psychological findings can contribute to instructors' understandings about how to effectively and optimally assist students in constructing knowledge and skills (e.g., Hacker, Dunlosky, and Graesser, 1998; Resnick, 1989).

In this chapter, we present a brief introduction to the research in cognitive psychology, including research on the importance of active processing for memory and learning. We also provide five cognitive learning principles, referred to as "building blocks of knowledge construction," which are supported by both laboratory and applied research in cognitive psychology. The research supporting these building blocks lends empirical support to constructivist approaches to classroom teaching.

Early Research in Cognitive Psychology

One goal of cognitive psychology is to develop a better understanding of human learning and memory (e.g., Healy and McNamara, 1996). Early in the history of psychology, concepts of learning and memory were driven by behavioristic principles. These initial principles revolved around notions of conditioning and the causal relationship between a stimulus and a response, stressing only the influence of the environment on an individual. Early behaviorism ignored the internal workings of the mind, referring to the mind as the "little black box," because such workings were unobservable and considered outside the realm of science (e.g., Gardner, 1985).

Despite their many valuable contributions, behavioristic principles failed to provide us with a framework for understanding the complexities of human learning and memory, not to mention principles of instruction. The notion of learning as the passive passage of information from one source to another was not helpful for understanding the type of knowledge construction human beings strive to achieve and to promote. However, the limitations found in behaviorist research spurred the birth of what today is referred to as cognitive psychology (e.g., Gardner, 1985).

A Key to Learning: Active Processing

Cognitive psychology progressed from the behaviorist emphasis on passive memorization to exploring active processing—the interaction between the learner and the new information. Numerous cognitive studies have supported the positive effects of active processing on memory and challenged behaviorism's notion of "the little black box," i.e., the unknowable, and, to behaviorists, uninteresting, mind. Research on active processing indicates that the more semantically complex (i.e., conceptually meaningful) the thought processes involved when learning new information, the greater the likelihood that the information will be integrated into long-term memory. Four useful notions under active processing are: semantic processing, the generation effect, encoding specificity, and mnemonics. Each can be explicitly applied to counselor education. Following is a brief description of these factors in active processing and their application to teaching and learning.

Semantic Processes

Craik and his colleagues were among the first to experimentally investigate the utility of semantic processing during learning (Craik and Lockhart, 1972; Craik and Tulving, 1975). Their experimental results indicated that semantic processing (i.e., having a meaningful context for an idea) involved greater depth than phonemic processing (i.e., thinking about the idea in terms of how it sounds), which in turn had a greater depth than structural processing (i.e., thinking about the idea in terms of how it looks when written). They found that the degree of active processing induced during learning predicted the probability of later recalling a target word. Most importantly, these researchers demonstrated that rote rehearsal (i.e., repeating information without thought to meaning) was the most ineffective method for learning (e.g., Craik and Watkins, 1973). In sum, the more semantically complex (i.e., conceptually meaningful) the thought processes involved when learning new information, the greater the likelihood that the information will be remembered and integrated into the individual's memory. Learners benefit from seeing the connections among ideas and the larger context that they fit into. Thus we can fit "cognitive-behavioral" therapy into the larger context of behaviorism.

The Generation Effect

The generation effect is another finding from cognitive research that points to the importance of active processing during learning. The generation effect refers to learners remembering self-produced information better than information that is simply copied or read (e.g., McNamara, 1995; McNamara and Healy, 1995; Slamecka, 1966; Slamecka and Graf, 1978). Slamecka and Graf established that when participants are given the task of generating a target word from a cue and a word fragment (e.g., hot—c_ld), they better remember the target words (i.e., cold) than if they simply read the intact words. In sum, when participants generate target information, rather than merely reading it, they recall it better afterward. Since Slamecka and Graf's landmark study, the generation effect has become well established across a wide range of stimuli types and experimental manipulations and is widely cited as a source of evidence for the critical role of active processing during learning. For example, in internship seminar, it is better for students to generate a case conceptualization than to be given one, at least some of the time.

Encoding Specificity

Encoding specificity is an important caveat to the generation effect (e.g., Jacoby, 1983; Tulving, 1983). This notion means that the match, in terms of mental processes involved, between a task, such as generating or reading information, and how memory for that task is tested impacts the degree of advantage displayed by each learning condition. For example, a "generation advantage" is more likely when the retention test taps into the same mental processes—retrieving or recalling the information—that were used during the generation task. On the other hand, a "read advantage" will be evident if the retention test taps into the same mental processes—reading—that were used during the read task. Instructors would thus do well to match testing procedures to learning procedures if they want a true reflection of the learning achievements (e.g., Healy and Bourne, 1995; Healy and Sinclair, 1996; Healy, King, Clawson, Sinclair, Rickard, Crutcher, Ericsson, and Bourne, 1995). For example, it behooves instructors of counseling skills to test progress via performance in interviews rather than on conceptual understanding of interviewing skills concepts.

Mnemonics

The importance of active processing is also reflected in the benefits provided by simple memory aids, called mnemonics. Cognitive research has repeatedly demonstrated the benefits of mnemonics for enhancing memory (e.g., Bower, 1970; Bower and Clark, 1969). Mnemonics are generally effective because they increase active processing of the words (or phrases) and render them more meaningful by linking them to familiar concepts in memory. In addition, mnemonics often use mental imaging (e.g., Bower, 1972). Images not only render the information more meaningful, but they provide an additional route for "finding" information in memory (e.g., Paivio, 1971). The more meaningful links exist to the information we need to remember, the greater the likelihood it can be retrieved. Lazarus's acronym "BASIC 10" immediately comes to mind as a useful mnemonic.

Types of Memory: Episodic, Semantic, and Procedural

The experiments which generated the above principles require translation into teaching practice. After all, how relevant for higher education is memory for word lists? In many of the studies discussed thus far, the participant received a single presentation of a word list, under laboratory conditions manipulated by the experimenter, and then was asked to recall the list within a relatively short period of time (typically within the same experimental session). These conditions hardly mimic those found in a standard educational setting.

The research on *types* of memory bring us closer to the teaching situation. Tulving (1972, 1983) identified three types of memory: *episodic, semantic,* and *procedural.* The last two are especially useful for educational endeavors. Remembering an episode, such as what you ate for breakfast yesterday, your tenth birthday, or a word within a list presented an hour ago, are all examples of episodic memory. Examples of semantic memory are knowing the appropriate foods to eat for breakfast, what a typical birthday includes, or the meanings of words in a presented list. Procedural memory concerns memory for how to do a task, such as riding a bicycle, composing a letter, or playing a musical instrument. All tasks (and knowledge) combine these three types of memory; but each task generally requires one type of memory more than another. Because episodic memories are more likely to be forgotten, the underlying goal of instruction should be to integrate course material within the student's semantic and procedural memory.

This research on active processing reminds counselor educators that they might incorporate semantic and procedural memory in assignments and classroom activities. Thus we might help students to form strategies or mental procedures to process new information (e.g., present an anecdote before launching into a discussion of an abstract concept), instigate multiple exposures to learning situations (e.g., "read, hear, see, try" in learning interviewing skills), and allow students to make errors during learning (e.g., have practice sessions with feedback). Research supporting the value of active processing for memory and learning implies that teaching abstract concepts without connecting those concepts to something the learners already understand, is fruitless for later professional application.

Five Building Blocks for Knowledge Construction

This brief review of research regarding the birth of and the empirical foundations for today's cognitive psychology highlighted one general principle—the importance of active processing. But how can we create opportunities for active processing? This section presents five general guidelines[1] which we have called building blocks for knowledge construction. Counselor educators might consider incorporating these five guidelines in their work. They are: (1) developing and using reinstatable cognitive procedures, (2) retrieving and testing information numerous times, (3) learning the same information in a variety of ways and settings, (4) increasing metacognitive processing, and (5) actively using prior knowledge.

Cognitive Procedures

Perhaps most important to knowledge construction is developing and using "cognitive procedures." Cognitive procedures are actions, mental or physical, that increase the distinctive meaning of the information by helping the learner relate the incoming information to prior experience. Such procedures illustrate one way to follow Chapter One's suggestion to personalize teaching. In essence, cognitive procedures help new information to attach itself to information already in memory. Without such attachment, the new information is only processed in short-term memory and will be quickly forgotten.

The *mnemonics* previously discussed are a familiar example of a cognitive procedure. Developing and accessing mnemonics and strategies, or other means of relating information to prior experience, contribute integrally to gaining skill in any domain and to demonstrating such skills in testing situations. Ample cognitive research demonstrates that when the learner links new information to prior knowledge, the information will be learned at a deeper, more meaningful level, and will be retained for a longer amount of time (e.g., Craik and Lockhart, 1972; Craik and Tulving, 1975; also see Kintsch,

---

[1]Here we only presented a subset of cognitive learning principles that seem most relevant to knowledge construction. For more complete reviews, along with explanations of the supporting research, see healy et al., 1995, and Healy and Sinclair, 1996.

1998 and Resnick, 1989 for discussions of this literature as it relates to instruction). However, demonstration of the effectiveness of such active processing depends on the match between the conditions of learning and the conditions required when testing the construction of knowledge (e.g., Healy and Bourne, 1995; Healy and Sinclair, 1996).

In order to link new information to prior knowledge, instructors may ask students to think of personal applications of the concepts being introduced during class. With larger classrooms and with "shy" students, students may be asked to write their thoughts down. In general, writing assignments encourage active knowledge creation. Counseling instructors might, for instance, present students with a case and ask them to write their evaluation of the case and techniques they might use to aid the client. In-class writing assignments, followed by sharing or peer evaluation, may contribute both to active learning and to reducing the time necessary for the instructor to grade writing assignments. Alternatively, weekly worksheets can be used concurrently with reading assignments to require the learner to actively engage the information and integrate new information into a prior body of knowledge.

Distributed Retrieval Practice

Retrieving and testing information numerous times is essential to learning (e.g., Healy and Bourne, 1996; Healy and Sinclair, 1996). The more times the information is tested (and thus retrieved), the better it will be remembered in the long-term, because every time the information is retrieved, its strength and stability in long-term memory is reinforced. In addition, retrieval practice should be distributed, that is, spaced out in time rather than done all at once (e.g., cramming). Further, practicing skills or retrieving information in random order—rather than in a fixed order—also increases long-term retention.

For counselor education, the need for retrieval practice can be translated into practice tests, worksheets, and quizzes. Moreover, counseling skills should be practiced (not just talked about). This practice might be achieved by acting out scenarios in class and by applying certain counseling theories to a variety of cases.

Heterogeneous Learning Experiences

Learners benefit from learning the same information in a variety of ways and settings, as the authors point out in Chapter One's Guideline Two. For example, a student learning school counseling principles may read about them, discuss them, observe them in a school setting, produce a drama demonstrating them, and debate them among classmates.

Heterogeneity of learning experiences provides a number of benefits. It improves the student's understanding of the material and maximizes the similarity between presentation of material and demonstration of knowledge or skill. It respects the fact that students learn in different ways, that they walk into our classrooms from a wide range of starting points, with different backgrounds, different skills, and different knowledge. Mixing up the content and teaching style may also be valuable in keeping students' attention. Further, different types of questions on exams will tap into different levels of understanding. Finally, including different types of questions on worksheets or exams ensures that each student will have an opportunity to convey their understanding of the material.

Metacognition

Increasing "metacognitive processing" is increasingly recognized as crucial to learning. Metacognition involves three basic processes. First, students need to develop an awareness of their own thought processes. Second, students need to become aware of whether or not comprehension has been successful. Finally, and most importantly, students need to use strategies to remedy comprehension difficulties.

Instructors can increase metacognitive abilities in several ways. First, instructors can create an "active learning environment" in order to focus students' attention on what is happening in the classroom. Counseling students, for example, can be encouraged to think about whether or not they understand a counseling technique well enough to utilize it with a client. They can further evaluate their understanding through attempting role plays and writing about concepts. Second, instructors can provide an atmosphere in which asking questions during class time is accepted and encouraged. Sometimes this requires simply stopping a lecture on difficult material and asking for questions. If met with silence, instructors simply wait for as long as it takes for the questions to emerge. Such interactive, multifaceted experiences allow students to identify areas that need more work. More clarification can take place as students ask questions in the classroom, request more "practice time" through role play, observe counseling situations outside the classroom, or ask for specific case examples of a technique being used with a client.

Prior Knowledge

One of the most important building blocks of knowledge is prior knowledge itself. For example, the comprehension of both written and verbally presented information depends in large part upon the reader's or listener's prior domain knowledge (e.g., Bransford and Johnson, 1972). Knowledge is particularly important for the understanding of instructional textbook material because textbooks rarely spell out everything needed for successful comprehension. This prior knowledge allows the reader to fill in contextual gaps within the text and to develop a better global understanding of the text (e.g., McNamara and Kintsch, 1996; McNamara, Kintsch, Songer, and Kintsch, 1996). The use of this knowledge also leads to a more active processing of the text. Readers who successfully understand text material have been shown to use their prior knowledge to process such things as the relationship between two separate sentences; the relationship between two separate paragraphs; the global purpose of the text; and how to integrate their prior knowledge with the text to develop a more complete understanding of the text. (e.g., Oakhill, 1984).

However, many students do not actively process text material or use their prior knowledge to understand and learn from the text, despite the fact that college courses require students to read articles or textbooks. Various training methods may be used to improve reading comprehension by inducing the reader to more actively process the text and to use prior knowledge to understand the text (e.g., Kucan and Beck, 1997). For example, less skilled comprehenders benefit greatly from inference training, that is, using prior knowledge to fill in conceptual gaps in a text (e.g., McNamara and Scott, 1999; Yuill and Oakhill, 1988). Prompting students to explain the text aloud to themselves while reading, stopping periodically to describe in their own words what they have just read, has also been found to enhance comprehension (e.g., Chi, de Leeuw, Chiu, and LaVancher, 1996). "Self-recitation" also induces greater comprehension. This means that while reading a text, students raise questions, seek answers, compare, contrast, and organize, and seek relationships among ideas. Students who engage in these types of study habits are more successful than those students who use such techniques as memorization or repetition (Walker, 1995).

Sometimes insufficient knowledge by the reader doesn't permit active processing. Such students may need an easier, more explicit textbook (e.g., McNamara and Kintsch, 1996; McNamara, et al., 1996). Instructors may need to have more explicit materials on hand to offer to struggling, less knowledgeable students in order to provide them with some basics before tackling the more difficult textbook. More explicit books may provide the students with a knowledge base to build upon during the course of the semester.

Speed of Acquisition versus Long-term Retention

Often educators and researchers are misled into considering an instructional technique effective when rapid acquisition of the knowledge or skill is observed. Also, in much cognitive research, the testing time is immediately after the intervention. Researchers and educators often don't have the luxury of observing longer-term retention or performance, only remaining aware of students' performance on a final exam rather than students' abilities to perform in the field six months after graduation.

A consequence of employing these learning principles may be a more time-intensive initial learning process. However, the benefits reaped in long-term retention and a deeper understanding of the material should be worth it. Research has shown that when information is acquired rapidly, it is also rapidly forgotten. On the other hand, when the learning requires time and effort, the information will be better retained and more useful in a wider variety of situations (see e.g., Healy, et al., 1995; Healy and Sinclair, 1996 for excellent reviews of this literature).

Conclusion

In summary, we have presented five building blocks of knowledge: (1) developing and using reinstatable cognitive procedures, (2) retrieving and testing information numerous times, (3) learning the same information in a variety of ways and settings, (4) increasing metacognitive processing and awareness, and (5) actively using prior knowledge. Such principles emphasize active processing of material, experiential and personalized learning, linking new information to information already stored in memory, engaging students in the learning process, encouraging questioning, posing questions that allow students to conceptualize information from different angles and to become comfortable with ambiguity, and creating a community of learners working together to create knowledge. These approaches to teaching and learning have been immensely successful and are currently accepted and used by an increasing number of teachers and schools (e.g., Brown and Palincsar, 1982, 1989; Palincsar and Brown, 1984).

Using these principles requires instructors to give up some control in the classroom. Instructors using a pure lecture format generally know what they will say, when they will say it, and how much information they will cover. Once students join in the teaching/learning process, instructors lose some of that control. However, our goal as instructors is, or should be, to assist students in constructing an understanding of the information, a deep, long-lasting understanding, that extends well beyond the classroom and the particular course's domain of study, even if we must give up some control.

Further, using these principles requires energy, genuine excitement about the material, and commitment to making new discoveries. These active learning approaches invite challenge in the classroom. Instructors need to be prepared to be questioned, to step down from the podium, to not always be the most knowledgeable person in the classroom. Once students start thinking, doubting, and worrying about learning, they will never again unquestioningly accept what instructors say. And that is good preparation for the fluid, dialectical experience that is professional counseling itself.

References

Bransford, J., and Johnson, M. K. (1972). Contextual prerequisites for understanding some investigations of comprehension and recall. *Journal of Verbal Learning and Verbal Behavior* 11: 717–726.

Brown, A. L., and Palincsar, A. S. (1982). Inducing strategic learning from texts by means of informed, self-control training. *Topics in Learning and Learning Disabilities* 2 (1): 1-17.

_____. (1989). Guided, cooperative learning and individual knowledge acquisition. In L. B. Resnick (Ed.), *Knowing, learning, and instruction: Essays in honor of Robert Glaser* (pp. 393-451). Hillsdale, NJ: Lawrence Erlbaum Associates, Inc.

Bower, G. H. (1970). Analysis of a mnemonic device. *American Scientist* 58: 496–510.

_____. (1972). Mental imagery and associative learning. In L. W. Gregg (Ed.), *Cognition in learning and memory,* (pp. 51-58). New York: Wiley.

Bower, G. H., and Clark, M. C. (1969). Narrative stories as mediators for serial learning. *Psychonomic Science* 14: 181-182.

Chi, M. T. H., de Leeuw, N., Chiu, M., and LaVancher, C. (1994). Eliciting self-explanations improves understanding. *Cognitive Science* 18: 439-477.

Craik, F. I. M., and Lockhart, R. S. (1972). Levels of processing: A framework for memory research. *Journal of Verbal Learning and Verbal Behavior* 11: 671-684.

Craik, F. I. M., and Tulving, E. (1975). Depth of processing and the retention of words in episodic memory. *Journal of Experimental Psychology: General* 104: 269-294.

Craik, F. I. M., and Watkins, M. J. (1973). The role of rehearsal in short-term memory. *Journal of Verbal Learning and Verbal Behavior* 12: 599-607.

Gardner, H. (1985). *The mind's new science: A history of the cognitive revolution.* United States: Basic Books.

Hacker, D. J., Dunlosky, J., and Graesser, A. C. (1998). *Metacognition in educational theory and practice.* Mahwah, N.J.: Erlbaum.

Healy, A. F., and Bourne, L. E. (Eds.). (1995). *Learning and memory of knowledge and skills: Durability and specificity.* Thousand Oaks, CA: Sage Publications, Inc.

Healy, A. F., King, C. L., Clawson, D. M., Sinclair, G. P., Rickard, T. C., Crutcher, R. J., Ericsson, K. A., and Bourne, L. E. (1995). Optimizing the long-term retention of skills. In A. F. Healy and L. E. Bourne (Eds.), *Learning and memory of knowledge and skills: Durability and specificity* (pp. 1-29). Thousand Oaks, CA: Sage Publications, Inc.

Healy, A. F., and McNamara, D. S. (1996). Verbal learning and memory: Does the modal model still work? *Annual Review of Psychology* 47: 143-172.

Healy, A. F., and Sinclair, G. P. (1996). The long-term retention of training and instructions. In E. L. Bjork and R. A Bjork (Eds.), *Memory. Handbook of perception and cognition* (pp. 525-564). San Diego, CA: Academic Press, Inc.

Jacoby, L. L. (1983). Remembering the data: Analyzing interactive processes in reading. *Journal of Verbal Learning and Verbal Behavior* 22: 485-508.

Kintsch, W. (1998). *Comprehension.* New York: Cambridge University Press.

Kucan, L., and Beck, I. L. (1997). Thinking aloud and reading comprehension research: Inquiry, instruction, and social interaction. *Review of Educational Research* 67 (3): 271-299.

McNamara, D. S. (1995). Effects of prior knowledge in the generation advantage: Calculators versus calculation to learn simple multiplication. *Journal of Educational Psychology* 872: 307-318.

McNamara, D. S., and Healy, A. F. (1995). A procedural explanation of the generation effect: The use of an operand retrieval strategy for multiplication and addition problems. *Journal of Memory and Language* 34 (3): 399-416.

McNamara, D. S., and Kintsch, W. (1996). Learning from Text: Effects of prior knowledge and text coherence. *Discourse Processes* 22: 247-287.

McNamara, D. S., and Scott, J. L. (1999). Training reading strategies. *Proceedings of the Twenty-First Annual Meeting of the Cognitive Science Society.* Hillsdale, NJ: Erlbaum.

McNamara, D. S., Kintsch E., Songer, N. B., and Kintsch W. (1996). Are good texts always better? Text coherence, background knowledge, and levels of understanding in learning from text. *Cognition and Instruction* 14: 1-43.

Oakhill, J. V. (1984). Inferential and memory skills in children's comprehension of stories. *British Journal of Educational Psychology* 54: 31-39.

Paivio, A. (1971). *Imagery and verbal processes.* New York: Holt, Rinehart and Winston.

Palincsar, A. S., and Brown, D. A. (1984). Enhancing instructional time through attention to metacognition. *Journal of Learning Disabilities* 20 (2): 66-75.

Pressley, M., and McCormick, C. B. (1995). *Advanced educational psychology for educators, researchers and policy makers.* New York: Harper Collins.

Resnick, L. B. (1989). *Knowing, learning, and instruction: Essays in honor of Robert Glaser.* Hillsdale, NJ: Erlbaum.

Slamecka, N. J. (1966). Differentiation versus unlearning of verbal associations. *Journal of Experimental Psychology* 71: 822-828.

Slamecka, N. J., and Graf, P. (1978). The generation effect: Delineation of a phenomenon. *Journal of Experimental Psychology: Human Learning and Memory* 4: 592-604.

Tulving, E. (1972). Episodic and semantic memory, In E. Tulving and W. Donaldson (Eds.), *Organization of memory* (pp. 381-403). New York: Academic Press.

_____. (1983). *Elements of episodic memory.* Oxford: Oxford University Press.

Walker, D. (1995). Integrative education. *Research Roundup* 21 (1): 5-10.

Yuill, N. M., and Oakhill, J. V. (1988). Understanding of anaphoric relations in skilled and less skilled comprehenders. *British Journal of Psychology* 79: 173-186.

Part Two

DESIGNING CONSTRUCTIVIST PROGRAMS

Part Two suggests the application of constructivist principles to the overall design of counselor education programs. The extensive use of democratic groups, cohorts, and narrative-generating activities are considered. Specific attention is given to reconstructing the admission and evaluation processes in a more dialogical, multicultural direction.

Chapter Four
Counselor Under Construction: Implications for Constructivist-Developmental Program Design
Pamela 0. Paisley and Richard L. Hayes, The University of Georgia

Meeting the demand to restructure counselor education in order that it be responsive to our post-modern, multicultural age raises a set of challenging questions about ourselves as counselors and as educators, about the content of our courses, and about our preferred teaching strategies. In addressing the broad concepts associated with program design, Paisley and Benshoff (1998) have suggested that transforming counselor education programs must involve a review of (a) the rationale for and the basic assumptions that underlie the proposed program; (b) the content of the curriculum and its program structure; (c) teaching methodologies; and (d) program evaluation. Further, restructuring counselor education to the extent suggested by the various authors in this text will require an intentionality on the part of program faculty that demands the careful integration of theory and practice in program structure, curriculum development, and summative evaluation (Hoshmond and Polkinghorne, 1992; Rest, 1986). In particular, transforming counselor education from an objectivism-based enterprise to a constructivist one will require that we accept the epistemological challenge to ground learning in the developmental experience of our students.

Toward a Constructivist-Developmental Counselor Education

During the past twenty-five years, numerous researchers have suggested that counselor educators take a cognitive-developmental approach to program development (see Aubrey, 1986; Hayes, 1994b; Ivey and Goncalves, 1987; Kohlberg, 1975; Mosher, 1979; Paisley and Benshoff, 1998, Sprinthall, 1981). Kohlberg (1975) advocated for a model in which: (a) counseling itself would be reconceptualized as an educational intervention intended to stimulate cognitive and affective development, and (b) counselor education would encompass training experiences to prepare counselors for these new activities. Over a decade ago, Ivey and Goncalves (1987) predicted a major shift in the focus of counselor education from an emphasis on theories of counselor actions to a new and revitalized focus on human development. More recently, a series of programs at the 1996 conference of the Association for Counselor Education and Supervision were devoted to the use of developmental principles, especially from a constructivist perspective, as a new paradigm for counselor preparation.

There is some evidence that such a paradigm shift is already occurring, as seen in the inclusion of developmental theories in the most recent preparation standards of the Council for the Accreditation of Counseling and Related Educational Programs [CACREP]. Nonetheless, the widespread application of a constructivist-developmental framework to counseling theory and practice is far from complete. Despite a longstanding claim by the counseling profession to be defined by a developmental orientation (Aubrey, 1986), many contemporary counselors struggle to integrate a developmental/wellness/preventive approach into a practice long-dominated by a medical/illness/deficit model (Hayes, 1994a). As a result, counselor preparation continues to be plagued by the same lack of guiding constructs and research that affect other areas of professional education (Sprinthall, Reiman, and Thies-Sprinthall, 1993).

The purpose of this chapter is to examine the implications of using developmental principles derived from constructivism to create a framework for program design, implementation, and evaluation. In keeping with the principles framing this text, we need, as authors, to name our own perspective—that place from which we tell our story. We present these ideas from the perspective of having been participants in restructuring one of our own master's degree programs. Our commitment has been to applying what we know about human development to the education of counselors and their clients (Hayes, Dagley, and Home, 1996).

In this chapter, we address the underlying assumptions and values that guide our work, and we outline the components of our program that can serve as examples for translating theoretical principles into practice. We do not claim to have "the true path" for all counselor educators to follow. We do claim a "direction," however, that is consistent with the principles espoused in this text and with our own personal and professional experiences in promoting the development of our students and their clients. In asserting these beliefs, we acknowledge that our program may not be suitable for every counselor educator or everyone who wants to be a counselor.

Basic Assumptions

Redesigning our counselor preparation program required us to re-examine our core values, to remind ourselves of the central purposes of our work as counselors, and to acknowledge what we believe about teaching and learning. Despite being willing collaborators on a four-person program faculty in a graduate department of fifteen tenure-track faculty, we are not of one mind about the fine details of our theorizing about development and change. Nonetheless, we all accept that we have a central responsibility to prepare counselors who are capable of the level of abstract thought, complex problem-solving, and self-reflective practice necessary to work in a rapidly changing, technologically sophisticated, multicultural society. The contribution that we make as professional counselors to the communities in which we live is reflected ultimately in the quality of the service provided by our students. As such, we are interested in preparing counselors who are up to the challenge of being effective social change agents, in enhancing the lives of their clients, and in improving the world community.

When we think of the best students we have had or the best counselors we have known, certain descriptors repeat themselves. These individuals tend to be flexible, tolerant of ambiguity, comfortable with a wide range of emotions, open-minded, self-directed yet collaborative, and enthusiastic learners. They embrace diversity and can be critical as well as creative thinkers. We believe that selecting such individuals at the outset for admission to our program holds the greatest promise for preparing the kind of counselors that we ultimately would like to graduate from our program. Further, we have some evidence that the higher the level of these qualities among the students we have admitted, the more likely the students are to achieve the goals of our program (Weitzman-Swain, 1995). A more detailed description of the admission process appears later in this chapter.

Our greatest challenge is to decide what to do with the students we have admitted during the two years they are with us. What activities will extend their considerable life experience in meaningful ways? What environments will build upon the knowledge, skills, and attitudes that inform their lives to this point? What type of educators will we have to be in order to realize our vision for their further development (as well as our own) as counseling professionals?

Major Assumption One

The answers to these questions are colored, in part, by what many of us believe about teaching and learning. First and foremost, we believe *that human development forms the basic conceptual framework for counseling theory and practice.* Although past counselor education models have stressed the necessity of conceptualizing counseling practice in developmental terms (Borders and Drury, 1992; Myrick, 1987; Paisley and Hubbard, 1989), our effort is to use what we know about human development to structure not only the curriculum but also the experience of our graduate students throughout the curriculum. Our graduate students are expected to achieve mastery of concepts and develop skills that are developmentally responsive to their clients. Equally important, the curricular activities of the program are intended to promote the development of the graduate students themselves (Bernier, 1980; Glassberg and Sprinthall, 1980; Oja and Sprinthall, 1978).

In our curriculum development, implementation, and evaluation, we have been guided by several theoretical models that are united by a constructivist perspective. In particular, we accept a developmental perspective that is informed by Jean Piaget's (1936/1954) approach to genetic epistemology, Lawrence Kohlberg's (1969) theory of moral development, John Dewey's (1916/1944) educational philosophy, and George Herbert Mead's (1934) theory of symbolic interactionism. The epistemological position embraced by these theorists is centered on the notion that development is characterized by increasingly complex and abstract modes of reasoning.

In particular, we take a systemic/constructivist perspective that is guided by the following assumptions: (a) development is contextual; (b) individuals are producers of their own development; (c) cognition is an active relating of events; (d) meaning-making is self-evolution; (e) reality is multiform; and (f) language constitutes reality (Hayes and Oppenheim, 1997). Constructivists propose that truth and knowledge are constructions within the mind of the individual and that meaning-making and valuing are based on those constructions.

Consistent with the constructivist position outlined above, we maintain that there are certain structuring tendencies inherent in human nature by which people attempt to make sense of the experiences within themselves and of the world in which they live (Bartlett, 1932; Hayek, 1952; Kelly, 1955; Piaget, 1960). The idea of transactions going on between people and their environments leads the constructivist to a particular notion of cognitive development. Each person's self-regulating system emerges as a consequence of new states of equilibrium that were created by the previous self-regulatory system. Therefore, disequilibration serves as a stimulus to development, while equilibration is its goal. Development can be seen from this view as the natural outcome of attempts to make stable sense of a changing world. As a result of this recurring cycle of equilibration-disequilibration-equilibration, development takes a path that may best be described by a spiral. The outer turns are analogous to the person's attempts to integrate novel experiences into existing structures. In each evolutionary turn, the spiral moves to a new level of organization analogous to the movement to a higher stage of development (Langer, 1969, pp. 95-96).

Although constructivists are not of one mind about the notion of stages, the term most generally refers to "*qualitative* [italics in original] differences in children's modes of thinking or of solving problems at different ages" (Kohlberg, 1969, p. 352). Where developmental stages are hypothesized, each of these stages is understood as providing a "structured whole" (Piaget, 1960, p. 14) that represents an individual worldview or frame of reference for meaning making. Each succeeding stage represents the capacity to make sense of a greater variety of experience in a more adequate way. Thus, each stage is a more differentiated, comprehensive, and integrated structure than the one before it. Development represents successively more complex attempts to make meaning of the facts of one's social experience, and learning is the outcome of organizing that experience.

From such a perspective, experience is not just the best teacher; it is the only teacher. If reality exists at all, therefore, it has meaning only after it is perceived. Rather than to educate in anticipation of practice, therefore, our aim is to build upon the growing experience of the graduate student in vivo, as part of a larger student development teams (Edmundson, 1990; Goodlad, 1990; Hoshmand, 1991; Hoshmand and Polkinghorne, 1992; Howard, 1986; Lieberman, 1992; Sprinthall, 1981; Su, 1990).

Further, if knowledge is a co-construction resulting from the interactive relationship between the observer and the observed, then teachers and their students are inseparable aspects of any curricular design. The constructivist's recognition that discourse on the world is socially constructed (Gergen, 1990) points to the problem of creating a mutual understanding of shared experiences across the boundaries of race, gender, ethnicity, or culture. Constructivism encourages the development of a "language of difference" that would permit one to understand the other as the self while also recognizing the inseparability of our knowledge of one another. The problem is that the self as a construction cannot see itself except as reflected in the reactions and responses of others (Mead, 1934). Thus, social problems can be understood as unsuccessful attempts to resolve interpersonal difficulties, pointing to both the potential for and the necessity of further dialogue and personal reflection in order to reach mutual understanding.

As a consequence, we believe that teaching must take place in a broad social context if it is to be effective. Recognizing that people are never "not themselves," we accept that it is our responsibility to be with our students as teachers in every contact we have with them. These contacts occur not only in core and specialty courses, but in the environments we structure, and in the experiences we share as co-constructors of a shared reality. Our teaching extends from the departmental website that describes our program to potential candidates, to the first telephone call inquiring about program details, through a two-year sequence of courses, through the exit interview, and to the graduation social.

In summary, a constructivist view of human development holds that people are able to reason in increasingly complex and abstract ways and that their understanding of experience is embedded in a social context. Therefore, teaching methodologies must vary both cognitively and contextually if we are to engage our students actively as participants in their own education. Similarly, as teachers we are obligated to be clear about our own beliefs, to be passionate about the subject at hand, and to be open to the diversity of perspectives presented by our students. Although we intentionally create educative experiences that will promote this tension between challenge and support, we are also keenly aware that teachable moments are readily available as long as we, as teachers, are prepared to seize them as developmental opportunities. For example, rather than our providing a carefully prepared lecture on ethics, we can utilize the authentic dilemmas that occur in practicum (e.g., documentation of records, reporting child abuse, confidentiality) as a rich arena for discussion of multiple related issues.

Major Assumption Two

A second assumption that directs our curriculum development is the recognition that *group work provides a natural vehicle for social construction and for encouraging collaboration in the empowerment of our students.* Small group interaction can help build the sense of community necessary for a comprehensive counselor preparation program and contribute to development (Dagley, Gazda, and Pistole, 1986; Glickman, Hayes, and Hensley, 1992; Hayes, 1991). Taking social construction a further step, we might conclude that democracy is the social structure that best provides the context for such development. As argued by Dewey (1916/1944): A democracy is "primarily a mode of associated living, of conjoint communicated experience" (p. 87). What Dewey is saying is that democracy begins in conversation because in conversation one must take the other into account. Acting in the context of a public decision-making process helps group members consider the opinions of others and places responsibility on members for the consequences of their actions (Haan, 1977). Asking students to consider the perspectives of their classmates in a discussion places the responsibility on each of them to clarify their reasoning.

An implication of helping future counselors to meet the challenges of a postmodern world (Kegan, 1994) is that counseling faculty need to become developmental educators who are involved in the creation of deliberate democratic institutions. The expansion of the self as a meaning-making system should be the proper aim of education and of a truly developmental counseling practice. By becoming developmental educators within a deliberate democratic community, con-structivist counselors accept the challenge to empower clients to work together to realize communities of their own making (Hayes, 1993).

We believe that some things are best learned from one another, such as collaboration, teamwork, and effective interpersonal relations. Whether through structured interaction in the classroom, task groups within the curriculum, regularly scheduled program meetings with area counselors, or informal social gatherings, group work is central to our efforts to build community (Lieberman, 1992; Newmann, 1993). Group work provides an authentic experience for collaborative problem solving, encourages self-reflection, provides role-taking opportunities, and helps students to test their perceptions of self and others. Our experience suggests that once students have learned to be more effective group participants through their own graduate experience, they are more likely to be willing to lead groups as practicing counselors.

Major Assumption Three

We are also committed to the principles of deliberate psychological education. As explicated by Mosher and Sprinthall (1971): *psychological concepts themselves can be taught as a means to promote human development.* Recalling from Assumption One, human development is characterized by successively more complex levels of reasoning that arise from experience in a social context. From such a perspective, the challenge for counselor educators is to serve as architects for appropriate educational experiences through which the probability for developmental advancement is most likely (Amerel, 1989; Dagley, 1987; Hayes, 1991, 1994b; Hoshmond and Polkinghorne, 1992; Kohlberg and Mayer, 1972; Kuhn, Amsel, and O'Laughlin, 1988; Schon, 1987; Sprinthall and Thies-Sprinthall, 1993; Weinstein and Alschuler, 1987). Sprinthall and Thies-Sprinthall (1983) have identified the components necessary for promoting such development: (a) opportunities for both significant role-taking and guided reflection related to that experience; (b) a balance of challenge and support; and (c) a sense of continuity.

Experience alone is not sufficient for change to occur. There must also be systematic opportunities to reflect upon and process that experience. Because the problems encountered by professional practitioners are frequently complex, Schon (1987) has argued that professional education should be centered on enhancing the practitioner's ability for "reflection-in-action." Because constructivism accepts the possibility of multiple realities, it is necessarily self-reflective. Faced with the recurring possibility of error, counselors—no less than clients—should engage in a process of continual self-reflection. Such critical self-reflection and ongoing dialogue among group members are central elements in democratic efforts to find unity in diversity. In effect, participation in democratic social structures is an ethical imperative for self-development and provides the conceptual link between our set of three assumptions.

In addition to encouraging students to reflect on their own reasoning, counselor educators can challenge their students to consider the reasoning of others. Placing students in situations that demand reflection upon their own reasoning, while simultaneously requiring them to understand the experience of the other *as the other*, has been shown to stimulate development (Kohlberg, 1985). The use of open-ended dilemmas for discussion, especially when grounded in the experience of the students in vivo, provides an opportunity for them to think through and to articulate their own reasoning about significant ethical decisions. Conducted in the context of the group as a whole, this process also gives students opportunities to hear the reasoning and be exposed to the ideas of others (Hayes, 1991).

Many experiences in educational and/or clinical settings provide authentic dilemmas for individual reflection and group discussion. Because educational groups typically provide a diversity of opinions and members who reason across at least two stages of development (Kuhmerker, Gielen, and Hayes, 1991), these authentic dilemmas provide excellent opportunities for exposing students to reasoning one level above their own preferred level-a factor that has been shown to stimulate development to higher levels of cognitive complexity (Turiel, 1966).

Although the challenge and the resulting state of dissonance are necessary and growth producing, they are not without pain or loss. Therefore, personal support for individuals facing such challenges becomes essential. The dynamic balance of challenge and support requires effective facilitators to monitor and adjust their interventions constantly so that students continue to move forward and embrace educational challenges without becoming overwhelmed by them.

Finally, deliberate psychological education does not provide a short-cut to human development. The continuity noted by Sprinthall and Thies-Sprinthall (1983) acknowledges that developmental change will most likely require a minimum of six months to a year of deliberate and sustained efforts. Brief interventions may be appropriate for sharing information or general awareness but not for promoting development (Kuhmerker, Gielen, and Hayes, 1991; Lickona, 1989; Mosher, 1980; Power, Higgins, and Kohlberg, 1989; Reimer, Paolitto, and Hersh, 1990).

Using these assumptions regarding human development, group work, and deliberate psychological education as a framework, we have endeavored to create a curriculum consistent with a constructivist perspective. In the sections that follow, we describe our model for program design related to selecting content for the curriculum, sequencing activities, and evaluating intended outcomes.

Content and Structure of the Curriculum

Our program is CACREP-accredited. As such, we use the CACREP standards as guidelines for the basic content of professional preparation, and we require coursework in basic helping skills, human development, lifestyle and career development, cross-cultural counseling, group work, individual assessment, research methods and design, counseling theories, and practicum and internship. A core content is required across program specialties (e.g., school, community, and rehabilitation counseling) as agreed upon by departmental faculty. Individual teaching style, instructional methodologies, classroom activities, and forms of evaluation are left to the academic integrity and creativity of the instructors.

The Cohort System

Consistent with the assumptions outlined above, we have centered our restructured program around group work with a cohort of students. A new cohort is admitted to graduate study annually to undertake a two-year, structured sequence of courses. Our rationale for the cohort system, unlike that of many other disciplines that use similar programs, is not "administrative convenience," although it does offer that. Instead, we use this system as a more authentic context for learning, as a supportive environment that provides role-taking opportunities and ongoing dialogue with others, and as a place for guided reflection on the experiences of graduate preparation.

The cohort also provides a vehicle for students to negotiate interpersonal and organizational issues over a sustained period. Aware of the chronic lament of developmental interventionists that "significant change might have been realized had we had more time," we have committed ourselves from the outset to a period of two calendar years. Such an extended period not only allows for sustained contact among the faculty and students, but it permits the student cohort sufficient time to develop into the type of learning community that can begin to direct its own education. Further, the use of a cohort group of master's students creates the expectation that they ought to collaborate with others and provides a model for later building of an empowered professional counseling staff (Goodlad, 1990; Human Services Policy Center, 1992; Su, 1990).

Building the Cohort

Community building begins with the admissions process. The reader will find parallels between our process and the "postmodern" admissions approach described by Disque and Robertson in another chapter of this volume. As Collison (1998) cautions: "Admission begins with mission" (p. 1). We have been careful to describe our program and its guiding vision for counselor education to prospective students. In being forthright about the type of program we have and the type of student for which we are looking, we believe that we have been able to more often attract the kind of student we want. More importantly, we also create an anticipatory mindset that both challenges and encourages our students to realize these goals.

We believe that past academic performance is one of several factors that contribute to the likelihood that applicants will be successful in our program. In an initial paper review, therefore, we consider undergraduate and graduate GPA, GRE, and/or MAT scores, and the quality of the applicant's previous educational programs. We also believe that what others say about the applicant is important, and that applicants should be able to identify people who can write a balanced and informative letter of support. Applicants are asked to submit a brief essay in which they identify their purpose for pursuing graduate study, including a description of their personal and professional goals and the most salient life experiences that have contributed to their development. We read applicants' written personal statements carefully and pay particular attention to their stated purposes for pursuing graduate education at this point in their lives. In addition to what these statements tell us about their competence as writers, we are especially interested in what their statements reveal about their level of cognitive complexity; and their abilities to consider multiple perspectives, to provide appropriate levels of self-disclosure, and to profit from past experiences. Although we do not specifically require it, we do prefer that students have relevant, pre-professional work experience, whether paid or volunteer, as evidence of both their commitment to and their familiarity with counseling as a profession.

From the paper review, we invite twenty to twenty-four of the most promising applicants to our campus for a day of interviews. Two groups of ten to twelve each join us for a series of group and individual interviews. The day consists of a group orientation, individual interviews, and an open group. The group orientation provides a basis for applicants' informed consent concerning continued interest in our program. Faculty members outline the program philosophy, requirements, and procedures.

Applicants also participate in two individual interviews with faculty members. While waiting for these individual interviews, applicants meet informally as members of an open group with doctoral students affiliated with the program and with currently enrolled master's students. This process provides a less structured setting within which to assess students on a variety of dimensions critical to their success in the program. We consider the interview day not only as a time for the program faculty to make final admissions decisions, but also for students to decide if the program is the best match for them. Consistent with our view of reality as socially constructed, these interviews provide an early opportunity for everyone to test emerging assumptions.

Although we cannot get a complete picture of every student under such abbreviated circumstances, we do look for confirming evidence of a set of personal characteristics consistent with the goals of our program. In particular, we try to assess the students on as many of the following characteristics as possible: (1) level of self-awareness; (2) capacity for self-reflection; (3) natural interest in and awareness of others; (4) interpersonal, coping, and learning styles; (5) areas of potential bias incompatible with program objectives; (6) obvious prejudices (e.g., racism, sexism); (7) awareness of self and impact on others; (8) appropriate level of self-disclosure; (9) honest commitment to diversity; (10) capacity to profit from and contribute to a group-oriented curriculum; (11) sense of humor, especially about self; (12) willingness to take risks interpersonally; and (13) flexibility and toleration of ambiguity.

As comprehensive as this list may appear, we recognize that people are complex and reveal themselves in multiple ways in selected circumstances. Our effort in these interviews is to provide a broad range of opportunities, with multiple audiences, for applicants to reveal themselves to us. The faculty and doctoral students then discuss all applicants until a consensus is reached about their prospects for success in the program. Ten to twelve applicants are ultimately invited for admission to the program and, based on our experience of the past few years, most accept.

Sequencing the Curriculum

As noted above, the curriculum consists of a planned six-semester sequence of courses through which the students progress as a cohort. In classes taught by the program faculty (e.g., foundations of the counseling specialty, professional development seminar, practicum, and internship), students are grouped and regrouped in collaborative problem-solving task groups as a means of providing the challenge and support necessary to development. Unused to working together, however, each new cohort of master's students encounters interpersonal problems that require new ways of relating. A benefit of these interpersonal problem-solving experiences is to enhance students' capacities to interact and to help them to overcome the isolation that is a widespread characteristic of professional counseling life (Lortie, 1975; Su, 1990). Toward these ends, we have adopted a team development model for sequencing the curriculum.

The sequence of courses is framed using the team development tasks under the rubrics of *awareness, conflict, cooperation, productivity,* and *separation,* as outlined by Kormanski and Mozenter (1987). During the first of their six semesters in the program, students take the basic helping relationships course, counseling theories, and the introductory course for their specialty. These courses provide a strong basis for grounding students in the profession and provide opportunities for them to understand themselves and each other better. This first semester is focused upon developing students' "awareness" of themselves and others and on their emerging understanding of what it means to be a professional counselor. The intended outcomes are a "commitment" to the broad values and goals of the program and of the field an "acceptance" of themselves and one another as members of the cohort.

During the second semester, students take eight to eleven credit hours of coursework, including courses in cross-cultural counseling, individual assessment, and a seminar in their program specialty. The second semester usually gives rise to some predictable interpersonal "conflict." Team building at this stage of the curriculum includes acknowledging and confronting the conflict and listening with understanding to the reasons that underlie stated differences. Desired outcomes for this stage are "clarification" of their roles and expectations for the group and a sense of "belonging."

In the third semester, students complete studies in lifespan and career development and group work, and complete a practicum. The third semester continues the tasks of promoting "cooperation" through open communication and of increasing cohesion among the members. The desired outcomes are "involvement" by everyone in the work of the group and "support" for one another in reaching mutually determined goals. Particularly in the context of the practicum, students become increasingly problem-focused as members encourage one another to contribute ideas and solutions. In this working stage of the group's development, "productivity" emerges as a central theme as students realize a sense of "achievement" with their clients and a growing "pride" in their work as counselors.

The fourth semester includes a research course and an elective. The final two semesters involve a half-time internship placement and an ongoing professional seminar. This period further refines the work of the cohort as a team. Problems once thought to be simple are now recognized as complex. In the internship seminar, goals are broken down by objectives, subgroups are formed to work on related tasks, and milestones are established both to motivate team members and to serve as points for celebration.

The sixth and final semester is focused intentionally on issues of "separation" for the cohort. "Recognizing and rewarding team efforts" become central objectives at this time. Students are encouraged to express their appreciation of one another and to share their experience of having been a member of the cohort for the past two years. Several opportunities are provided for processing, both formally—through in-class activities and an individual exit interview—and informally—through activities at a graduation party.

Evaluation

In intentionally designing a graduate program to promote development as well as provide content knowledge and skill development, we realized that our program evaluation would require special attention. If we accept promoting development as a goal for counselor preparation, then program evaluation needs to assess related variables (Paisley and Benshoff, 1998). Rest (1986) suggested the construction of a research agenda for assessing development that would include relevant instruments to: (a) appraise entering students; (b) evaluate the effectiveness of educational programs; and (c) ascertain the competence of and developmental status of graduating professionals.

Using this model, we are interested not only in the traditional student satisfaction reports and assessments of student competency in counseling, but also in changes in levels of cognitive development and in-depth qualitative reports of the students' experiences in the program. Therefore, we use a multifaceted approach to capture both the outcomes and relevant processes.

All students complete a quantitative survey of satisfaction as well as a comprehensive examination related to the core and specialty content areas. The comprehensive examination is a multiple choice exam modeled after the National Counselor Exam. The satisfaction survey uses a Likert scale to assess the adequacy of preparation and a ranking to determine the significance of various aspects of the program in preparing them to be effective in their current work site. On this form, students are specifically asked to provide a numerical rating and narrative feedback evaluating their practicum and internship experiences and the effectiveness of the supervision they received. In addition to these paper and pencil assessments, each student also completes an exit interview with one of the doctoral students affiliated with the program. The exit interviews are usually one to two hours in length and consist of fifteen open-ended questions about student experiences. These interviews are taped and then reviewed qualitatively by a departmental research team looking for themes and for deeper understandings of the quantitative results. Aside from assessment data, the exit interviews provide an excellent method for student reflection on the experience of graduate preparation and a natural vehicle for closure.

We are also interested in whether our program meets its intent of promoting development. We have chosen to use the Hunt (1975, 1978) Paragraph Completion Test, the Rest (1979) Defining Issues Test (DIT), and The Washington University Sentence Completion Test (Loevinger, Wessler and Redmore, 1970) to assess conceptual level, ethical reasoning, and ego development, respectively. We administer each test as students enter the program and as they exit. Preliminary results indicate positive trends in conceptual level and ego development and statistically significant results in ethical reasoning.

Program evaluation and analysis of data is on-going. We use the results to inform our restructuring of both the process and content of our curriculum. Because we recognize that the preparation program is actually continually co-constructed with our students, we also acknowledge that the ever-changing nature of the two years creates a unique experience for each cohort.

Concluding Remarks

In closing, we are aware of the challenges attendant on the creation of a constructive-developmental, deliberate psychological education model that purports to enhance personal and professional development in the preparation of self-reflective practitioners. In particular, we recognize that implementation of such a curriculum is an ongoing, iterative process that demands constant attention. As part of our efforts to construct a model counselor education curriculum, we are prepared to make multiple revisions before we say that we have our curriculum "developed." Such a goal itself may be unattainable. As Mosher (1979) pointed out, development "is an alternating cycle of reflection designed to produce a more comprehensive understanding of how by systematic educational experience to effect specified knowledge, skill, or development in students" (p. 313).

We have learned that this kind of program development is very difficult: it is time-consuming, has few immediate rewards, demands extraordinary patience, and tests one's commitment to closely cherished values about democratic involvement, participatory decision-making, honoring diverse perspectives, and the need as counselors to be empathic and understanding. More than anything, it demands a sophisticated use of the larger system's resources and a commitment to the process of collaborative inquiry. We also, however, have known the personal challenge, excitement, and reward the process brings. We often find ourselves stretched beyond our current capacity for teaching and learning, and yet grateful to be on this journey with our colleagues and with our students.

References

Amerel, M. (1989). Some observations on a model of professional training: The developmental teacher education program. *The Genetic Epistemologist* 17: 31-38.

Aubrey, R. F. (1986). The professionalization of counseling. In M. Lewis, R. L. Hayes, and J. Lewis (Eds.), *An introduction to the counseling profession* (pp. 1-35). Itasca, IL: Peacock.

Bartlett, F. C. (1932). *Remembering*. Cambridge, England: Cambridge University Press.

Bernier, J. E. (1980). Training and supervising counseling: Lessons learned from deliberate psychological education. *The Personnel and Guidance Journal* 59: 15-20.

Borders, L. D. and Drury, S. M. (1992). Comprehensive school counseling programs: A review for policymakers and practitioners. *Journal of Counseling, and Development* 70: 487-498.

Collison, B. (1998, January). Active admissions: You get what you look for. Paper presented at a training session for The Education Trust, Inc., Washington, D.C.

Dagley, J. (1987). A new look at developmental guidance: The hearthstone of school counseling. *The School Counselor* 35: 102-109.

Dagley, J., Gazda, G., and Pistole, M. C. (1986). Groups. In M. Lewis, R. L. Hayes, and J. Lewis (Eds.), *An introduction to the counseling profession* (pp. 130-166). Itasca, IL: F. E. Peacock.

Dewey, J. (1944). *Democracy and education.* New York: Free Press. (original work published 1916).

Edmundson, P. (1990). A normative look at the curriculum in teacher education. *Phi Delta Kappan* 70 (9): 717-722.

Gergen, K. (1990). Toward a postmodern psychology. *The Humanistic Psychologist* 18: 23-34.

Glassberg, S., and Sprinthall, N. (1980). Student teaching: A developmental approach. *Journal of Teacher Education* (2): 31-38.

Glickman, C., Hayes, R., and Hensley, F. (1992). Site-based facilitation of empowered schools: Complexities and issues for staff developers. *Journal of Staff Development* 32 (2): 22-27.

Goodlad, J. (1990). Studying the education of educators: From conception to findings. *Phi Delta Kappan* 70 (9): 698-701.

Haan, N. (1977). Two moralities in action contexts: Relationships to thought, ego regulations, and development. *Journal of Personality and Social Psychology* 36: 286-305.

Hayek, F. A. (1952). *The sensory order.* Chicago: University of Chicago Press.

Hayes, R. L. (1991). Group work and the teaching of ethics. *Journal for Specialists in Group Work* 16: 24-31.

_____. (1993). A facilitative role for counselors in restructuring schools. *Journal of Humanistic Education and Development* 31: 156-162.

_____. (1994a). Counseling in the postmodern world: Origins and implications of a constructivist developmental approach. *Counseling and Human Development* 26 (6): 1-12.

_____. (1994b). The legacy of Lawrence Kohlberg: Implications for counseling and human development. *Journal of Counseling and Development* 72: 261-267.

Hayes, R. L., Dagley, J. C., and Horne, A. M. (1996). Restructuring school counselor education: Work in progress. *Journal for Counseling and Development* 74: 378-384.

Hayes, R. L., and Oppenheim, R. (1997). Constructivism: Reality is what you make it. In T. Sexton, and B. Griffin, (Eds.), *Constructivist thinking in counseling practice, research, and training* (pp. 19-40). New York: Teachers College, Columbia University Press.

Hoshmand, L. (1991). Clinical inquiry as scientific training. *The Counseling Psychologist* 19: 431-453.

Hoshmond, L., and Polkinghorne, D. (1992). Redefining the science-practitioner relationship and professional training. *American Psychologist* 47: 55-56.

Howard, G. (1986). *Dare we develop a human science?* Notre Dame, IN: Academic Publications.

Human Services Policy Center. (August 1992). Training for interprofessional collaboration for client responsive, integrated services. Unpublished manuscript, University of Washington, Seattle.

Hunt, D. (1975). Person-environment interaction: A challenge found wanting before it was tried. *Review of Educational Research* 45: 209-230.

Hunt, D. E. (1978). Theorists are persons, too: On preaching what you practice. In C. Parker (Ed.), *Encouraging student development in college*. Minneapolis: University of Minnesota Press.

Ivey, A.. E., and Goncalves, O.F. (1988). Developmental therapy: Integrating developmental processes into the clinical practice. *Journal of Counseling and Development* 66: 406-413.

Kelly, G. A. (1955). *The psychology of personal constructs.* New York: Norton.

Kohlberg, L. (1969). Stage and sequence: The cognitive-developmental approach to socialization. In D. Goslin (Ed.)., *Handbook of socialization theory and research* (pp. 347-480). Chicago: Rand McNally.

_____. (1975). Counseling and counselor education: A developmental approach. *Counselor Education and Supervision* 14: 250-256.

_____. (1985). The just community approach to moral education in theory and practice. In M. M. Berkowitz and F. Oser (Eds.), *Moral education: Theory and application* (pp. 27-88). Hillsdale, NJ: Erlbaum.

Kohlberg, L., and Mayer, R. (1972). Development as the aim of education. *Harvard Educational Review* 42: 449-496.

Kormanski, C., and Mozenter, A. (1987). A new model of team building: A technology for today and tomorrow. *The 1987 Annual: Developing Human Resources.* La Jolla, CA: University Associates.

Kuhmerker, L., Gielen, U., and Hayes, R. (1991). *The Kohlberg Legacy for the helping professions.* Birmingham, AL: R.E.P. Books.

Kuhn, D., Amel, E., and O'Loughlin, M. (1988). *The development of scientific thinking skills.* San Diego, CA: Academic Press.

Langer, J. (1969). *Theories of development.* New York: Holt, Rinehart, and Winston.

Lickona, T. (1989). *Educating for character: How our schools can teach respect and responsibility.* New York: Bantam Books.

Lieberman, A. (1992). The meaning of scholarly activity and the building of community. *Educational Researcher* 21 (6): pp. 5-12.

Loevinger, J., Wessler, R., and Redmore, C. (1970). Measuring ego development. San Francisco: Jossey-Bass.

Lortie, D. (1975). *Schoolteacher: A sociological study.* Chicago: University of Chicago.

Mead, G. H. (1934). *Mind, self, and society.* Chicago: University of Chicago Press.

Mosher, R. L. (1979). Funny things happen on the way to curriculum development. In R. L. Mosher (Ed.), *Adolescents' develop-*

ment and education: A Janus Knot (pp. 306-326). Berkeley, CA: McCutchan.

Mosher, R. (1980). *Moral education: A first generation of research and development.* New York: Praeger.

Mosher, R., and Sprinthall, N. (1971). Psychological education: A means to promote personal development during adolescence. *The Counseling Psychologist* 2 (4): 3-82.

Myers, I. B., and McCaulley, M. H. (1985). *Manual for the Myers-Briggs Indicator: A guide to the development and use of the MBTI.* Palo Alto, CA: Consulting Psychologists Press.

Myrick, R. (1987). *Developmental guidance and counseling: A practical approach.* Minneapolis, MN: Educational Media Corporation.

Newmann, F. (1993). Beyond common sense in educational restructuring: The issues of content and linkage. *Educational Researcher* 22 (2): 4-13, 22.

Oja, S., and Sprinthall, N. (1978). Psychological and moral development in teachers. In N. Sprinthall and R. Mosher (Eds.), *Value development as the aim of education* (pp. 117-134). Schenectady, NY: Character Research Press.

Paisley, P. (1990). Counselor involvement in promoting the development of beginning teachers. *Journal of Humanistic Education and Development* 29: 20-31.

Paisley, P., and Benshoff, J. (1998). A developmental focus: Implications for counselor education. *Canadian Journal of Counselling* 32: 27-36.

Paisley, P., and Hubbard, G. (1989). School counseling: State officials' perceptions of certification and employment trends. *Counselor Education and Supervision* 29: 60-70.

Piaget, J. (1954). *The origins of intelligence in children.* New York: International Universities Press. (Original work published 1936).

_____. (1960). The general problem of the psychological development of the child. In J. M. Tanner and B. Inhelder (Eds.), *Discussion on child development: A consideration of the biological, psychological, and cultural approaches to the understanding of human development and behavior* (Vol. 4). New York: International Universities Press.

Power, C., Higgins, A., and Kohlberg, L. (1989). *Lawrence Kohlberg's approach to moral education.* New York: Columbia University Press.

Reimer, J., Paolitto, D., and Hersh, R. (1990). *Promoting moral growth from Piaget to Kohlberg* (2nd ed.). Prospect Heights, IL: Waveland Press.

Rest, J. (1979). *Development in judging moral issues.* Minneapolis: University of Minnesota Press.

_____. (1986). Moral development: Advances in research and theory. New York: Praeger.

Schon, D. (1987). *Educating the reflective practitioner.* San Francisco: Jossey-Bass.

Sprinthall, N. (1981). A new model for research in the service of guidance and counseling. *Personnel and Guidance Journal* 59: 487-493.

Sprinthall, N. A., and Thies-Sprinthall, L. (1983). The teacher as adult learner: A cognitive developmental view. In G. Griffin (Ed.), *Staff Development* (pp. 13-35). Chicago: National Society for the Study of Education.

Sprinthall, N., Reiman, A., and Thies-Sprinthall, L. (1993). Role-taking and reflection: Promoting the conceptual and moral development of teachers. *Learning and Individual Differences* 5 (4): 283-299.

Sprinthall, N., and Thies-Sprinthall, L. (April 1993). Teacher development and democratic schooling: Necessary conditions for school reform. Paper presented at the Russian-American Conference on the Contemporary School, Moscow, Russia.

Su, Z. (1990). The function of the peer group in teacher socialization. *Phi Delta Kappan* 70 (9): 723-727.

Turiel, E. (1966). An experimental test of the sequentiality of developmental stages in the child's moral judgments. *Journal of Personality and Social Psychology* 3: 611-618.

Weinstein, G., and Alschuler, A. (1987). Educating and counseling for self knowledge development. *Journal of Counseling and Development* 64: 19-25.

Weitzman-Swain, A. (1995). *The influence of interactive journal writing on the self-development, self-reflective ability, and empathy ratings of counselors in training.* Unpublished doctoral dissertation, The University of Georgia, Athens.

Chapter Five

The Storying[1] of Professional Development

John Winslade, Kathie Crocket, Gerald Monk and Wendy Drewery,
University of Waikato, New Zealand

A question we are sometimes asked as counselor educators is, "Do you have a professional practice?" It is a valid question, asking whether we continue to practice counseling as well as teach it. At issue is our credibility in relation to what we teach. To be sure, we do need to continue to find opportunities, as time allows, to keep in practice as counseling practitioners in order to keep our teaching up-to-date.

However, we have gradually become more concerned with what this question excludes. The question assumes that the work of counselor education is not itself a practice. George Bernard Shaw's aphorism, "He [sic] who can, does; he who can't, teaches," (Shaw, 1946) hovers behind such an assumption. In the background of such a question lies a discourse in which sharp distinctions are made between theory and practice. From this frame, teaching is assumed to be about the presentation of ideas, rather than about their implementation. Teaching lies more in the domain of theory than the real work of counseling, which lies in the domain of practice. A consequent assumption is that the teaching practitioner need have little concern with what the student is learning and with how this learning is being applied. What would follow would be a practice of counselor education that features unidirectional instruction rather than two-way engagement or relationship.

---

[1]We have deliberately used the word *storying* as a verb rather than an expression like "tell a story" or "narrate a story." The verb suggests an ongoing process which is never complete and is constantly subject to revision, rather than a singular product which is produced on one occasion.

An Alternative: Discourse

Behind our view of counselor education is a larger discourse on the nature of learning and knowledge construction. Discourses offer people positions from which to negotiate subjective experience (Davies and Harre, 1990). However, such positions can also be rejected. The position we are called into by the discourse that lies behind this question about our professional practice might be considered an "irritant" for the field, one that asks for a fuller articulation of the practice of counselor education. We would like to articulate some ideas about the practice of counselor education, a task that can be conceived of as the "storying" of this work. The verb *storying* is used intentionally, indicated an unfinished, and unfinishable, conversation that we all are engaged in on our educational practice.

Developing an account of a practice inevitably leads to several things. First, it invites us to theorize this work at some level. Secondly, theorizing, or making generalized meanings, leads us into a different relationship with the practice itself. Our practice becomes more conscious or intentional and develops further. These developments then become material about which to make further meaning or tell further stories.

Making such meaning and trying to organize it so that it makes sense to others might be all that theory is (in counselor education, as in counseling itself). We take a narrative perspective on counseling theory and counselor education, viewing theories as cultural products, rather than as grander or more enduring claims to truth. In the activity of counseling itself, all counselors are, we would assume, engaged in the process of theory development as well as theory implementation, even if only for their own benefit.

Like counseling practice, counselor education itself can be most usefully thought of primarily as a practice. This perspective weaves together thinking and doing, or theory and practice, rather than separating them out into different domains of activity performed by different people. We want to articulate therefore an account of the practice of counselor education that builds upon the ideas we are teaching our students.

A Narrative Perspective

At the University of Waikato, we have committed ourselves to the development of a narrative perspective in counseling (White and Epston 1992; Monk, Winslade, Crocket and Epston, 1997; Winslade, Monk and Drewery, 1997). Briefly, the narrative perspective believes that it is through stories that people make sense of their lives. Moreover, human beings "act into" as well as "act out of" their stories about experience. In other words, they at the same time both produce and develop a professional identity and also base their decisions on the most compelling stories available for characterizing their sense of their own competence. Through the performance of stories, we give meaning to the world and create identity for ourselves. Over time, stories develop and take on lives of their own, sometimes seemingly dragging us along with their momentum. In the process of storybuilding (or living), we never, however, start with a clean slate. We receive the materials with which to build from the discourse that dominates in the cultural world in which we live. At the same time we constantly partake in the shaping of our cultural world through the choices we make about how we will live.

This is not the place to develop a full explanation of this narrative perspective. Suffice it to say, however, that we have found that this perspective mines a rich vein of opportunity for creative professional practice, at which we and our students have been working.

Counselor Education as a Storying Process

How do we teach this perspective in a way that does not conflict with the perspective itself? In other words, how can we give an account of the practice of counselor education that is similarly informed by a narrative metaphor? We have been conceptualizing the task of counselor education as that of developing a professional identity of "counselor" in our students. The task of counselor education then becomes one of co-authoring (students and counselor educators together) a story of professional identity development. In order to develop such an identity, certain skills must be learned, certain thinking must be done in relation to current theoretical conversations, and certain relationships must be formed with a community in which counseling can be practiced. In using the word *identity*, we remain conscious of the internal process that students must go through, but also of the social or cultural authentication processes around the individual. The practice of counselor education provides a context of acknowledgement in which such identity development can take place. This context consists of the many interactions that take place among faculty and students in the counselor education program. What we are exploring are the advantages of thinking about students' (and indeed faculty members') professional development in terms of an unfolding story.

Stories are made up of plot developments, characterizations, and thematic elements. Each of these features of stories can be applied in the development of a story of professional identity. Events exist in the life of a counseling student that can be storied and rendered significant in the telling. Descriptions of a student (such as confident or nervous, warm or rigid, outgoing or withdrawn, calm or panicky, perceptive or vague) will be entertained in the minds of students and faculty alike, and these descriptions shape the conversations that take place between them Development of a professional identity involves fostering self-descriptions consistent with the performance of the values and skills of counseling practice. Thematic or philosophical assumptions can be learned, made more explicit, embodied in practice more richly, and articulated more systematically in the process of counselor education.

The story of professional identity development as a counselor might take a number of paths, not all of which should or could be planned for or programmed. Therefore, the authoring process cannot be completely programmed and best proceeds in relation to the unique developments of a particular character's (student's) plot trajectory. However, we believe it is possible to structure a context that provides opportunities for such storying and keeps us, as practitioners of counselor education, alert to the moments that can arise for story development. What follows are descriptions of a few ways in which we are seeking to build a context of professional development in a narrative frame. These ways are: admissions accounts, mid-year interviews, the teaching of interviewing skills, second-year learning plans, final portfolios, supervision visits, reflecting teams, faculty-as-counselor and self-disclosure, and peer self-reflective interviews.

Admissions and Mid-Year Interviews

When people apply to enter our program, they give an account of their personal, professional, and academic development to date. At various points in the program, we create opportunities for them to add developments to these plots. These opportunities include mid-year interviews with each student, faculty mentors for each student to oversee the developing plot of their progress, and written assignments in which students examine and deconstruct plot events in their own lives in relation to social constructionist theory.

By deconstruction we mean the analytical process of rendering visible the taken-for-granted aspects of discourse that shape the myriad aspects of experience. Deconstruction involves developing a curiosity about how things are and wondering about how they might be otherwise (White, 1991). If student counselors do this work in relation to their own lives, we believe they are better in a position to help their clients do the same. Social constructionist theory offers us some linguistic tools with which to make sense of the events of our lives; for example, concepts like "discourse," "deconstruction," and "positioning." (For definitions, see Monk et al., 1997.) These concepts can sit usefully alongside, and often replace, the conceptual tools of humanistic psychology, such as empathy, congruence, self-actualization, or self-awareness.

Storying Skill Development

We also seek to story carefully with our students the development of their counseling skills. This takes place in the process of microskills training sessions and in debriefing their first experiences of counseling members of the public[2]. The skills we are referring to are: careful listening (including the kind of listening that is sensitive to the constitutive, or meaning- and action-instigating, effects of discourse on people's experience); reflexive negotiation of counseling relationships to avoid a "colonizing expert" (Anderson and Goolishian, 1992) stance; instigating "narrative-externalizing" conversations that

---

[2]In our Master's program, students begin early on to work with members of the public in a small way. In the second year they enter into a major internship experienced in a school or community setting.

separate the person from the problem (White and Epston, 1992); and the kind of questioning skills that open up space for alternative stories to develop (Winslade, Crocket and Monk, 1997; Winslade, Monk and Drewery, 1997). Feedback from faculty and other students about the use of such skills is interwoven with the self-talk that student counselors report about their own work. In this way these early experiences of counseling receive significance and later efforts become important for the developments they afford.

Learning Plan

At the start of their second year in the master's program, students write a learning plan for themselves which foreshadows the developments that they are seeking to create in their professional identity. We then invite students to reflect upon their practice in light of this plan during the course of the year, with a view to opening up space for envisioning the next developments.

Portfolios as Products of Story Development

At the completion of the program, students produce a portfolio of work which summarizes their progress to date in their story development. The portfolio includes examples of their work with clients, an account of their overall conception of a professional practice, and an account of the learning processes engaged in to get to these points. In other words, students construct a story of their own development. Here are a few sample questions we ask students to assist their writing of this portfolio:

1. What particular experiences have contributed to your developing understanding of your work as a counselor?

2. In what ways have you noticed yourself being curious about developments in your work? What have been the outcomes of that curiosity?

3. In what ways have you noticed others responding differently to you as you have developed your work as a counselor?

4. How would you make sense of these developments in ways that recognize your own contribution?

Supervision as the Storying of Practice

Clinical supervisors also produce a version of this story of development. When we visit students at their placement sites (in the middle and again toward the end of our program), we ask questions designed to co-author with the student and the supervisor a story of how the placement has been working out: "What have been the high points of the plot? What new aspects of character development has the placement called forth? What denouements might be predicted from the story so far?" and so on. In these conversations, and in social constructionist fashion, we seek out appreciative audiences for the developments that have been taking place. Possible audiences who might be able to contribute to this appreciation and the elaboration of the student's development include colleagues, administrators, clinical supervisors, and clients and their family members. Sometimes we ask a student to reflect upon the significance of comments that they have heard others make about their work. Or, we might actually ask a school principal, for example, to speak about and acknowledge the work that a student has been doing in the school. Here are some sample questions we ask supervisors to answer in the reports they write about students' development:

1. What has been most satisfying to you in supervising this student's work?

2. What particular developments in the student's work have you addressed in supervision?

3. What particular strengths and attributes would you be likely to recommend if called upon to refer a client to this person?

4. From your experience of supervision with this person this year, what experiences of supervision might you expect them to seek next year?

Central to the process of plot development (i.e., of the student's professional identity story) is asking questions that instigate the verbalization of the story. Otherwise, elements of the story can remain fragmented and go unnoticed. In the process of conversation, previously unstoried elements can be captured and built into a coherent account, which might otherwise not be available. Thus, skill developments are viewed as "unique outcomes" (White and Epston, 1992) around which an account is made explicit, in the expectation that action that gets storied will be more likely to be repeated and elaborated in the future.

Reflecting Teams

White (1996) and Andersen (1990) provide models of reflecting team practice that we employ. White's four-stage reflecting team process is one that we find particularly useful for training purposes. The four stages of the reflecting team process that we use include:

1. Beginning with a conventional counseling interview, while a team of listeners observes behind the one-way mirror.

2. Then, rather than allowing the team of listeners to remain hidden behind the screen looking in on other people's lives, the reflecting team switches places with the "client" and the counselor, so that "client" and counselor observe from behind the screen the reflecting team talking about their observations on the session. The reflecting team members—now being observed—are not to set themselves up as objective observers or expert commentators on the work of either the counselor or the client. Instead they should concentrate on:

• sharing personal responses to what the client has said (e.g.: *I was quite moved by the courage X [the client] was showing in standing up against these problems.*)

• interviewing each other about these responses in order to situate these responses as part of a personal perspective rather than as an expert pronouncement (e.g.: *So what do you think made those expressions of courage stand out so much for you and seem so moving?*)

• expressing curiosity about things that were not explored by the counselor in a way that opens up the dominant discourses shaping the client's problems to further deconstructive scrutiny (e.g.: *I was wondering about how all the cultural expectations that influence mothers might have been making it difficult for X to respond any differently to her son in that situation.*)

• wondering about the significance of other possible avenues to explore in the development of alternative stories (e.g.: *I wonder if there would be anyone in X's life who would not be surprised to see her struggling to overcome these problems, someone who has known about her courage all along perhaps.*)

3. Then the counselor and the client again swap places with the reflecting team. The counselor then interviews the client about the personal significance of what the reflecting team has said.

4. Finally everyone gets together and debriefs the process. Debriefing may include expressing curiosity about the counselor's thinking or behavior and asking questions of the client about the effects of the counselor's responses.

Use of reflecting teams in this manner has many advantages. Chiefly, everyone participating removes themselves from the typically modernist role of "neutral observer" of the counselor. Being "observed" can be counterproductive to the counselor's development of confidence and competence, because it invites counselors to view themselves from the outside. Such an external view brings into play the internalized products of the "gaze" (Foucault, 1977), such as self-doubt or feelings of inadequacy. We interpret Foucault's ideas about gaze to refer to the proliferation of processes of "normalizing measurement" in modern society, against which we are frequently invited to assess ourselves, often because we are in fact being assessed, or at least imagine ourselves being assessed, by others in authority. The effect is an internalized social control mechanism that renders people docile by undermining their sense of their potency as they defer to normalizing measurement. Objectivity can be, in this analysis, an enemy of the expression of personal agency. We seek to avoid this kind of personal undermining by avoiding the use of neutral observers who comment from positions of disembodied objectivity.

Instead of the role of neutral observer, both counselors and counselor educators are recruited by the reflecting team process into role of supportive co-participants with both the counselor and the client. From this position they can add to the work done by the counselor (and to the story of this work), rather than critiquing it. To add in this way, the reflecting team has to be "thinking themselves" into the position (and the identity) of "counselor" all the time. For all involved, we find this process to be more productive than taking on an observer role.

We also use reflecting teams to supervise the work done by students in the community. In this process, a faculty member interviews a student in each class meeting about some aspect of their professional practice. Then other students act as a reflecting team for this conversation, concentrating on "appreciative elaboration" of this aspect of identity development. In other words, the reflecting team expresses interest in the developments the student is making in his or her work, and uses questions as opportunities to explore these developments further. The reflecting team again avoids objective evaluation. In the process, plot developments in a counselor's professional identity are co-authored.

At times, such conversations might begin with a focus on a problematic element in such a story. For example, students might discuss the influence of self-doubt or confusion on their work. Or they might map out confidence-sapping turns of events. They might externalize and give expression the "voice of self-criticism" as separate from the person whom it has been maligning, and might deconstruct (unpack) its "thin" conclusions (White, 1998) about a student's abilities. This process of externalizing the problem gives voice to a linguistic device (often an extended metaphor) in which the problem is granted an existence of its own, even a personality, quite distinct from the person. The person is cast as the victim of the problem's malevolent designs, before being asked if they want to take up a position of agency and protest against these designs. In line with this narrative practice of externalizing conversation, the students work to separate themselves from the storyline that produces such problematic stories and to enter more fully into a counterplot which features preferred themes, like competence, acknowledgement, and appreciation. They then connect these themes with storylines that embody them in action. To this end, the reflecting team process works to mine moments of achievement and provide acknowledgement for these by storying them in exquisite detail. In this way the reflecting team constructs a richer or "thicker" description (White, 1998) of a student's work, one which features further entry into a preferred professional identity (that is, one that is preferred by the students themselves rather than prescribed by the teaching faculty).

Similarly, when students bring video recordings of their work with clients to share in seminar sessions, we seek to find ways to get the whole class to respond from the position of (identity of) the counselor. To this end, the class might make a recording of their reflecting team discussion about the counseling interview, which the counselor can then take back and show to the client. Or each member of the class might write a letter to the client for the counselor to take to the next counseling meeting. Such activities enrich the counseling process as well as add to the counselor's resourcefulness. In a sense, the counselor takes back into the counseling room the appreciation and support of her colleagues in class. But there is also a sense that the class members take forward into their professional development an involvement in this counseling relationship.

Putting Ourselves on the Line

Increasingly, we are more willing as counselor educators to put ourselves forward as both clients and counselors while teaching the microskills counseling classes. Such a stance seems to contradict some ethical codes which warn against entering into a counseling relationship with students. In addition, many would argue that it is highly irregular for a counselor educator to become the client of a student in a counselor education class.

However, we think there is a legitimate purpose for the counselor educator to be both counselor and client in classroom work. Being a client enables us to join with the students as members of a community finding our way in the world. Like the people we teach, we wrestle with unresolved challenges, we ask questions that don't always have answers, we have ragged edges, and we struggle with competing discursive demands. We are not modeling the one true way to live, or posing as gurus who have become free of all human impediments. Rather than parading as dispassionate all-knowing instructors, we overtly "get alongside" our students as people, working like everyone else to create a life in the face of powerful dominating discourses.

This teaching approach gives students opportunities to try things out, to take more risks, and to become less restricted by the imperative of getting everything right. We can also offer feedback from the perspective of directly experiencing the effects of their counseling efforts. One caveat: as clients, we are careful not to burden beginning counselors with huge unresolved problems that leave us vulnerable and reliant on the student counselor's skills to assist us to function.

When playing the role of counselor, we also make our professional identities more vulnerable. While we can model the skills we are teaching, we will not always be completely effective, nor perfect exemplars of the counseling methods that we are teaching. In reflecting teams, students are encouraged to elaborate on aspects of the clients' stories that we have not touched on, or pick up on cues that we might have missed. In the process, we are joining with the students as learners.

Peer Interviewing: Questions to Encourage the "Performance" of Professional Identity

In class, we seek to create occasions for conscious development of the characterization of "counselor" in each student's identity performance. One way to do this is assigning pair, small group, or whole class conversations in which students are asked to interview each other, beginning with the following questions:

1. What was the best moment in your placement so far?
2. What's the most moving experience you have had in your counseling work this year?
3. What is an experience of your work as a counselor that you would like to perform more often or live more into?
4. When have you found yourself thinking of yourself as "a counselor"? What enabled such thoughts to develop?
5. In your best counseling interviews, what do you notice happening inside yourself and in the relationship? In your most difficult counseling interviews, what do you notice?
6. What sorts of feedback have you had about your work in recent months? What meaning have you made of this feedback?
7. What sorts of self-talk have you found yourself getting caught in that might undermine your confidence in your work at times? What might be some of the discursive origins (in which discourses) of this kind of talk?
8. What is the ideal counselor like? How do the notions of an ideal counselor influence you in ways that get you to measure yourself in your work? Is this helpful or not?
9. Have you in any way rebelled against any of the ideal specifications for a counselor in ways that you feel pleased with?

10. How does "the gaze" operate on you as a counselor? What sorts of gaze are you susceptible to? How do you separate yourself from these effects?

11. What ways are you developing as a counselor that particularly please you?

12. Has anything you have been saying or doing or hearing in your counseling sessions surprised you?

13. What particular successes from your practicum work would you like to share with others in the group?

14. When during your practicum work have you surprised yourself, achieved something challenging, or described yourself in a new way.

These questions open a conversation. They are not an interview schedule. In asking their peers for an elaboration of each of these questions, students practice the narrative skills of counseling (curiosity, deconstructive listening, appreciative elaboration, "thickening the plot") while they are the subject of the conversation.

In the practice of asking such questions and of developing the conversations which emerge, we believe we are participating in the construction of a narrative of professional identity. The more intentionally we think about our task in these terms, the more focused our practice becomes. In the end, it feels as though the practice of counselor education becomes isomorphic with the practice of counseling. In counselor education, we are working with students on their professional identity development projects, provided that we include a full range of skills, concepts, and experiences in our understanding of what constitutes a counselor's professional identity. In counseling, we are working with clients to develop personal identity projects through which the possibilities of their lives are enriched. However, professional identity development projects are not, in process terms, too different from personal identity development projects. Therefore, the central focus of counselor education, that is, the process of constructing a conversation which instigates a rich description of professional identity, is not too different from the practices that counseling is about.

Concluding Remarks

When we are asked the question about whether we have a practice or not, the answer that we increasingly want to give refers to the related practices of both counseling and of counselor education; our answer does not assume these practices are separate and unrelated. Our answer amounts to an assertion that future dialogical counseling practice is crafted in conversation among counselor educators and students during the program of study. Our experience is that our counselor education work becomes more satisfying the more we produce our decisions about how to act out of the narrative ideas that we want to teach. In the process, these ideas cease to be just a technology. They also cease to be just a way of thinking alone. They become increasingly a way of acting in the world. As our students come to understand this, they often catch the spirit of this approach to storying the profession. Those that do catch the spirit of this work can easily get caught up in enthusiasm for the journey. We find that they then begin to do wonderfully creative things in their practice. Even as we describe this stance in this chapter we are called further into this way of being, since how we describe things, from a narrative perspective, is a product of our acting, as well as an action in the world.

References

Andersen, T. (1990). *The reflecting team: Dialogues and dialogues about dialogues.* Broadstairs, UK: Borgmann.

Davies, B. and Harre, R. (1990). Positioning: The discursive production of selves. *Journal for the Theory of Social Behaviour* 20 (1): 43-63.

Foucault, M. (1977). *Discipline and punish.* New York: Pantheon.

Monk, G., Winslade, J., Crocket, K. and Epston, D. (1997). *Narrative therapy in practice: The archaeology of hope.* San Francisco: Jossey Bass.

Shaw, G. B. (1946). *Man and superman: A comedy and philosophy.* Middlesex: Penguin.

White, M. (1991). Deconstruction and therapy. *Dulwich Centre Newsletter* 3: 21-67.

_____. (1996). *Re-authoring lives.* Adelaide: Dulwich Centre Publications.

_____. (1998). *Narratives of therapists' lives.* Adelaide: Dulwich Centre Publications.

White, M. and Epston D. (1992). *Narrative means to therapeutic ends.* New York: Norton.

Winslade, J., Crocket, K., and Monk, G. (1997). The therapeutic relationship. In Monk, G. Winslade, J., Crocket, K., and Epston, D. (Eds.), *Narrative therapy in practice: The archaeology of hope* (pp.53-81). San Francisco: Jossey Bass.

Winslade, J. Monk, G. and Drewery, W. (1997). Sharpening the critical edge: A social constructionist approach in counselor education. In T. Sexton and B. Griffin (Eds.) *Constructivist thinking in counseling practice, research, and training* (pp. 228-248). New York: Teachers College Press.

Chapter Six
A Postmodern Approach to Counselor Education Admissions

J. Graham Disque, Patricia E. Robertson, and Clifton W. Mitchell
East Tennessee State University

During the last decade the counseling profession has begun to incorporate a postmodern worldview that offers an alternative to the objectivist, reductionistic metaphor of modernism (Goncalves, 1995; Neimeyer and Mahoney, 1995). Constructivism and social constructionism (Hoffman, 1992) are being presented as expressions of the postmodern paradigm. They represent efforts to dismantle a long-held belief in the human capacity to know an objective reality. In contrast, within the postmodern paradigm knowledge is viewed as a process of interpretation and invention, or what Smith (1997) has called "perspectival knowing"—knowing that is defined by the perspective from which it is viewed. This shift in paradigms from modern to postmodern has a profound, and unsettling for many, influence on both personal and professional understanding of such "essential" concepts such as truth and knowledge.

Postmodern Discourse: Inevitably Social

Postmodernism has an inherently social dimension, suggesting that, in Sexton's words (1997, p. 11) ". . . the primary location of the truths we have empirically sought is based in the realm of social interaction rather than in the intrapsychic world of the individual or the true nature of reality. Consequently, choices and decisions that are thought to be made on the basis of truth and facts can be understood instead, as Smith (1997, p.5) puts it, ". . . as saying that a sufficient community currently accepts this information as 'true' or 'real.'" Boughner, Davis, and Mims (1998, p. 3) add the unsettling dimension of this paradigm, "Social construction invites inquiry into the historical and cultural foundations of our views of reality, and the ways of life that these afford."

Foucault (1980) referred to these culturally created ideas of truth and reality as "discourse." He was particularly concerned with the negative and destructive practices that can emerge from professional discourses. Foucault described the process of aligning oneself with a dominant social discourse as "subjugation." In a similar vein, White (1992) and Hoffman (1992) refer to this process as "colonization." Here is Hoffman: "Once people subscribe to a given discourse, . . . they promote certain definitions about which persons or what topics are most important or have legitimacy" (1992, p. 14). Individuals and groups then feel compelled or obligated to live by or even police themselves or others in order to be in compliance with the definitions and standards of the dominant discourses (Monk, 1997).

Postmodernism and Admissions

The aim of this chapter is to share with the reader our efforts to reduce the negative effects of adherence to the dominant discourse on the admissions process, by examining the limitations of the modernist paradigm and discussing our local struggles to develop a postmodern alternative. The importance of this shift for us lies in this fear: As counselor educators, we are susceptible to the ascendancy of our own personal and professional discourses, which creates the danger of devaluing the discourses of already-marginalized groups. Indeed, as participating members of counselor education's dominant discourse, we may not be aware of the embedded definitions or "truths" that we take for granted and the subsequent influence that they have on our thinking and actions. In the area of admissions practices, it is our view that a postmodern/social constructionist paradigm encourages us to seek out, question, and challenge what we have come to accept as common practices in our profession and the socially generated truths upon which these practices are based. From a postmodern perspective, the option is no longer available for us to choose an admissions modus operandi with the security that it has been based on empirical evidence. We must examine the larger social context and also the local discourse in which this knowledge is situated and explore the relationship between what is known and us as the knowers.

In addition, a postmodern view sensitizes us to local variation: different counselor education programs exist in different contexts than ours. Each program carries with it various expectations and interpretations about what constitutes good counselor education or appropriate academic practice. Therefore, it is not our intention to convince the reader about a better way for you to do counselor education admissions, but to ask you to examine your own admissions process by considering it to be a locally situated discourse. We hope to stimulate a dialogue among counselor educators by sharing our "reflexive" admissions process and invite others to consider the benefits of initiating a similar questioning process in their own programs.

Paradigms: Romantic, Modernist, and Postmodernist

Monk (1997) has suggested that counseling approaches can be conceptualized as emanating from three dominant paradigms, the romantic, modernist, and postmodernist. These three paradigms have emphasized self, causality, and meaning, respectively.

The Romantic Paradigm

The romantic paradigm is reflected in our culture in the common, everyday use of the word "self." It has an attachment to a notion of an authentic and dissoluble self which is separable from the taint of social convention. As such, romanticism is wedded to an individualistic ethos. We take the concept of self for granted and might be surprised to find that it is used in very different ways and to very different degrees in cultures that emphasize group and community. In counseling, the romantic paradigm includes existential, humanistic, developmental, analytic, and other theories that emphasize the growth, development, understanding, and expression of the self.

In admissions, a romantic paradigm includes interview questions designed to identify the strengths and weaknesses of the candidate's self. For example, the decision to admit Sue may depend on the way she carries her self, presents her self, or asserts her self. Self-focused interviewers would formally or informally be utilizing a list of terms to describe the characteristics of a desirable counselor. They would be interested in how candidates compared with the list. Such a list might include such constructs as courage, integrity, and perseverance. The self of the interviewer would also be accentuated because the romantic perspective strongly emphasizes looking through the self-focused lens. In addition, the relational aspects of counseling would be valued, particularly the candidate's potential to form therapeutic relationships. The interviewers would rely on their phenomenological experience of the candidate for admissions information. They might ask, "Does she seem like someone that I would enjoy getting to know?" "Could I see myself referring a client to her in the future?"

The Modernist Paradigm

A risk is involved in the use of the romantic lens: it may cite parameters of self as desirable which are narrow or limited. However, this danger can be somewhat reduced by including a diverse population of observers and deciding to value a broad range of characteristics. Nevertheless, the modernist lens goes several steps further toward the goal objectivity. A modernist perspective would reject this type of interviewing as nonscientific, subjective, and lacking in reliability and validity (and legally nondefensible).

The modernist paradigm, in Monk's usage, represents the scientific approach, focusing on cause and effect links between variables that can be accurately observed and measured. The modernist lens for inquiry and description focuses on various aspects of objective assessment and diagnosis. In counseling, modernist approaches include family therapy models based on circular causality and general systems theory, and behavioral theories.

If a modernist paradigm dominates the admissions process, relationship and self-oriented information might be absent, candidates would very likely not be interviewed, and they would be judged largely on academic ability. Admissions would emphasize previous performance and standardized measures. If candidates are interviewed, emphasis would be placed on responses to concrete, evaluative questions. Questions asked by modernist interviewers would generate from predetermined "knowledge" about best responses, much like testing situations in which the responders demonstrate their knowledge or expertise in a certain area.

The Postmodern Paradigm

In contrast to the romantic and modernist paradigms, the postmodern paradigm explores the way in which meaning is created and recreated and the influence that particular meanings have on individual choice and experience. From this perspective, no core self striving for congruent expression exists (i.e., the romantic perspective), nor are people merely a link in the stimulus-response cycle of questions with assumed answers (i.e., the modernist perspective). The postmodernist model is concerned with the fit between the observer and the observed. From a postmodernist lens, the modernist and romantic paradigms lack attention to contextual and ecosystemic factors that address the complexity of reciprocal interactions and diverse interpretations of the same events.

The postmodern umbrella covers approaches that emphasize the influence of broader meaning systems such as culture, community, family, and other contextual factors. Postmodern approaches include social constructionist and constructivist theory and are applied to counseling through approaches such as feminist therapy, narrative therapy, and collaborative language systems.

Postmodern approaches encourage us to take a participant-observer perspective (Amatea, Sherrard, and Rafuls, 1998). The participant-observer position puts observers inside the equation, consciously taking into account their impact on the individuals being observed. Participant-observers continually monitor how they are influencing those being observed and how those being observed are influencing them.

We have found it helpful to acknowledge our position as participant-observers in the admission process. From the participant-observer perspective, faculty members take into account the personal beliefs or agendas that influence their experience of the candidates, the influence of their questions on the candidate, and how the candidates influence them. For example, we have observed that some counselor educators bring with them preconceived negative ideas about candidates who have been affiliated with the military, organized religion, or physically aggressive athletics. Other interviewers acknowledge the positive significance they give to certain personal characteristics, such as "grit," "moxy," or "brass." These anticipatory positions influence the observer's responses and perceptions of candidates and may privilege certain groups. When taking a participant-observer role, faculty acknowledge and discuss these influences as part of the decision process, rather than assuming that such influences don't exist or trying to objectively omit them from the interactions and subsequent decisions. Another way to combat these potential biases is to include a variety of people—current students, graduates of the program, community professionals, and faculty from other disciplines—in the interview process. Including a variety of people in the interview process assures a more balanced, less exclusive perspective.

The postmodern perspective has been criticized on the grounds that favoring subjectivity over objectivity results in an "anything goes" approach. Our experience is quite the opposite. We prefer to see postmodernism as a "we do not have to do the same old thing again and again" approach, and a "we can actually do something better if we aren't locked into reductionistic, rule-bound models" approach. When taking into consideration the linguistic, subjective, and consensual nature of reality, postmodernism compels us to be vigilant about the ways in which preferred knowledge or practices can marginalize alternative voices and thus privilege certain populations. Adherence to one paradigm limits the development of and information available from alternative paradigms is often inaccessible or ignored.

With the romantic, modern, and postmodern paradigms in mind, we examined the admissions process in our counselor education program with a curiosity about how such paradigms have been influencing our practices. We believe that our thinking about and practice of admissions had been dominated in the past by the use of the romantic and modernist paradigms. We wanted to make an effort to design an admissions process based on a postmodern paradigm, specifically, a social constructionist approach, hoping that new experiences and alternatives might open up.

Our Journey Toward Postmodernism in Admissions

Part of what attracted us to developing a postmodern approach to admissions was the sense that it was congruent with what we were already trying to do with students in our classes. As counselor educators, we encourage our students to embrace a collaborative and reflexive stance toward the personal and professional discourses that influence the practice of counseling. We would like our behaviors as counselor educators to be isomorphic with the beliefs we espouse and the efforts we ask of our students.

If we were to accept the challenge of switching paradigms, it would require asking and answering questions from different belief systems than those that generated the original solution, or "deconstruction" of the usual belief systems. Deconstruction is the examination of commonly held beliefs and the search for exceptions and unique outcomes that may challenge the accepted truths of those views and their related actions (Freedman and Combs, 1996). As can be imagined, such deconstruction and the shift to a more postmodern paradigm might generate resistance in well-established academic systems.

Deconstructing GRE Scores and GPA

One of the first factors we examined in the deconstruction of the admissions process was the use of GRE scores and undergraduate grade point average (GPA) as means to predict successful counseling ability. GRE scores and GPA have been a mainstay for admissions in most academic institutions. Yet even if one chooses to use first year graduate GPA as an outcome measure, only about 23 percent of first year academic performance is predicted by undergraduate GPA and GRE scores taken together (Educational Testing Service, 1997). Of course, the very criterion variable of first year graduate GPA in and of itself may predict little about the overall performance of a successful counselor. We wanted to build a stronger link between admissions criteria and ultimate performance as a counselor.

By challenging the assumption that truth is known only through a rigorous method of quantitative analysis (a modernist assumption), we opted to listen more carefully to what postmodernists refer to as the voice of "subjective reality." We began to look more closely at our own experience regarding GRE scores and GPA as predictors of student success. Our experiences indicated that GRE scores and GPAs did not account for contextual factors which affected grades, such as life experience and age. We also were not convinced from our own experience that grades relate so clearly to counselor effectiveness. GRE scores may predict some types of student success, but they don't seem to offer enough information about success as a practitioner.

Exploring the Concept of "Fit"

As we reviewed our experiences with students, we suggested that the most compelling predictor of who would become productively employed counselors and would be most helpful to clients was "goodness of fit" between the graduate and the place of employment. How well the graduate fits with a work environment seemed to be at least equal to, if not more important than, any ability, knowledge, or characteristic they appear to possess.

Further, the concept of fit seemed more aligned with our efforts to explore the use of a postmodern paradigm in revamping our admissions processes. Once we started viewing the world from a position of fit, we favored this contextual notion as a basis for an admissions decision. We did not seek an essential or critical truth about ability. But the task remained: How could we pay more attention to the relationship, or fit, between individuals and their program environments? How would we go about building an admissions process based on such a concept? How would we measure for fit? How would fit be defined or conceptualized?

Maintaining a "not knowing" stance about what criteria were important for admissions was disconcerting. We found ourselves wishing for objective, reliable, and valid paper-and-pencil tests that assessed affective qualities such as relational abilities more than the GRE and GPA might. We looked at quantitative methods for assessing empathy. We thought that at least this could alleviate our anxiety and stand up to the challenge about the objectivity of our methods. However, from a postmodern perspective this did not feel quite right. It was a bit like suggesting that one be more like a man to survive in a patriarchal society. The pull to return to what is familiar (modernism and romanticism) when experiencing a lack of equilibrium was evident.

"Not Knowing" as a Characteristic for Candidates Who "Fit"

We began to wonder if perhaps social constructionism was useful in the classroom for encouraging reflexive and critical thinking but not applicable as a model for making decisions. As Karl Tomm (1998) points out, "Social constructionism is an extremely valuable resource in supporting expansion . . . because it provides a means for generating alternative realities . . . [however] . . . there is no clear basis within the theory to select and act on one possible reality rather than another. In other words, the strength of social constructionism in making alternative realities possible is also it weakness" (p. 183). The question for us became one of how to utilize a model of divergence and expansion for a process of making a judgment that seems to require a model of convergence and reduction.

We realized that a postmodernist approach to the admissions process would require stepping out of our roles as experts who might take positions of certainty. We found it hard to let go of the need to be in full control of the process of making a proper decision, given enough information. Recognizing the relativity of a "good" or "right" decision constituted a significant shift in our efforts. The focus of our attention was transformed from trying to avoid uncertainty and "not knowing" to an acceptance of uncertainty and "not knowing." Indeed, we began to consider how we could embrace and value a "not knowing" position. If we could tolerate the contradiction and ambiguity that would accompany such a position, perhaps we could learn something new about admissions rather than searching for alternative methods for validating our current belief patterns.

Once we embraced this uncertainty we began to pay attention to our own process of not knowing and the effects that it was having on us. We noticed that by reconsidering what it was we thought we knew, specifically about admissions, the faculty began to disagree and, at times, passionately so. Not knowing created a struggle both within us and among us. However, there was a quality about this struggle that felt exciting and creative. Perhaps we were engaging in what Bruner calls the "problem of authenticity" or the "shifting from role taking to role making" (Bruner, 1993). We noted the isomorphic nature of this process with what clients experience. At first we wanted to end our confusion and conflict with a simple solution. However, our experience with clients tells us that growth or clarity often comes only after more confusion. Often it is the increase in anxiety, not the reduction of it, that leads to change. We had been operating under a belief system that at times appeared to value clarity at the expense of growth, a belief that what we already knew might take precedence over what we were willing to learn.

We realized that, if taking a position of not knowing and curiosity is a process that we have found to be valuable, why not look for candidates' own abilities to engage in a similar process of open-ended engagement. By paying attention to our own group processes rather than looking outside of ourselves, we were able to see new possibilities. We shifted our attention from what candidates had previously demonstrated as knowledge or competence to how candidates could learn together with us.

Engaging "Fit" as a Relational Concept

The concept of "fit" might be used to make judgments about whether candidates mesh with our ideas about what is important. This model could result in simply admitting those that fit with our thinking and rejecting those that do not. How could we keep our notions of fit from discriminating against worthy candidates?

Social constructionist theory conceptualizes knowledge as the ongoing result of a relational process and not as the possession of direct access to the "truth." If we were to consider fit as a relational process, then we would be willing to bring ourselves into the admissions process in a way which left us open to be influenced by the interaction. For example, candidates themselves might have some ideas about admissions that had not been considered in the past. However, we are not suggesting turning admissions decisions over to the candidates. We are instead suggesting that we allow candidates a voice about what is important and let that voice influence what we think and how we will decide on who is admitted. Such an approach, based on dialogue, requires the faculty and candidates to identify parameters for a relationship of fit in an emergent way rather than their relying on historical patterns or on one party's expertise.

Our Current Perspective on "Fit"

Gianfrancco Cecchin (1992) has offered a perspective that articulates our current ideas about fit. In Cecchin's terms, fit is a state of activity between two or more people rather than an objective statement about one person—i.e., that one person fits or does not fit. The effort to look for "relational patterns" and not for objective evidence of desired behaviors is what constitutes fit. This relational concept of fit requires faculty to be aware of and sensitive to the influence of their own beliefs and values on how they assess fit, without considering the absence of these values to be the goal. We believe it is inevitable that our actions are reflecting a stand or belief in something, whether we are aware of it or not. It is the process of reflexively noticing our own views and values and at the same time putting our position in a larger context that creates a relational and fluid rather than an objective and static notion of the admissions process. Cecchin (1992, p. 93) reminds us, "Such a position also permits . . . that healthy state of mild irreverence towards (one's) personal truths no matter how much hardship it took to conquer them."

It should be noted that we are not arguing against the notion of using standardized tests or efforts to be as objective as possible. We are instead proposing a larger frame: that we examine the positions we are taking and question some of the assumptions hidden in those position. We are asking ourselves to think about who might be affected by our beliefs and to consider that any one interpretation is only part of the story. We are inviting you as a counselor educator to consider that the stance you are taking towards admissions has no inherent truth or validity to it. We ask that you recognize the risk of modernism: adherence to procedures that have consensual agreement and acceptance from your professional community but which drown out the voices of marginalized populations and ideas. We find that, ". . . becoming free of the co-optive nature of consensual belief," (Cecchin, 1992, p. 94) encourages us to explore alternative possibilities.

Overarching Values

With the freedom to step outside of the confines of consensual belief comes the responsibility for acting on the new, flexible principles that we have committed to. We as faculty began to generate questions about how students being interviewed demonstrated a number of characteristics, such as: reflexivity, critical social consciousness, the awareness of the relationship that they have to the status quo, an ability to approach learning from a position of expansion rather than contraction, patience with ambiguity, a willingness to contradict themselves, openness, tolerance for confusion, capacity for both/and thinking, irreverence, flexibility, adaptability, indeterminacy, complexity, perseverance, stepping outside one's self, improvisation, creativity, and variability. We recognized that these were our biases, and that we would have to love them as we engaged in creating this postmodern admissions process. We then set about the task of creating that process. The following are some ideas we have developed to approach the "how" of admissions from a postmodern perspective. Our experience is that, with paradigms, when we use a different "how" we get a different "what."

The Interview Process

Most of our efforts to reconstruct our admissions process have centered around developing an interview with exercises that allow us to assess the characteristics we feel are most critical for fit with the program and, ultimately, with successful counseling. Toward this end we currently employ four hours of group and individual interviews. What follows are the currently used group interview exercises, as well as some newly developed individual interview questions.

The Admissions Criteria Exploration Exercise

We begin to implement the concept of fit in our interviews by inviting the candidates to share with us their ideas about what is important to consider in the admissions process. Candidates are separated into discussion groups of five to seven people. They record their ideas on large sheets of paper that are later displayed and discussed with the whole group. Through these discussions applicants have suggested that their colleagues will be better fitted for the program and profession if they are: open minded, passionate about wanting to be a counselor, accepting, respectful, ethical, willing to take risks, persevering, communicative, appreciative of diversity, well-balanced, courageous, flexible, supportive, sensitive, and experienced in that will enhance their work as a counselor.

Groups quickly conclude that many of the ideas they have identified as important are not easily measured or quantified. For example, they often suggest that empathy is an important quality for a counselor. We then ask how they would suggest that we assess or provide an opportunity for candidates to demonstrate empathy.

By doing this Admissions Criteria Exploration Exercise as the group interview begins, candidates develop some sense of ownership of the interview process. They tell us what they think is important and how we can create an environment that will give them a chance to demonstrate who they are and what they believe in. Our experience has been that there is a qualitative difference in interviews when candidates are provided a forum that invites them to express themselves rather than one in which candidates are focused on trying to figure out what the interviewers want.

To further create an atmosphere of collaboration, we feel it is important to share with the candidates our ideas about what qualities we think are important in a counselor. This sharing quickly demonstrates the diversity among the faculty and helps dismiss the notion that there is a single right answer to any question that will be asked. The faculty's disclosure also reduces the secrecy, anxiety, and hierarchical nature that typically dominates interviews.

The following are comments that we have collected at the end of interviews anonymously from candidates. We think they represent the interview atmosphere. "I think that this type of interview process is really great. My first thoughts of a 3.5 hour interview sent a bad feeling throughout me. As the process went on I realized it was a very comfortable environment. The interview was also very challenging. I do believe that the faculty could really get to know the applicants in an ideal setting (as a group and individual)." "I think that your interview was a great way to get at those difficult things to measure." "I applied to six different universities (three of which I've already been accepted) and ETSU was the only one that attempted to get to know me as a person not just a student. I am excited to learn about the program and excited that I may become part of it in the fall."

The Admissions Criteria Exploration Exercise gives us a feeling for candidates' values and broadens our perspectives on the criteria that we use to make decisions. We also hope that it sets the tone for the kind of relationship that we anticipate having with students who are admitted: that is, a relationship in which their opinions and ideas are valued and in which they are active participants in the learning process. Further, we anticipate that an interview process that clearly and candidly reflect the beliefs of the faculty helps the candidates themselves make better-informed decisions about how this program will fit with their needs.

Externalization Exercise

During the Criteria Exploration exercise candidates typically identify "understanding of other people's points of view" and "empathy" as important admission criteria. We follow up on their ideas by explaining our belief that flexibility and the ability to take multiple perspectives are directly related to empathy. We then introduce an exercise called "Externalization" to give them the opportunity to demonstrate their ability to see multiple sides of any given issue.

During Externalization, students choose from a series of concepts that are written on small pieces of paper, folded, and placed in a container. Some of these concepts are "power," "love," "feminism," "intelligence," and "addiction." The students inform the group of the concept they draw blindly from the cup. Candidates then talk to the group as if they are that concept. We inform them not to talk about their experience of the concept they have picked or how it relates to them, but instead they are to envision the concept as something that exists outside or external to people. We ask them to consider the concept as a social phenomenon rather than as a personal characteristic. Portraying concepts in this manner requires students to operate out of what Ivey (1986) has described as a dialectic/systemic developmental perspective.

The other candidates, who are receiving the presentation of the concept, are asked to empty their minds of any preconceived ideas about the concept being presented and to ask questions from a position of "not knowing" and curiosity. If it helps them, they can imagine themselves to be researchers from another planet coming to learn about human beings. The listeners are advised that we may inquire about the source of their questions and how it relates to their personal life. For example, we might respond to someone who is asking "Power" a question in this way: "You asked Power about how it manifests itself differently in men and women. Is your question based on some experience of your own that suggests there is a difference?"

We choose concepts that we believe reflect social values and lend themselves to a variety of interpretations. The following is a list of concepts that we use in the externalization exercise: power, academia, responsibility, love, risk, sexuality, patriarchy, feminism, money, safety, beauty, intelligence, privilege, expertise, control, kindness, marriage, mental health, anxiety, trust, depression, spirituality, righteousness, addiction, playfulness, and respect. We explain to the candidates that we focus on their process of flexibility and multiple perspective taking and not on the content of their answers.

To illustrate: when a candidate picks the word *love* the exercise tends to unfold something like this: "I am Love. I am very important to people. They long to have me as a part of their life. I make people feel good about each other. If people would let me into their lives the world would be a better place. There would be no more wars, no more divorce or violence. I may come to you when you least expect it and change your life around." This typifies the responses we hear as the teller identifies strongly with either a positive or negative side of the concept.

Tellers tend to talk about the word from an individually oriented perspective; that is, something that a person has or something that becomes a part of them. We ask and encourage questions that challenge the teller's assumptions and require viewing the word from a social perspective. Examples of questions would be: "I've heard people say that they love things such as their car or even an idea? Are you different when it comes to people and things?" "Have people used you in negative ways?" "I am assuming that you have been around for a long time, how has your role in the world changed?" "What is your relationship with jealousy?" "Do some people have greater access to you because of some distinguishing factor such as gender, race, cultural or national origin?" "How does the idea that you are all that people need influence their reactions to poverty?"

The majority of candidates are able to participate in this exercise with comfort after they see it modeled. Others have struggled. A recent candidate drew the concept of "rejection." She struggled to see anything positive about rejection. She was asked if there were any ideas or practices society embraced and accepted that she would like to see reconsidered for rejecting. She was not able to come up with anything.

At the end of each person's turn, we ask him or her to share what the experience was like for her or him. If it was easy or difficult, we want to know what was easy or difficult about it. Some students have indicated that their concept related to them personally and the exercise gave them a new way to think about it. The following are some responses made by candidates about the process. "The externalization exercise was a great way to bring out people's true thoughts and feelings and also to see how well we are able to feel what others feel and understand their emotions." "I thought the externalization exercise was effective in sharing thoughts and ideas, as well as different perspectives. It provided interaction and eased the stress of the interview." We never use this exercise as information to stand on its own in making a decision, but taken with other factors it has proven to be useful in demonstrating the ability to understand abstract concepts from different perspectives.

Imagery Exercise

We also utilize an imagery exercise in the interview process. The imagery exercise assesses some of the characteristics typically identified by students as important to being an effective counselor, such as empathy, appreciation of diversity, and the ability to understand others.

We begin the imagery exercise by asking candidates to close their eyes, if they are willing, and to get as comfortable as they possibly can. Then, one of our faculty members reads the following:

Please close your eyes . . . relax . . . imagine the world that I will be describing. You live in a world where people of color have the control. African-Americans, Native Americans, Latina/os, Asian-Americans are the leaders, they make the laws, they control the economy. People of color are our senators, our congresspersons, and the CEO's of major corporations. They are our university presidents, our school administrators, and most of our religious leaders. The President of the United States (as with all previous presidents) is a man of color and 90 percent of his cabinet is composed of people of color.

Our neighborhoods and our communities are made up of people of color. There are small, isolated pockets of white communities— usually in the poorer sections of the towns and cities.

People of color are everywhere. When you go to your bank, you know a person of color is in charge and will make the decision about your loan. When you take your clothes to the dry cleaner, your shoes to the repair shop, when you put gas in your car, it is a person of color with whom you are interacting for these services. Indeed, almost everyone you encounter outside of your neighborhood in the course of your day-to-day routine is a person of color.

The exercise continues to describe a hegemonic "world of color." After the exercise, candidates are asked to talk about their experience with this exercise. We ask, "What are the feelings you are having now and were having during the exercise?" Our particular program is located in the mountains of east Tennessee. That area of the country is predominantly populated by European-Americans. Most of our applicants are from the region, so most are White. The imagery is especially powerful and effective in this area of the country. Those students from the dominant culture often respond that they feel "invisible," "angry," "afraid," "insignificant," "powerless," "hypervigilant," "sad," "eager to please; afraid not to." It is often expressed that this is the first time they have thought what it might be like for people of color to live in this area of the country. The candidates of color often express feelings such as "relief," "happiness," "safety," "not wanting to open my eyes— I didn't want to come back from this place." The exercise also helps us observe and listen for the ability to step into someone else's experience and genuinely begin to understand white privilege. Perhaps even more importantly, it lets candidates know that appreciation and celebration of diversity is important in counselor education at East Tennessee State University.

Individual Interview Questions

Until we entered into the deconstruction of our admissions process, we conducted individual interviews that consisted of the usual getting-acquainted, "socially correct" introductions, followed by rather common interview questions. Such questions included, "Why do you want to be a counselor?" "What are your plans upon graduation?" "What are your plans for the next five, ten years?" "What are your strengths and weaknesses?" "Have you had any experience in the field?"

Unfortunately, while the answers were not completely without merit, they often provided little information on the characteristics we deemed to be important in determining an appropriate fit with the program. More specifically, most applicants answered in predictable ways. They desired to be a counselor because they want to "help people;" they planned to get a job in counseling after graduation and beyond; their weakness is "math" (They are worried about the research/statistics course they know they will have to take); and their strengths are that they are a "good listener" and that their friends often come to them for advice. We would not be surprised to find that most counseling programs that conduct interviews have encountered applicants with similar profiles.

In order to generate more helpful responses we set out to develop interview questions which would shed light on characteristics which we felt appropriate for a good fit. Here again, we had to work to see beyond the typical interview format and take a chance that what might appear somewhat unrelated or inappropriate may be fruitful. After a bit of experimentation, we are currently using three main questions in our individual interviews:

1. "What is it that you fear most?"
2. "What circumstance, issue, or crisis has occurred in your life which has challenged your coping abilities and how did you cope?"
3. "Many people who are in pain have been affected by what is outside of them in their environment. We can be affected by racism, sexism, and homoprejudice. Could you talk about racism, sexism, and homoprejudice?"

While we have a general idea of the benefit of these questions, an exact explanation of why we have chosen these questions is difficult to offer. These questions stimulate a direction in our conversations with applicants which was not formerly encountered. Applicants are more likely to reveal whether their approach in handling problems includes the ability to abstractly reason, empathize, and perceive and deal with multiple perspectives of the problems. Interestingly, the question addressing racism, sexism, and homoprejudice, while very straightforward, has worked well in assessing applicant attitudes and opinions concerning the influence of culture on individual problems. Perhaps the lesson is that sometimes the most direct approach is ultimately still the most effective.

While these questions are currently serving us well, we will undoubtedly continue to experiment in the future. Better interview procedures may be waiting to be discovered. Experimenting with interview questions provides an easy place to start for those who are looking for something more from their interview process.

Summary

What we have presented is a postmodern way of thinking about admissions. We have specified alternative ways of gathering information about candidates. Having this information may not lessen our anxieties about making difficult admissions decisions. In fact, greater tension within and among faculty members may generate, oscillating between the freedom to go in a new direction and the security of staying with what is already known. Rather than making counselor educators' lives easier by providing them with fixed solutions, we may have made it more difficult by offering new dilemmas with which to struggle.

We are not suggesting that counselor educators simply mix all of these ideas together, any more than artists should mix all the colors available to them together or chefs mix all of their spices together. What we hope we have done is to shed some light on options which represent a more reflexive paradigm. We hope each counselor education program will be encouraged by this chapter to create an admissions process that best reflects their collective and diverse preferences. We hope we have assisted in bringing other educators to a place where they can "look at their looking" and see how it has been influenced by different paradigms. The ideas we have offered may have raised the question: "Will we continue to base admissions on criteria that are representative of the status quo and the dominant discourse, or are we going to take some steps toward designing a new process?" If that question is asked, we will have achieved our goal.

References

Amatea, E. S., Sherrard, P. A. D., and Rafuls, S. E. (1998). Discovering a choice of lenses: A postmodern approach to couple and family counselor training. In J. D. West, D. L. Bubenzer, and J. R. Bitter (Eds.), *Social construction in couple and family counseling* (pp. 135-172). Alexandria, VA: American Counseling Association.

Boughner, S., Davis, A. S., and Mims, G. A. (1998). Social construction: A family perspective for the twenty-first century. In J. D. West, D. L. Bubenzer, and J. R. Bitter (Eds.), *Social construction in couple and family counseling* (pp. 3-20). Alexandria, VA: American Counseling Association.

Bruner, E. M. (1993). Epilogue: Creative persona and the problem of authenticity. In S. Lavie, K. Narayan, and R. Rosaldo (Eds.), *Creativity/anthropology* (pp. 321-334). Ithaca, NY: Cornell University Press.

Cecchin, G. (1992). Constructing therapeutic possibilities. In S. McNamee and K. J. Gergen (Eds.), *Therapy as social construction* (pp. 86-95). London: Sage.

Educational Testing Service. (1997). *GRE: 1997-98 guide to the use of scores.* [Brochure]. Princeton, N.J.: Author.

Foucault, M. (1980). *Power/knowledge: Selected interviews and other writings.* New York: Pantheon.

Freedman, J., and Combs, G. (1996). Narrative therapy: The social construction of preferred realities. New York: Norton.

Goncalves, O. F. (1995). Hermeneutics, constructivism, and the cognitive-behavioral therapies: From the object to the project. In R. Neimeyer and M. J. Mahoney (Eds.), *Constructivism in psychotherapy* (pp.195-230). Washington, DC: American Psychological Association.

Hoffman, L. (1992). A reflexive stance for family therapy. In S. McNamee and K. J. Gergen (Eds.), *Therapy as social construction* (pp. 7-24). London: Sage.

Ivey, A. E. (1986). *Developmental therapy: Theory into practice.* San Francisco: Jossey-Bass.

Monk, G. (1997). How narrative therapy works. In G. Monk, J. Winslade, K. Crocket and D. Epston (Eds.), *Narrative therapy in practice: The archaeology of hope* (pp. 3-31). San Francisco: Jossey-Bass.

Neimeyer, R., and Mahoney, M. J. (Eds.). (1995). *Constructivism in psychotherapy*. Washington, DC: American Psychological Association.

Sexton, T. L. (1997). Constructivist thinking within the history of ideas: The challenge of a new paradigm. In T. L. Sexton and B. L. Griffin (Eds.), *Constructivist thinking in counseling practice, research and training* (pp. 3-18). New York: Teachers College Press.

Smith, C. (1997). Introduction: Comparing traditional therapies with narrative approaches. In C. Smith and D. Nylund (Eds.), *Narrative therapies with children and adolescents* (pp. 1-52). New York: Guilford Press.

Tomm, K. (1998). Epilogue: Social constructionism in the evolution of family therapy. In J. D. West, D. L. Bubenzer, and J. R. Bitter (Eds.), *Social construction in couple and family counseling* (pp.173-187). Alexandria, VA: American Counseling Association.

White, M. (1992). Deconstruction and therapy. In D. Epston and M. White, *Experience, contradiction, narrative and imagination: Selected papers of David Epston and Michael White, 1989-1991* (pp.109-152). Northfield, South Australia: Dulwich Centre Publications.

Chapter Seven

Counselor Portfolios: An Example of Constructivist Assessment

Debra C. Cobia, Jamie S. Carney, and David M. Shannon
Auburn University

Judging whether counseling students understand theory, research, and other course-related content is a fairly straightforward process. Traditional approaches to assessment allow us to test for knowledge and even comprehension of counseling content. However, counselor educators face greater challenges when assessing whether students can then judge how and under what conditions to apply that knowledge (Carney, Cobia, Shannon, 1996). During the 1990s, numerous calls have arisen for more flexible and holistic means to evaluate the learning of mental health professionals-in-training (Carney, Cobia, and Shannon, 1996; Goldman, 1992; Ryan and Kuhs, 1993). Such calls were not new. As early as 1969 the National Assessment of Educational Progress called for alternatives to multiple-choice formats of testing as a means of assessing learning (Drummond, 1996).

The debates in education and other social sciences about subjective versus objective assessment have also existed for a long time (Peavy, 1996). From an objectivist perspective, one strives for assessment procedures that produce consistent results across individuals and groups. Goldman (1992) described some of the arguments consistently presented by objectivists who are opposed to subjective, holistic, or qualitative approaches to assessment. They most frequently mention concerns about validity and reliability. Such critics of what we will here call constructivist, or qualitative, evaluation, often cite the absence of technical manuals with statistics supporting the use of these evaluation methods. Similarly, Goldman cites the absence of printed booklets, answer sheets, number scores, and norm equivalents in constructivist evaluation, which may imply scientific objectivity.

In contrast, critics of objective assessment methods claim that, while such methods allow for specific comparisons across individuals, their "view" is often limited (Scriven, 1988). For instance, objective measures usually do not assess skills or knowledge in a "real world" context (Shannon and Boll, 1996). Constructivist assessment proponents suggest solutions to the limitations of objectivist evaluation.

Constructivist assessment refers to evaluating the performance of realistic tasks or activities related to a particular domain (Drummond, 1996). Goldman (1992) suggested six advantages of constructivist assessment, and also described the nature and types of qualitative assessment methods counselors might find useful with clients. We believe these six advantages hold true for assessment of counselors-in-training, as well.

First, qualitative assessment methods demand a more active role on the part of participants, which extends their learning throughout the course of the assessment process (Goldman, 1992). Qualitative assessment also occurs in context (real life situations), which allows students to reflect both on the decisions and choices they make and on their real life implications. Constructivist assessment further takes into account the interactions among the various facets of the social situation or context in which the counselor/student finds him or herself, while standardized measures are typically unidimensional. For example, a standardized measure of knowledge of counseling theory does not provide a vehicle for understanding how a student's interests, personality, and skills interact with individual theories.

From our perspective, one of the most meaningful advantages identified by Goldman is that constructivist methods tend to operate within a developmental framework; they provide an opportunity to learn about one's current functioning as well as to prepare for one's subsequent personal and professional growth. Additionally, the assessment process cannot be separated from the learning process. Each assessment "result" leads to an opportunity for self-reflection and additional learning on the part of the student (Nelson and Neufeldt, 1998). This advantage holds true for groups as well as for individuals, which is clearly congruent with the constructivist view that learning takes place in a social context (Nelson and Neufeldt, 1998). As groups of students describe in dialogue what they have experienced and learned about themselves, a cycle of reflectivity may be generated for group members. Finally, Goldman (1992) points out that constructivist methods are flexible enough to apply to people from different populations and widely variant backgrounds.

Our purpose for the remainder of this chapter is to describe a specific method of constructivist assessment for counselor education: the individual counseling portfolio. As an assessment strategy, the portfolio has the potential to make evaluation a developmental process, providing a record of the individual's progress, strengths, and accomplishments over time (Peavy, 1996); and involving the student as a co-evaluator.

Developing and Implementing Portfolio Assessment

Many counselor education programs have begun to consider or implement portfolios as a form of student assessment (Baltimore, Hickson, George, and Crutchfield, 1996; Carney et al., 1996). These efforts are often linked to the widespread use of portfolios in colleges of education to evaluate teachers-in-training (Baltimore et al., 1996; Barton and Collins, 1993; Ryan and Kuhs, 1993; Shannon and Boll, 1996). Portfolio assessment developed, in part, out of the criticism that standardized measures failed to capture the complex nature of teaching and the interrelationship between content and professional aptitude (Collins, 1990; Scriven, 1988). They provide an opportunity to assess a student's ability to both apply knowledge and demonstrate acquired skills in a 'real world context' (Wolf, 1991; Shannon and Boll, 1996). Portfolios also allow students the opportunity to be more directly involved in the evaluation process.

Goals and Values of Portfolio Assessment

Most critical to the successful use of portfolio assessment procedures is establishing the goals and purposes of the portfolio (Carney, et al., 1996; LeMahieu, Gitomer, and Eresh, 1995; Shannon and Boll, 1996). Prior to implementation, faculty need to determine how the evaluation will be used, who will be involved in the process, and what indicators of student and program success will be considered. Faculty might begin by reviewing and evaluating extant assessment methods and becoming aware of the strengths and limitations of current measures. In some instances, portfolios may be added to the existing methods in order to add the dimensions of assessing progress over time, engaging students in self-assessment, and determining the student's level of success in applying skills in a counseling context

(Carney, Cobia, and Shannon, 1995). In other instances, portfolios may completely replace existing methods.

Portfolios include information which spans "courses, time, clinical experiences, and contexts" (Carney et al., 1996, p.124). Therefore, the process of establishing the purposes of the portfolio includes consideration of how specific courses and requirements fit within the overall evaluation process. A review of course syllabi, assignments, and requirements can be first conducted in order to provide vital information for the goals of the evaluation as well as about the variety of teaching and assessment tools which will be needed to achieve these goals. Such a review may also encourage the involvement and input of faculty and students in developing and implementing the portfolio assessment process (Carney et al., 1996; Shannon and Boll, 1996). Further, one of the primary strengths of portfolio assessment is promoting reciprocal learning among faculty and students. As students discover what faculty deem meaningful, faculty in turn benefit from learning from students and colleagues what they find most meaningful.

One of the true values of portfolios is their role in empowering students by increasing their involvement in the construction of knowledge (Baltimore et al., 1996; Wolf, 1991; Shannon, Ash, Barry, and Dunn, 1995). Because portfolios are not only an evaluation tool but a means of enhancing student learning, students need to be involved in implementing the portfolio assessment procedures themselves. For example, students may serve on committees involved in investigating and implementing portfolio assessment (Carney et al., 1995; 1996). Students may be asked to identify assignments or tasks from specific courses that helped them apply skills, use critical judgement, or challenge their own beliefs. Further, during final oral exams students may be asked what experiences were beneficial to their development as counselors and professionals. In addition to providing information about the portfolio process, these activities may initially inform students' choices about the nature and content of their portfolios.

Portfolio Domains and Components

The process of establishing the purposes and goals of the portfolio lays the foundation for the structure of the portfolio. Wolf (1991) states that the creation of a portfolio should not be simply an "amassing of papers," but instead should be a "selective, reflective, and collaborative" collection of materials that provide evidence of a student's progress and accomplishments (p. 2). To accomplish this goal, some structure is needed to define and organize the final product. Portfolio "domains" provide this structure.

Domains are the areas or specific sections to be included or addressed in the portfolio. Wolf (1991) suggests that portfolio domains reflect the established competencies or requirements of a profession. These domains should also reflect the overall goals and purposes established for the portfolio. We have developed a portfolio model (Carney et al., 1996) whose domains reflect the core areas identified by CACREP (Council for the Accreditation of Counseling and Related Programs, 1994). While we agree with Sexton (1998), that the CACREP standards are grounded in ". . . prevailing professional beliefs" and thus inevitably have limitations, we maintain that the standards are a helpful organizing structure for the portfolio. Because the portfolio model is flexible, portfolio domains may be adjusted to reflect any new beliefs that emerge through professional consensus building about core knowledge in counselor education programs.

We include the nine core CACREP knowledge and competency areas as domains in our model; that is, Human Growth and Development, Social and Cultural Foundations, Helping Relationships, Group Work, Career and Lifestyle Development, Appraisal, Research and Program Evaluation, Professional Orientation, and Clinical. For each of these domains, students include demonstrations of their skills and knowledge, according to specific criteria. For example, we specify the following criteria for the "professional orientation" domain:

Professional Orientation components will demonstrate knowledge and counseling skills related to professional development, ethical and legal principles, history and roles, organizational structures, professional standards and credentialing (Carney et al., 1996, p.132.)

Other programs may choose to identify domains using other sources, such as mission statements, program goals and objectives, program requirements, or course objectives. As in the above example, it is important to identify both the domains and their defining criteria.

Portfolio components offer "evidence" of students' competence and skills in the specific domains. Faculty, supervisors, and students work collaboratively to decide what materials best demonstrate such competence (Wolf, 1991; Shannon and Boll, 1996; Worten, 1993). Faculty might provide component options or examples and general guidelines pertaining to quantity and type of components. A review of current course assignments and requirements may also contribute to identifying potential portfolio components (Baltimore et al., 1996; Carney et al., 1996). Portfolios may vary widely among students in terms of what types of student work or self-assessments best demonstrate competence. Examples of materials that might be included are provided below (Carney et al., 1996):

1. *Artifacts:* materials normally produced or developed in courses or training (group session plans, career counseling plans, theories or research papers).

2. *Reproductions:* materials that demonstrate actual practice or skills (audiotapes or transcripts of counseling sessions or role-plays of counseling sessions).

3. *Reflections:* materials that demonstrate thoughts or self-assessment, critical thinking, personal growth, or professional development (journals, critiques, self-assessments of skills).

4. *Attestations:* evaluations from practicum or internship site supervisors, letters or notes regarding special services rendered, or notification of acceptance of professional presentations or publications (Barton and Collins, 1993).

Faculty may require for all student portfolios certain components that most directly correspond to professional and program competencies or requirements. Requiring some faculty-identified components in the portfolio increases the overall reliability of the final portfolio product (Shannon et al., 1995; Shannon and Boll, 1996). Faculty may provide students with an overall outline of these required components or may identify the components during individual courses. The latter option provides faculty with some flexibility in component development and selection. For example, all students enrolled in our counseling theories courses write a paper describing their "theory(ies) of choice." All students may be asked to include this paper in their portfolios. Additionally, some students may decide to provide a reflective statement about how they have changed their theoretical position during their program of study and what contributed to the change.

In addition to faculty-required components, students need some flexibility in determining which portfolio components best reflect their growth, development, and achievement. Faculty challenge students to reflect upon what components best demonstrate their acquisition of skills and their personal and professional development (Carney et al., 1996; Wolf, 1991). Such reflection also helps students to consider how they construct knowledge and to anticipate how they will respond to diverse clinical experiences (Shannon and Boll, 1996). This constructive process promotes the development of self-assessment skills, which are critical to lifelong counselor development. Thus, what this level of flexibility loses in reference to reliability, it gains in validity (Shannon, et al., 1995, Valencia, 1990). Importantly, students receive criteria guiding component selection, but have latitude and flexibility with regard to materials included.

A Trial Period

During the early phases of adopting portfolio assessment and establishing guidelines, faculty may use a trial period to generate examples of student portfolio components and completed products. This trial period provides faculty with an opportunity to examine ways to implement the process and structure the compilation of portfolios. Furthermore, later students benefit from specific portfolio examples and from guidelines for establishing and creating their own portfolios.

One area to consider during this trial period is ethical and legal concerns relating to such an evaluation process. As with all forms of student assessment, students need to be informed about the stages of the evaluation process, evaluation criteria, how evaluation information will be used, and students' rights in the evaluation process (American Counseling Association [ACA], 1995). For the portfolio, specifically, students should be provided not only guidelines about required and self-selected components, but how such components might be differentially weighed during the evaluation process.

For instance, reflection components require that students share information about their own growth and development. Students may feel vulnerable in disclosing information that identifies their limitations, concerns, or deficits. Faculty must consider how they will use information from reflection components and convey this information to students. More importantly, faculty need to create a safe environment where such self-assessment is nurtured and encouraged. In the service of this goal, faculty may talk about their own professional development or lead class discussions in which students share concerns about their competencies or professional development.

Other ethical or legal issues relate more indirectly to the evaluation process and need to be considered when developing guidelines for component selection (Carney et al., 1996). For instance, client rights and welfare need to be protected when selecting artifact and reproduction components that rely on the use of client data (ACA, 1995). Students need to acquire informed consent from clients when they intend to use client information or tapes. This includes providing clients (and field supervisors) with explicit details about the use of client materials, with information about who will have access to the materials, and what steps will be used to protect client confidentiality (Carney et al., 1996). For instance, students may delete names of clients on their materials and may obscure the client's image on videotapes in order to ensure confidentiality. Clients need the freedom, based on such information, to decide whether any of their information may be used in the student's portfolio.

Portfolio Evaluation

Evaluating portfolios is often more challenging than evaluating traditional written tests. However, credible and valid evaluation strategies are possible (Shannon et al., 1995; Shannon and Boll, 1996; Wolf, 1991). Several authors recommend establishing a scoring rubric that is tied directly to the criteria and domains identified for the portfolio (Shannon and Boll, 1996). In our portfolio model, the scoring rubric corresponds to the CACREP standards (CACREP, 1994). Others' scoring criteria correspond to stages of counselor performance or development. For example, Baltimore et al. (1996) recommend a scoring system based on "Stoltenberg's levels of counselor complexity . . . novice, apprentice, proficient, and expert" (p.119).

In developing a scoring system or process, faculty need to clearly establish the methods that will be used to document reliability and validity (Carney et al., 1996). They may clarify how the scoring system is linked to the portfolio criteria, establish multiple points of evaluation (e.g., annual evaluation, final evaluation), and include multiple sources of evaluation (e.g., advisor, student committee members, site supervisors).

However, evaluating a portfolio should not rely solely on the use of a scoring system. Faculty should first view the portfolio from a holistic, developmental perspective, look at the final product in totality, and then consider the specific requirements or evaluation criteria for components or domains (Carney et al., 1995; Haertel, 1991). This holistic process may be most important for the reflection components. As discussed earlier, it is difficult to evaluate reflection components, and such evaluation needs to attend closely to the established criteria and intent for using reflection components. Usually reflection components provide students with the opportunity to 'evaluate' their own progress. Faculty may thus evaluate student development as manifested in how well students evaluate themselves.

The task of reviewing students' portfolios can seem daunting, but there are steps that may decrease the time involved. For instance, if required components of the portfolio are selected from course assignments, they will already have been evaluated by course faculty (Carney et al., 1995; 1996). The course instructor's previous evaluation can then be used as part of the overall portfolio evaluation (Wolf, 1991). Advisors or student committees (e.g., thesis committees, faculty advisement committees) can also review portfolios prior to a final evaluation as part of annual student evaluations. Earlier evaluations may provide a context for final evaluations, allow students some input into how they are evaluated, and provide students with ongoing direction about the portfolio. While evaluation at these earlier stages may not be as involved as in the final evaluation, earlier evaluations offer advisors or committee members concrete information about a student's progress in the program. Such information helps faculty during individual advisement to inform students about their progress, professional identification, or areas for remediation (Baltimore et al., 1996, Carney et al., 1996). In addition, adding an earlier stage of evaluation and encouraging the use of multiple sources of evaluation (e.g., advisor, committee members, faculty) increases the overall reliability of both the portfolio and the evaluation process (Shannon and Boll, 1996).

The final portfolio evaluation process may go beyond the review of the portfolio. Students may be asked to present their portfolio in an oral comprehensive exam or discussion (Carney et al., 1996; Wolf, 1991). Orals may include questions requiring students to reflect on and evaluate the portfolio process and the program, and to reflect on indicators of their progress or development. Although orals may currently only include the student's committee or other faculty, programs may want to consider the benefits of opening orals presentations to all students. For instance, open presentations allow other students to learn about the portfolio process and to vicariously benefit from their peers' experiences.

Conclusions

We believe that individual counseling portfolios provide the flexibility necessary to conduct meaningful formative and summative assessment activities. Portfolios allow evaluation to become a more developmental process and take into account individual differences. Portfolios are, by definition, individualized (personalized). During reflection on portfolio development, students select those materials that clearly reflect their growth and development for inclusion. The structure of the portfolios can vary in order to include artifacts representing academic and clinical program areas and personal reflections. As has been described, these artifacts may be highly structured components, such as course assignments, or less structured components related to students' individual experiences.

Peavy (1996) describes competence as an emerging capacity at least partially "constructed" by the individual through relations with others and the environment. Similarly, Nelson and Neufeldt (1998) assert that constructivism is rooted in the notion that one's beliefs and assumptions are products of the meanings one makes in social contexts. Therefore, students must be active participants in ". . . socially coconsidering, questioning, evaluating, and inventing information" (p. 79) if the information is to be meaningful to them. The portfolio assessment process encourages, and in fact requires, such active meaning making.

References

American Counseling Association. (1995). *Code of ethics and standards of in the practice.* Alexandria, VA: Author.

Baltimore, M. L., Hickson, J., George, J. D., and Crutchfield, L. B. (1996). Portfolio assessment: A model for counselor education. *Counselor Education and Supervision* 36 (2): 113-121.

Barton, J., and Collins, A. (1993). Portfolios in teacher education. *Journal of Teacher Education* 44 (3): 200-210.

Carney, J. S., Cobia, D. C., and Shannon, D. M. (1996). The use of portfolios in the clinical and comprehensive evaluation of counselors-in-training. *Counselor Education and Supervision* 36 (2): 113-121.

_____. (April 1995). *Portfolios in counselor education: Clinical and comprehensive evaluation.* Poster session presented at the annual meeting of the American Counseling Association, Denver, CO.

Collins, A. (1990). *Transforming the assessment of teachers: Notes on a theory of assessment for the 21st century.* Paper presented at the annual meeting of the National Catholic Education Association, Toronto, Canada.

Council on Accreditation of Counseling and Related Programs. (1994). *CACREP accreditation standards and procedures manual.* Alexandria, VA: Author.

Drummond, R. J. (1996). *Appraisal procedures for counselors and helping professionals* (3rd ed.). Englewood, CA: Prentice Hall.

Goldman, L. (1992). Qualitative assessment: An approach for counselors. *Journal of Counseling and Development* 70: 616-621.

Haertel, E. (1991). New forms of teacher assessment. In G. Grant (Ed.), *Review of research in education* (pp. 3-29). Washington, DC: American Educational Research Association.

LeMahieu, P. G., Gitomer, D. H., and Eresh, J. T. (1995). Portfolios in large-scale assessment: Difficult but not impossible. *Educational Measurement: Issues and Practice* 14 (3): 11-16, 25-28.

Nelson, M. L., and Neufeldt, S. (1998). The pedagogy of counseling: A critical examination. *Counselor Education and Supervision* 38 (2): 70-89.

Peavy, R.V. (1996). Constructivist career counseling and assessment. *Guidance and Counselling* 11 (3): 8-15.

Ryan, J. M. and Kuhs, T. M. (1993). Assessment of preservice teachers and the use of portfolios. *Theory into Practice* 32 (2): 75-81.

Scriven, M. (1988). Duty-based evaluation. *Journal of Personnel Evaluation in Education* 1 (4): 319-334.

Sexton, T. L. (1998). Reconstructing counselor education: Supervision, teaching, and clinical training. *Counselor Education and Supervision* 38: 2-5.

Shannon, D. M. and Boll, M. (1996). Assessment of preservice teachers using alternative assessment methods. *Journal of Personnel Evaluation in Education* 10 (2): 117-135.

Shannon, D. M., Ash, B. H., Barry, N. H., and Dunn, C. (April 1995). *Implementing a portfolio-based evaluation system for preservice teachers.* Paper presented at the annual meeting of the American Educational Research Association, San Francisco, CA. Valencia, S. (1990). A portfolio approach to classroom reading assessment: The whys, whats, and hows. *Reading Teacher* 43: 338-340.

Wolf, K. (1991). *Teaching portfolios: Synthesis of research and annotated bibliography.* San Francisco, CA: Far West Laboratory.

Worten, B. W. (1993). Critical issues that will determine the future of alternative assessment. *Phi Delta Kappan* 74 (6): 444-454.

Part Three

APPLYING CONSTRUCTIVISM TO TEACHING: EXEMPLARS OF BEST PRACTICES

Part Three offers illustrations of mental health training course designs that use constructivist principles.

Chapter Eight

Transforming Diversity Training in Counselor Education

Marilyn Montgomery, Florida International University
Aretha Marbley, Raquel Contreras, Texas Tech University,
and William M. Kurtines, Florida International University

For leaders and educators in the field of counseling, the focus on diversity is by now a very familiar one. Over the past few decades a growing recognition of the social and cultural foundations of our work and of the profession's tendency toward ethnocentrism with respect to these issues has emerged. Upon observing the underutilization of counseling services by people of minority races and ethnicities and the small proportion of nonmajority individuals in counselor education programs, many in the profession have become convinced that counseling is, knowingly or unknowingly, engaging in a form of marginalization. Further, many have become convinced that counselor education has not been supplying the type of training necessary to prepare students to provide multiculturally competent services. According to this view, the profession engages in "active neglect" by not effectively addressing cultural, racial, and ethnic diversity in training, practice and research. The result of this neglect is not only the exclusion of nonmajority people from participating in counseling as clients (Sue and Sue, 1977, 1990), but also from participating as professionals and colleagues (D'Andrea and Daniels, 1995).

Within the field, the recognition of the profession's tendency toward ethnocentrism gathered momentum during the 1970s and the 1980s. Cultural factors are now widely recognized as having a powerful influence on our effectiveness as counselors (Marbley, 1998). Consequently, efforts have been made to respond to these influences in a positive way. In 1991, for example, the Association for Multicultural Counseling and Development (AMCD) approved a document outlining the need and rationale for a multicultural perspective in counseling, the culmination of work begun two decades earlier (Sue, Arredondo, and McDavis, 1992). More recently, an American Psychological Association task force composed Guidelines for Practice, Education and Training, and Research; these include multicultural competencies and have been discussed and endorsed by a growing number of division memberships (Fouad, 1999). Both documents reflect the growing recognition of the importance of cultural competence and the need for the profession to become more inclusive of nonmajority individuals.

In addition to these changes of the last decade in the counseling field, dramatic parallel changes (sometimes called "paradigm shifts") have also taken place outside the field—in the culture and other academic disciplines. These changes raise questions about the ethnocentric biases of the theoretical and practical foundations of the profession and about the nature of "truth." For instance, the "critical" philosophical tradition points out that the Western theoretical traditions were constructed by dominant groups and, consequently, implicitly favor the needs and views of these dominant groups (Derrida, 1976; Habermas, 1971, 1979, 1981, Lyotard, 1984). From the perspective of these new understandings (e.g., postmodernism, postpositivism, etc.), "truth," instead of being "universal and objective," is relativized as a constructed understanding that makes sense at a particular time, in a particular context (Rorty, 1979, 1985; 1992; Weinrach and Thomas, 1998).

The recognition that traditional psychological theories are biased and limited guides has given birth to a new, broad-based theoretical tradition in counseling. Variously identified as cross-cultural counseling, multicultural counseling, and diversity-sensitive counseling, this new tradition has been designated as "A Fourth Force" in Counseling. It has been asserted that its influence is commensurate with the traditional theoretical orientations of psychoanalysis, behaviorism, and humanism (Pedersen, 1990). These emerging emphases on the importance of diversity and difference in counseling approaches, along with the emergence of an epistemological tradition that emphasizes the "local and particular" nature of knowledge (Derrida, 1974; Lyotard, 1984), highlight the importance of recognizing the diversity of human experience in our practice and of including many voices in the professional dialogue.

This "critical" shift calls into question all narratives, especially any "metanarratives" which might aspire to universal truth. In this sense, any narrow definition of multiculturalism itself is questioned. Some have raised serious concerns about the past and future success of the diversity-sensitive counseling movement in coming up with viable theories to supplement those that fall short, as well as concerns about potential limitations of affirmative action as a strategy for rendering the profession more inclusive (Weinrach and Thomas, 1996, 1998). We as a field are thrown into the "culture wars" as the power and limits of various versions of diversity-sensitive counseling are debated.

So what's a good counselor educator to do? In the face of these challenges, what are our alternatives? One place to start is in de- and reconstructing some of the ways we are proposing to do diversity-sensitive counseling. It is our view that enhancing our cultural competence will require the development of training approaches grounded in an epistemology that can bridge the gap between traditional theories—ones that view knowledge as "mind independent"—and emerging theories—ones that view knowledge as the outcome of a co-constructive process (Kurtines, Azmitia, and Alvarez, 1992). We need training approaches that are broad-based enough to be adapted to local and particular contexts. That is, we must create approaches that welcome all marginalized and under-represented trainees, including those who have alternative conceptions from ours of the work they wish to do. We will illustrate this point later in this chapter.

In this chapter, we share with the reader what we have been doing toward these ends. We begin by discussing the response of counselor educators to the call for sensitivity to diversity in general and our own response in particular. In doing so, we describe some of the problems and paradoxes that emerge in implementing the current dominant approaches to diversity sensitivity training. We also describe our own efforts to address these problems by way of our re-evaluating what we are doing and why we are doing it. Finally, we share with you the approach to diversity sensitivity training that emerged out of our efforts at re-evaluation. Specifically, we offer a theoretically grounded approach to multicultural counselor education, one which is characterized by the use of participatory learning experiences and transformative activities in diversity sensitivity training (with both majority and nonmajority trainees). This approach to multicultural counseling training highlights both counseling and social activism, but with an eye to the trainee's world view and goals.

The Response to the Call for Diversity Training

When the AMCD approved, in 1991, the document outlining thirty-one cross-cultural competencies and standards (i.e., in the three areas of multicultural awareness, knowledge, and skills), it was hoped that these would become the ingredients for curriculum reform and the training of helping professionals. In this document, the authors argued that teaching these competencies would enhance the effectiveness of counseling interventions by helping counselors identify and overcome racial and ethnocentric biases in their understanding and treatment of others. Further, the document issued a call to the profession to remedy its active neglect of culture and oppression and instead "take a proactive stance in incorporating standards of practice that reflect the diversity of our society" (Sue, Arredondo, and McDavis, 1992, p. 479). Thus, according to these standards, training programs should orient new counselors toward social action to reduce the injustices that continue to exist in contemporary social forms.

The response of counseling programs to this call for action has been strong but uneven, at least with respect to developing and implementing diversity-sensitivity training programs (Hills and Strozier, 1992). In an effort to transform trainees' cultural competence, many counseling programs added an overview "multicultural" counseling course. Others experimented with weekend intensive courses or with introducing relevant cultural issues into courses across the counseling curriculum (the "infusion approach"). Multicultural training efforts typically emphasize one of three distinct teaching approaches (Reynolds, 1995):

1. Awareness approaches concentrate on participants' discovery of personal biases, exploration of personal racial and ethnic identity, increased sensitivity to multicultural issues, and development of greater tolerance and acceptance of cultural differences.

2. Oppression-focused models utilize a socio-political framework to help participants 'unlearn' oppression. Such training confronts participants' world-views and perceptions, challenging their notions of

power and the status quo, and sensitizing them to the realities of racism, sexism, heterosexism, and classism.

3. An integrative training focus seeks to foster multicultural attitudes, knowledge, and specific skills in the participants. Often incorporating features of both of the previous models, an integrative focus also aims to have changes in attitudes and knowledge result in changed (more culturally appropriate) behavior, such as seeking consultation from indigenous helpers, accurately comprehending non-verbal cues and conversational meta-messages, etc. (e.g., Brown, Parham, and Yonker, 1996; Lee, 1996).

Research on diversity training programs is still in its infancy (Ridley, Mendoza, Kanitz, Angermeier, and Zenck, 1994; Nuttal, Sanchez, and Webber, 1996). Because little data exists to guide the development and delivery of diversity training, a lack of consensus exists about what types of training are most needed or most effective (D'Andrea, Daniels, and Heck, 1991). As a result, counselor educators have tended to choose course content based on personal familiarity with concepts and their own instructional preferences. Our own efforts began similarly. However, we were humbled to discover that improvements were necessary.

The Paradox of "Requiring" Sensitivity to Diversity

Convinced of the need for multiculturally competent counselors, we began by implementing curriculum-driven approaches to training for diversity. One of our basic working assumptions was that if we delivered educational interventions guided by the AMCD competencies our students would acquire, through our efforts, increased awareness, knowledge, and skills. It was not to be that easy, however. In using curriculum-based approaches to teach sensitivity to diversity we encountered a curious problem: the use of such approaches created a paradox that often resulted in student resistance; both majority and minority students found aspects of the multicultural "canon" to be narrow and limiting.

Other educators have similarly noted the occurrence of student resistance that arises in multicultural initiatives. Usually the resistance (and the accompanying discomfort, anxiety, and ambivalence that students express) has been attributed to students' personal developmental issues or cultural identity issues (Ottavi, Pope-Davis, and Dings, l994; Sabnani, Ponterotto, and Borodovsky, l991). However, an equally plausible alternative (or perhaps collateral) hypothesis, we reasoned, was that the nature of the instructional process might itself contribute to the students' resistance. A critical examination of our teaching methods and assumptions appeared to provide support for this latter view.

Curriculum-based teaching models are based on the (usually implicit) assumption that if educators deliver the correct intervention to change students' sensitivity to and appreciation of diversity, students will become more multiculturally competent. However, a paradox arises when valuing diversity and sensitivity to diversity are required as instructional outcomes. Students resist when they sense that a class that ostensibly teaches the valuing of diversity insists that everyone adopt a particular value, even when that value is consistent with their own values.

For example, oppression-focused teaching strategies aim to help students become sensitive to "oppression" (the abuse of power by means of the use of force, intimidation, manipulation, deception, etc.) by confronting and challenging students' world views in order to sensitize them to the realities of racism, classism, sexism, etc. The problem is that in programatically confronting and challenging students, we are in effect using (sometimes not so subtle) forms of oppression (e.g., intimidation, manipulation, etc.). Consider the following journal entry from one of our students:

My reaction to the first two chapters of the text, the film, and the class discussion were troubling. I felt trapped, powerless. I feel as if anything I say or respond to will be invalidated, will be discounted, because I am a white male. It feels as if there is nothing that I can say that will be construed in a constructive manner. . . . I feel stereotyped. I am as angered as any person might be by someone who has not lived where I have lived, walked where I have walked, who has not had my experience but who has the audacity to define me. . . . If the intent of the film was to help me understand people of other cultures, it failed. I could not hear the message because the labels that were being assigned to me drowned out the words.

For this majority counselor-trainee it is not clear whether the perception of being portrayed as an oppressor had the positive effect of deepening his sensitivity to diversity or the negative effect of strengthening his resistance to the concept. He experienced the educational intervention as challenging (in offering a new interpretation of power) but in no way supportive (because it attacked his sense of personal worth). He was open to transforming his awareness, knowledge, and skills, but he felt dismissed as a person while the "right way" of seeing the world was being forced upon him. Could he learn multiculturally oriented counseling this way? Constructivist theory (as outlined in Chapter One of this book) emphasizes that students can take the best advantage of our educational interventions when they are both challenged and supported in the process. We realized that notions of "parallel process" suggested that if we expected our students to themselves provide clients with therapeutic environments via a growth-producing balance of support and challenge and respect for their clients' diverse attitudes, we could hardly expect ourselves to do any less in the classroom.

A similar paradox arises when a counselor educator provides multicultural training for a student who clearly and self-consciously chooses a largely monocultural professional goal; in other words, one who prefers developing skills for working with a particular underserved group rather than "to learn basic elements of several cultures" (see Fouad, 1999, p. 5). Indeed, the very survival of some ethnic and cultural groups has been assured only through exclusive values, rituals, and practices. What is a counselor educator to do when a student has more interest in preserving and protecting, for example, a nonmajority way of life than in learning about and appreciating an unfamiliar cultural perspective? For example, should we insist that a rural Diné (Navajo) counselor who wants to help tribal children discover and explore traditional values become multicultural? What does it mean to promote multicultural counseling values to a Spanish-speaking counseling student in Miami who has the goal of working with Cuban immigrants in Little Havana? These students are preparing to work in largely monocultural settings as (much-needed) helpers; ironically, they sometimes believe that "multicultural" attitudes and knowledge and skills are not what they most need to learn to serve their own minority populations. This leads to another alarming question: is it possible that (especially minority) trainees experience our version of multiculturalism as culturally oppressive?

As we pondered these questions we discovered that a similar paradox was described by Ewing and Allen (1996), who wrote about the dilemma that arises when feminist research includes participants who are opposed to feminist ideas and/or do not view themselves as oppressed. As feminist researchers who study conservative Christian women, Ewing and Allen concluded that "finding ways to keep the tensions flowing—not buried or enraged" is an essential part of the process, and that personal journaling, reflective conversations, and openness with participants have been effective tools for taking responsible steps towards nonoppressive methods. They suggest that sharing the results of such methods allows them to be more transparent as they seek to uncover and deal with their potential biases, power differentials, and the tentative resolutions of these (1996, pp. 184).

Perplexed by the tensions (sometimes buried, sometimes public) that we regularly encountered in our diversity training efforts, we too sought to explore, with our students, a deeper understanding of classroom process. We sought a more isomorphic, consistent pedagogy. We realized that in order to promote the value of inclusiveness, we must genuinely listen to our students (both majority and nonmajority). Through weekly journaling, reflective conversations, and openness with our students about our own struggles with making sense of the paradox, we began to wonder: Who should determine the diversity training curriculum? If the instructor determines the curriculum and sets forth the competencies that will be achieved, is this an implicitly "oppressive method"? If so, what could we do to ensure that, in our own classrooms, the "local and particular" voice was heard?

To fully address this paradox and the questions it raises, we need approaches to diversity training in which our students are active co-participants in the creation of the learning context and process. The use of "participatory learning" helps to resolve this paradox because it offers a model of teaching and learning that is collaborative rather than didactic. And in keeping with the notions of "parallel process," it is also more consonant with the collaborative counseling relationship that we find most empowering for clients (see Steward, 1998). Rather than using a fixed curriculum model that dictates the endpoint, participatory learning processes directly involve students in determining what is to be included in the training curriculum. We believe that this is the best approach for transforming our profession into one that is truly inclusive. In the next section, we articulate our reasons for adopting a "transformative pedagogy."

Transformative Pedagogy

Transformative pedagogy is adopted from the pedagogy of liberation in general and the transformative pedagogy of Paulo Freire (1970/1983) in particular. Friere's approach was found to be useful in developing a non-oppressive, participatory learning process in recent work at the Adolescent and Adult Development Program at Florida International University (Ferrer-Wreder, Cass Lorente, Kurtines, Briones, Bussell, Berman, and Arrufat, 1999; Milnitsky, Ferrer-Wreder, Briones, Berman, and Kurtines, 1997). We have adapted and extended this work to multicultural training in this chapter.

Freire sought to empower the marginalized by offering them the opportunity to enhance their "critical consciousness" about their own exclusion from mainstream normative institutions (political, economic, legal, etc.). While working to empower marginalized peasants in Brazil, he found, for example, that the individuals who were disempowered and marginalized by poverty did not learn well from classic lecture formats that were detached from their reality. According to Freire, the use of a didactic approach only served to emphasize the peasants' sense of "incompetence," in contrast to the "competence" of the knowledgeable expert who was dictating the lesson. In his book, *Pedagogy of the Oppressed* (Freire, 1970/1983), Freire offers an alternative: an approach that is participatory and transformative.

Freire referred to such a transformative pedagogy as a pedagogy of dialogue and considered it distinct from a pedagogy of instruction. It is a "problem-posing" and participatory learning model in which the marginalized take an active role in the educational process. The teacher works with the students to collaboratively explore and critically examine the meaning and significance of their marginalization.

Transformative pedagogy extends beyond identifying problems to action-oriented problem solving. It does not seek to carry out constructive transformations for the oppressed, but with the oppressed. While intentionally identifying problems and following through by engaging in successful "transformative activities" to solve these problems, students learn "to see a closer correspondence between their goals and a sense of how to achieve them, gain greater access to and control over resources and . . . gain mastery over their lives" (Zimmerman, 1995; p. 583). As a consequence of these experiences, they not only become the experts on their own "local and particular" situation but they also take control of their transformative activities. They become empowered as they develop a greater sense of control and responsibility in their lives and the life of their communities.

In drawing on Friere to create participatory and transformative learning experiences, our goal with minority trainees has been to open them to the possibility of transforming (rather than enduring) the circumstances that negatively impact their personal and professional lives and the life of their communities. Our goal with majority trainees has been to open them to the possibility of taking social action to reduce the injustices that continue to exist in contemporary social forms. Thus, in posing problems and in following through with transformative activities to solve these problems, students acquire a greater critical understanding of themselves (as racial, cultural persons) and of the contexts (of privilege or marginalization, or both) in which they live. Doing so in the context of the training program empowers students to continue transforming themselves and to eventually transform their profession and their communities.

A Transformation-Oriented Training Program

Our three-phase transformation-oriented training program was designed to be flexibly adapted to diverse populations and problems, goals, and institutional and cultural settings. The phases are: (1) a preliminary group cohesion-building phase, (2) participatory learning experiences, and (3) student-directed transformative activities. The duration of the program and sequence of the phases can be adapted to specific course formats. In addition, as discussed below, the program can be variously targeted at individual, institutional, or societal change.

Preliminary Phase

During the preliminary phase of the training we work at developing group cohesion within the training group (for example, use ice breakers, mutually establish group rules, etc.). This process is influenced by the ethnicity, academic level, and personal styles of the group members. Of course, genuine cohesiveness does not automatically result from getting people together as a group; it results from the ongoing building of connections between people in ways that are culturally and contextually most appropriate. The sense of cohesion contributes to genuine exploration of self and the world of others. Once sufficiently established, the focus shifts from establishing group cohesion to the participatory learning phase.

Participatory Learning Experiences

During the second phase of the program, students engage in a series of participatory learning experiences which are aimed at enhancing their multicultural awareness, knowledge, and skills. In contrast to training approaches which rely on directive and didactic processes, participatory learning experiences emphasize cooperative and mutual learning contexts. Mutual sharing of knowledge and reciprocal learning take place between the students and the teacher. For example, from the instructor, the students can learn about diversity-sensitizing concepts for the delivery of counseling services. From the students, the instructor can learn what life has taught them about the practical and political issues of getting along and getting ahead in their own cultural settings.

We use *exploration and problem posing* to accomplish training goals. The class group becomes a starting point from which both students and the teacher can *explore* their own multicultural competence. As the group becomes more cohesive and inclusive, members challenge one another to think critically about:
• their awareness and sensitivity to diversity,
• the assumptions, motivations, and cultural agendas they bring to the counseling context,
• their level of knowledge about cultural issues that are "local and particular"(e.g., immigrant issues, local ethnic politics, etc.), and

• their level of general cultural skills, local and particular cultural skills, and competencies for dealing with clients.

The members of the group support one another as they gather information, encounter resistance, uncover surprising (distressing or encouraging) facts, and draw new conclusions. Group exercises encourage each student to genuinely and active participate. Some students are comfortable with all exercises; others become quite anxious (and less able to profit from the experience in a constructive way) with some exercises. Offering opportunities for choices in participation, however, allows students to locate the level of challenge where they are optimally "stretched," rather than bored or broken.

The exercises. We find five exercises useful in facilitating the acquisition of multicultural awareness, knowledge, and skills. We drew these exercises from those commonly used in diversity training, but we adapted them to fit the participatory goals of our training program. We describe them in the sequence that we have found useful, but the selection (number, type, content, etc.) of the exercises can be adapted for particular contexts.

The first two exercises focus on enhancing *awareness*. In Exercise One, *Awareness Of One's Own Culture*, students explore and discover the roots of their own cultural values and share information about their cultural tradition with others in the group. For instance, they identify attributes characteristic of their culture; family traditions related to holidays, music, food, occupation, religion; their genogram and family geographic associations. Because Exercise One is a time-intensive exercise, we recommend that instructors use several three hour lab times for the exercise, and that during the labs the class be divided into discussion groups no larger than eight.

Many students experience this exercise as extremely meaningful. Students have been very creative with their sharing. One person, for example, brought a poster with her "life in pictures," from baby pictures until the present. Another person brought a special type of bread that had special memories from childhood. This person served the bread to each participant, as it was her cultural tradition for women to serve meals. Another person brought very old albums of music that had special relevance to her culture. Yet another person brought a handout with brief description of her religion and used her time to explain how her faith shaped her values.

Exercise Two, *Awareness of Differences*, raises consciousness about differences. Students select one form of diversity, develop an operational definition, and define anchors along the continuum for this form of diversity. We recommend starting with less emotionally laden forms of diversity such as birth order (oldest, youngest, middle), residential background (urban, suburban, rural), or gender. We recommend that emotionally laden forms of diversity such as ethnicity or sexual orientation not be explored until the class has reached a high level of acceptance of diversity and until the instructor is willing to process individual reactions, even outside of class.

One neutral continuum of diversity that we often use as an example is diversity of clothing on a cold day—Wearing a coat, vs. sweater, vs. neither. The objective is to place people into meaningful categories that are not shame-based or painfully prejudicial so that people can come to accept diversity as a way of life. Since the "benign" forms of diversity proposed by the exercise are typically not painful, or even subject to change, it allows people to become comfortable with displaying and discussing diversity. We like to close the exercise by introducing the idea that, in contrast to the forms of diversity used in the exercise, other forms of diversity are defined pejoratively, to some extent, by forces outside the individual. These pejorative evaluations can limit the individual that possesses the devalued characteristics.

Exercise Three, *Increasing Your Knowledge about Local and Particular Ethnic Groups*, increases student's *knowledge* about the ethnic groups of class members by using guided imagery about what it would be like to be a member of those ethnic groups, including stereotypes and typical labels used for members of those ethnic groups. Rather than focusing on the content of every group's culture, this exercise provides the opportunity for the students to share in the experience of being a member of particular nonmajority ethnic groups. This exercise can be repeated for as many ethnic groups as are locally relevant. It can also be broadened to include other types of cultural or lifestyle diversity.

Exercises Four and Five increase students' diversity *skills*. Perspective-taking skills are essential to the helping professions and these exercises sharpen their use in multicultural counseling contexts. Traditional role-taking and role-playing exercises help trainees to experience the cultural world of others and to develop skills for interacting with individuals who experience different modes of being in the world. Exercise Four, *Assuming Another's Ethnic Identity*, uses role taking and role playing to focus on the "ethnic identity" of another. Students divide into dyads with someone they don't know well who is of a different ethnic identity. Each pair takes turns sharing information about themselves (within the limits of comfort) with their partner. The students finish the exercise by "taking the ethnic identity" of their partner while self-disclosing to the group. This exercise may be broadened to include other kinds of cultural or lifestyle diversity.

Exercise Five, *Experiencing Another's Ethnic Identity Through the Expressive Arts*, uses role-taking and role-playing exercises that are rooted in the expressive arts. The expressive arts offer verbal and visual chances to experience the world of others and are designed to be powerful and influential experiences. In this exercise, small groups present a novel or film to the rest of the students through dramatic readings or enactments of particularly poignant portions of the novel or films. The group then discusses these renditions.

Problem posing. After group members explore their own cultural awareness and knowledge, they engage in *problem posing* as a means of identifying cultural problems in themselves, their community, or the profession. Freire (1970/1983) stresses *problem posing* as the foundation for transformative activities. He recognized that deciding on what the problem is was necessary if problem-solving, transformative activities were to be effective. That is, he recognized the need to solve the "right" problem and to not be deflected or distracted by solving the wrong problem. "Problem solving" skills alone, consequently, would not be sufficient for successful transformative activities.

Each student poses a specific problem or set of problems for the group's consideration. We find it helpful to focus on problems for which the group might genuinely contribute to a solution. More specifically, we suggest that members of the group focus on the negative consequences of intolerance of diversity for themselves personally (as members of marginalized groups, e.g., ethnic, gender, social class, etc.), their profession (e.g., as students, as future counselors, etc.), or their community in the broadest sense (e.g., neighborhood, city, nation). We find that many students experience the process of problem posing as extremely meaningful and also often find the problems they identify to be personally compelling. As a result, they learn to take a proactive stance toward social justice.

As might be expected, students sometimes direct these critical competencies toward the profession for which they are training itself. It would be hypocritical of us not to welcome such a challenge to any narrowness or blindness in our vision or practice of multiculturalism. Instead, one of the best things we can hope for is that our students leave our class with a critical sensitivity to the harm that results when any persons inflict their versions of "the right way to be" upon one another. When our students realize the limitations that might be disguised even in our attempts to be multiculturally skilled, we have indeed come far. In the last entry of the semester, the same student who began the course feeling excluded on the basis of his "majority" status wrote:

I would like to share an awareness that has come as a result of the semester's work. Over the holidays, while recuperating from feasting and football, my wife and I watched the movie *My Fair Lady* on one of the network channels. As I re-watched this story of the "gutter snipe" being transformed into a lady, I was impressed by the similarity of what we are asked to do in counseling, especially from a multicultural perspective. We are often asked, either explicitly or implicitly, to help an individual to fit into a culture different from their own. And therein lies the conflict. At one point in the movie, Liza Doolittle understands that in spite of all the preparation and all of the hard work, she cannot assume the position of a "lady" in that society, but she also realizes she no longer "fits" in her old world, either. We, as counselors, need to be aware of the potential consequences of our interventions. By being insensitive to the demands of cultures, don't we also run the risk of placing our multicultural clients in "no man's land," betwixt and between, rejected by two cultures? I'm not in a position to say yes or no with authority, but the prospect of doing harm counsels caution. (And it's either a good sign or a bad sign when the things you study in your multicultural class creep into a viewing of *My Fair Lady!*)

We think this is a good sign. This student's awareness of and sensitivity to multicultural issues has been transformed. He sees himself as responsible for critically evaluating not only his own culture, but also the culture of his own profession, as he strives to interact with all individuals in sensitive and helpful ways.

The above participatory learning processes provide the foundation for the next phase of our program, namely, the student-directed transformative activities. Through these self-directed transformative activities and the success of these activities in solving real problems, students become empowered and develop a sense of control of (and responsibility for) the choices and decisions they make as professionals in the community. For individuals from backgrounds that have limited access to social or professional power, the experience of gaining influence is particularly important.

Transformative Activities

AMCD's cross-cultural competencies and objectives for counselors include institutional intervention skills and active efforts to eliminate biases, prejudices, and discriminatory practices. Consequently, in this third phase of the program, *participants do more than talk about problems; they do something about them.*

During this phase, students choose to intervene in their communities and their profession in ways that are personally most meaningful to them, as a group or as individuals. The class provides a supportive context for students who tackle the problems that have an impact on their lives, the profession, and the life of their community. For example, a class taught by a minority faculty member illustrates how awareness and problem posing became the foundation for a subsequent transformative activity. During a field trip to a minority neighborhood school, students became aware of the lack of a facility for students at risk in their community schools. After considerable exploration and problem posing, the class decided that their "transformative activity" would be writing a grant to establish a special multiethnic school. At the end-of-semester, they had produced an excellent first draft of a grant. A number of students decided to make this transformative activity more than a class project. So, in collaboration with the faculty member, they continued to work on the grant, and it was eventually funded. Not only was the multiethnic school started, it was maintained throughout the funding period, and was eventually taken over and operated by the public school system.

Other students prefer to target problems in their own personal and professional lives. The case of Amelia illustrates the type of personal difference that successful mastery experiences can make in the lives of individuals and in the life of a community. Amelia was a counseling student in her last semester in a master's program at a university in West Texas. She commuted from a distant farming community that had a high percentage of Mexican migrant workers. Herself a daughter of migrants, Amelia had gathered her courage to become a teacher, and then a school counselor, for two reasons: "because my people need me" and because her husband insisted that she develop a professional skill (since his medical condition made it likely that she will someday have to support their four children alone).

When she first began taking counseling classes, Amelia was very uncomfortable. The beginning of each semester brought a new crisis of confidence. She felt torn by her long commute, being away from her family, and being expected to speak out and talk about her experiences.

For Amelia, being urged to see herself as devalued and oppressed by a majority culture was unhelpful. "Everybody knows about oppression first-hand, in my community," she said. Instead, her own "liberation," as she described it, was to sort out for herself whether she could be a good and proper Hispanic wife and mother and become a counselor, too. What she experienced as holding her back was not the dominant white culture but certain values of the minority members of her extended family and community. Her goal was to return to those in her community who had little hope for a good future and convince them that "you can do it, too."

Near the end of her last semester, Amelia sought and obtained a job in her community as a counselor; in fact, she was the first non-majority counselor ever hired by her school district. Most recently, she joined her state association of school counselors and secured an agreement from her district to fund her trips to their annual meeting. Thus, over several years and with a great deal of personal commitment, Amelia took action on her own behalf and, by being a model, is in the process of also transforming her community.

As a counselor educator, would you think of Amelia as one of your successes or your failures? She was sympathetic to other minority groups, but did not feel the need to deeply understand a variety of other ethnicities. Amelia was not very interested in racial identity models or in "consciousness-raising." Amelia insisted that adopting an oppression-focused viewpoint in relation to the majority culture was not what she or the students in her small town needed most. Instead, she disclosed to her group that she found the existential theoretical tradition to be the most useful guide for her own development and for helping her Hispanic, poor, and rural students see that they did have choices about how to improve their lives. Amelia changed, but in a way that was consistent with her own values and her own understanding of her ethnicity. And she effected a landmark change in her community's school system.

Would it be in keeping with multicultural values to view Amelia as unenlightened, resistant, or at a lower level of ethnic identity development because of her views? That would be so only if we teach from the perspective of having our students adopt our version of multicultural competence. Instead we tried to meet her at her current readiness. When Amelia had the freedom to choose the issues that meant the most to her, and was supported as she worked in the ways that were most comfortable for her, she did no less than change local history.

Constructing a Way of Working with Difference

Whether we address diversity issues in one class or in many, counselor educators hope for change: change in our students' (and our own) ways of understanding, feeling, practicing counseling, living as citizens in our communities, and participating in the profession. We hope our students, both nonmajority and majority, will choose greater sensitivity to diversity and greater cultural competence in providing services. We hope they will also choose to increase their proactive participation in our profession. As educators and mentors of future practitioners, our goal is to engage counselors proactively in dialogues and endeavors that enhance the level of sensitivity to diversity in individual counselors, in the helping professions, and, ultimately, in the countries and communities in which we all live.

Of course, students have their own goals with respect to diversity issues. They also have their own preferred ways of learning. Although true in any class, the importance of students' perspectives is heightened when the basic goal of the curriculum is to promote respectful approaches to difference. The irony is not lost on our students if we insist that they adopt our version of cultural competence, through our preferred educational process, whatever those may be.

Thus, the curriculum for diversity training needs to parallel the skillful respect for individuality and difference that we hope to nurture in our students. We see the process of fostering students' growth in awareness of cultural diversity as parallel to the process of students' growth in skillful and respectful counseling. Many of the ways we support clients' growth processes are isomorphic with facilitating a climate in which the students' multicultural competence can grow. In this way, individuals' diverse voices will be supported and encouraged, adding to the richness, dialogue, and equity in our communities and our profession.

References

Brown, S. P., Parham, T. A., and Yonker, R. (1996). Influence of a cross-cultural training course on racial identity attitudes of white women and men: Preliminary perspectives. *Journal of Counseling and Development* 74: 510-516.

D'Andrea, M., and Daniels, J. (1995). Promoting multiculturalism and organizational change in the counseling profession. In J. Ponterotto, J. M. Casas, L. A. Suzuki, C. M. Alexander (eds.), *Handbook of multicultural counseling*, (pp. 17-33). Thousand Oaks, CA: Sage.

D'Andrea, M., Daniels, J., and Heck, R. (1991). Evaluating the impact of multicultural counseling training. *Journal of Counseling and Development* 70: 143-150.

Derrida, J. (1976). *Of grammatology*. Baltimore, MD: The Johns Hopkins University Press.

Ewing, J. A., and Allen, K. R. (1996, November). *Reflecting on our process: Ethical issues in doing feminist research when participants are opposed to feminist ideas.* Paper presented at the Theory Construction and Research Methodology Workshop, National Council on Family Relations, Kansas City, MO.

Ferrer-Wreder, L. Cass Lorente, C., Kurtines, W., Briones, E., Bussell, J., Berman, S., and Arrufat, O. (1999, under revision). Promoting identity development in marginalized youth. *Journal of Adolescent Research.*

Fouad, N. A. (1999). Diversity and the public interest. *Division 17 Newsletter (American Psychological Association, Division of Counseling Psychology)* 20 (2): 3-5.

Freire, P. (1970/1983). *Pedagogy of the oppressed.* New York: Continuum.

Habermas, J. (1971). *Knowledge and human interest.* Boston: Beacon Press.

_____. (1979). *Communication and the evolution of society.* Boston: Beacon Press.

_____. (1981). Modernity versus post-modernity. *New German Critique* 22: 3-14.

Hills, H. I., and Strozier, A. L. (1992). Multicultural training in APA-approved counseling psychology programs: A survey. *Professional Psychology: Research and Practice* 23: 43-51.

Kurtines, W., Azmitia, M., and Alvarez, M. (1992). Science, values and rationality: Philosophy of science from a critical co-constructivist perspective. In Azmitia, M., Kurtines, W., and Gewirtz, J. (Eds.). *The role of values in psychology and human development,* (pp. 1-34). New York: John Wiley and Sons.

Lee, C. C. (1996). MCT Theory and implications for indigenous healing. In Sue, D. W., Ivey, M. B., and Pedersen, P. B. (Eds.), *A Theory of Multicultural Counseling and Therapy,* (pp. 86-111). Pacific Grove, CA: Brooks/Cole.

Lyotard, J. F. (1984). *The postmodern condition: A report on knowledge.* Minneapolis: University of Minnesota Press.

Marbley, A. F. (1998). *Factors affecting underutilization, negative out-comes, and premature termination of minority clients: The voice of ethnic/racial minority counselor-educators-in-training.* Unpublished doctoral dissertation, University of Arkansas, Fayetteville.

Milnitsky, C., Ferrer-Wreder, L., Briones, E., Berman, S., and Kurtines, W. (1997, November). Making life choices: Encouraging critical and responsible decision making and problem solving—The Brazilian and American experience. Symposium presented at the Association for Moral Education Conference, Atlanta, GA.

Nuttal, E. V., Sanchez, W., and Webber, J. J. (1996). MCT theory and implications for training. In Sue, D. W., Ivey, M. B., and Pedersen, P.B. (Eds.), *A Theory of Multicultural Counseling and Therapy,* (pp. 123-138). Pacific Grove, CA: Brooks/Cole.

Ottavi, T. M., Pope-Davis, D. B., and Dings, J. G. (1994). Relationship between racial identity attitudes and self-reported multicultural counseling competencies. *Journal of Counseling Psychology* 41: 149-154.

Pedersen, P. B. (1990). The constructs of complexity and balance in multicultural counseling theory and practice. *Journal of Counseling and Development* 68: 550-554.

Reynolds, A. L. (1995). Challenges and strategies for teaching multi-cultural counseling courses. In Ponterotto, J. G., Casas, J. M., Suzuki, L. A., and Alexander, C. M. (Eds.), *Handbook of multi-cultural counseling* (pp. 312-330). Thousand Oaks, CA: Sage.

Ridley, C. R., Mendoza, D.W., Kanitz, B.E., Angermeier, L., and Zenck, R. (1994). Cultural sensitivity in multicultural counsel-ing: A perceptual schema model. *Journal of Counseling Psychology* 41: 125-136.

Rorty, R (1979). *Philosophy and the mind as the mirror of nature.* Princeton, NJ: Princeton University Press.

_____. (1985). Solidarity or objectivity? In J. Rajchman and C. West (Eds.), *Post-analytic philosophy* (3-19). New York: Columbia University Press.

_____. (1992). *Consequences of pragmatism: Essays 1972-1980.* Minneapolis: University of Minnesota Press.

Sabnani, H. B., Ponterotto, J. G., and Borodovsky, L. G. (1991). White racial identity development and cross-cultural counselor training: A stage model. *The Counseling Psychologist* 19: 76-102.

Steward, R. J. (1998, April). PAR: A theoretic model for self-assessment and practice toward multicultural counseling competence. In *Integrating theory, research training, and practice toward multi cultural competence.* Symposium conducted at the American Counseling Association World Conference, Indianapolis, Indiana.

Sue, D. W., Arredondo, P., and McDavis, R. J. (1992). Multicultural counseling competencies and standards: A call to the profession. *Journal of Multicultural Counseling and Development* 20: 64-88.

Sue, D. W., and Sue, D. (1977). Barriers to effective cross-cultural counseling. *Journal of Counseling Psychotherapy* 24: 420-429.

_____. (1990). *Counseling the culturally different: Theory and practice* (2nd ed.). New York: John Wiley.

Weinrach, S. G., and Thomas, K. R. (1996). The counseling profession's commitment to a diversity-sensitive counseling: A critical reassessment. *Journal of Counseling and Development* 74: 472-477.

_____. (1998). Diversity-sensitive counseling today: A postmodern clash of values. *Journal of Counseling and Development* 76: 115-122.

Zimmerman, M. A. (1995). Psychological empowerment: Issues and illustrations. *American Journal of Community Psychology* 23: 581-599.

Chapter Nine
Constructing the Course of Human Development
Jean Sunde Peterson, Purdue University

Two years ago a middle-aged student, in his evaluation of a large-ly experiential Human Growth and Development course, said, "Excellent integration of reading, discussion, interpersonal experiences, presentations, and writing assignments. I expected a dull, dry academic experience. The continual personalization of the material and the connection to the counseling experience made for a lively and interesting semester." That comment was gratifying. The course's learning process, as I teach it, often demands that students be willing to stretch themselves beyond what is familiar, preferred, and comfortable. That year a somewhat younger student offered another positive perspective: "I grew personally. Every aspect of the course was valuable."

Not all reviews were unqualified. A student in her late twenties said: "The self-study paper was beneficial, but I found it difficult due to my bottled-up personality. Some issues surfaced during writing that I realized I had not dealt with." Comments of the youngest students, just out of undergraduate studies, varied from "This course provides students with a real picture of what we will need to deal with" to "Would prefer more discussion of the text" and "I think class time could have been used in a more efficient way."

These varied comments represent a typical range of evaluative feedback for this experientially based course and may, of course, reflect differences in age, life experience, personality, and temperament. Similar student statements led Perry (1970) to devise a scheme which portrayed such responses as differences in constructive capacity. He proposed nine "positions" of intellectual development through which adults progress. An instructor, then, could face potentially nine ways of knowing in a class. The evaluative comments from my course remind us not only that graduate students can represent a wide range of cognitive developmental levels and preferred and nonpreferred learning styles, but also that counselor educators must be prepared to respect and respond nonjudgmentally to such individual differences (Komives, Woodard, and Associates, 1996).

To further complicate matters, Lamborn and Fischer (1988) have suggested that individual students tend to operate within a *range* of developmental stages. Helms (1995) argues for a "phasic" view of "stages," with stages representing "interactive themes rather than mutually exclusive categories" (Helms, 1995, p. 183). It is clear that in any one course there are many "audiences," all varying in readiness and style. Is it therefore imperative that we label students' development and preferences before we teach them, so that our instruction might match their cognitive development and learning preferences? Komives, Woodard, and Associates offer a qualified "No." They suggest that educators should beware of labeling students as though they "possess only one set of talents, skills, or sensitivities [and focus on helping students] effectively adapt their methods of learning to the specific tasks and contexts at hand" (1996, p. 231). Thus the pure matching of development and instruction is not realistic. However, the use of multiple methods can encourage students to exert themselves and practice new strategies for learning (McMillan and Forsyth, 1991). And students are motivated in part by activities that help them meet their developmental needs.

In this course, with these perspectives in mind, I attempt to address multiple needs, using personalized, experiential dimensions of constructivist teaching, not only to raise awareness about human development in general, but also to enhance motivation. Toward those ends, the students are purposefully bombarded with ambiguity, incongruity, multiple perspectives, and incompleteness, four additional tenets of constructivist teaching.

When I was first assigned the course, I recognized that enrolled students would represent a wide range of social, psychological, and intellectual developmental levels. I knew I did not want to merely "cover the content," even though I felt responsible for preparing them for the human development portion of the NBCC exam. I wanted the course to help them develop a framework for understanding themselves and their future clients. I wanted them to learn inductively, constructing their own knowledge, knowledge that would be meaningful because it would represent a "connection between what they are learning and their overall life experiences" (hooks, 1994, p. 19). With Kegan's (1994) "self-authorizing" way of knowing in mind, I considered that I wanted them to learn to read in an active, questioning way and to be self-directed in their learning. I wanted them to write "to parts of themselves, conducting an inner conversation" (p. 284), not just to write to me for my approval. I hoped some might experience, as a prelude to working with future clients, a respectful discovery of others' worlds, while accepting their own vulnerability to discovering another world within themselves as a result (p. 312).

Yet I knew that there would be students who would be preoccupied with my approval and directed toward that end, at the expense of the kind of self-direction and self-authoring I had in mind, and with no transformation to a broader, more flexible way of knowing. I wanted to generate honest self-examination and therefore needed to respect each student, regardless of their cognitive capacity, offering a bridge that "must be well anchored on both sides, with as much respect for where it begins as for where it ends" (Kegan, 1994, p. 62). I needed to provide an appropriate mix of challenge and support to encourage continued intellectual growth (cf. Perry, 1981). I also wanted to create an environment in which students could embrace their relational ties (i.e., for confirmation and cooperation) while simultaneously adopting a new, more developmentally advanced, "self-authorizing" perspective on them (cf. Kegan, 1994, pp. 243, 294) in the interest of applying such new understanding in their future work.

My own preferred teaching and learning style is experiential. I do not learn well auditorially, and thus, possibly as a result of projective identification, I have never been comfortable lecturing at length to students. I was aware that an individual often teaches in a style that matches his or her own learning style (Delworth, Hanson, and Associates, 1989), and that students who are taught in a style that is incompatible with their own often have difficulty succeeding (Kolb, 1984; Witkin, 1976). I therefore wondered how best to accommodate both my own and my students' needs as I attempted to move them toward reflective thinking (see King and Kitchener, 1994) and constructing their own knowledge, and away from relying on knowledge received from another source (cf. Komives et al., 1996).

Developing a Course That Transforms

The methodology and format of what became a largely experiential course, involving "examined experience," have evolved with transformation in mind—not only nudging students toward new ways of thinking and new ways of thinking about the nature of knowing and about human development, but also transforming those experiences into becoming a different kind of counselor. Students are altered in many ways during this course, according to their feedback at the end of this personalized learning experience.

The course varies in structure. Students apply developmental concepts to themselves in writing, they regularly interact with individuals representing various developmental phases, and they conduct a written dialogue with me through "response paragraphs" after each experience. The experiential dimensions are meant to move students away from emphasis on passive reception of "objective" knowledge to active engagement in integrating and applying diverse understandings, as well as increased tolerance for ambiguity and incompleteness.

Through direct contact with persons from the entire lifespan, most students appear to gain comfort with populations they previously thought were "off limits," newly considering them in terms of counseling practice. Some who have taken the course late in their program have called it their "most vital" experience in becoming a counselor. By contrast, a few have been frustrated and stressed by the nearly weekly experiential dimensions, perhaps because of being challenged too much (cf. Widick, Parker, and Knefelkamp, 1978).

Cognitive dissonance can occur as individuals move to correct a "too-subjective view of 'you'" (Kegan, 1982, p. 100) at each stage of development. For instance, for students who are at Kegan's third order of consciousness in their internal interpersonal evolution, which might be seen as a "merged self," there is "projected ambivalence" about "you." In other words, they have not yet authored "a self which maintains coherence across a shared psychological space and so achieves an identity" (p. 100). From the perspective of the third order of consciousness, ideas that differ from theirs and lack external structure may cause discomfort, and may challenge the developing sense of self. For example, needing certainty, students might find not having an outline to guide an interview to be threatening. Needing "truth," they might find it difficult to tolerate an interviewee's political or religious views which differ from their own.

Despite these challenges, this experientially based course continues to receive strong support from the vast majority of students who take it. At the end of the course, I see students who appear to have changed in both subtle and obvious ways. Through extensive interaction, they have bonded with one or more fellow students, and almost invariably they and I have developed comfortable rapport. They no longer make quick and stereotyping pronouncements about either human development or particular age groups or populations. They recognize many more of their own "issues." And they seem to be more comfortable with ambiguity and, consequently, with client surprises. In short, they have moved significantly forward in the process of becoming counselors. What follow are the constructivist principles that guide this human development course: personalized learning, experiential learning, hearing student voices, and encouraging multiple perspectives.

Constructivist Principles at Work

Personalized Learning

The teacher. A teacher's personality and self-presentation are among the social factors that contribute to classroom atmosphere and, ultimately, to student learning (cf. hooks, 1994, pp. 129-166). Above all, as a teacher I am also a learner, and I see my students as well as my clients as my teachers, as they share their thoughts and experiences and "make sense" of their lives. I communicate my fascination with the complexity of human nature. And I present real but anonymous clients from my own counseling practice, applying both systems and developmental perspectives. These personal references help me to demonstrate the use of a developmental template, whether stage, phase, position, or continuum, when forming hypotheses about clients.

I rarely "lecture" in class. Exceptions include presentations of findings from my own developmental research. The fact that these findings are my own studies seems to invite challenge and discussion, and I hope such presentations communicate that I am a lifelong learner, excited about pursuing questions of interest to me, and eager for continued learning through thoughtful feedback.

I do offer self-disclosure, choosing carefully what I share, in the interest of modeling appropriate professional discretion. That kind of risk-taking on my part, a professor's "linking confessional narratives to academic discussions so as to show how experience can illuminate and enhance our understanding of academic material" (hooks, 1994, p. 21), may give students permission for similar risk-taking. I intend to communicate that I am a complex and unstatic human being.

Self-disclosure can take other and less obvious forms, of course. I frequently employ immediacy in responding to students' comments and nonverbal behaviors, and I try to model openness to learning and to multiple perspectives by communicating genuine interest in their comments which are incisive and/or divergent from mine and others.' I am aware of the impact of an instructor's personal involvement and commitment in teaching, and I am continually self-reflective about the teacher-learner relationship (cf. Schon, 1987), always assuming that it contributes to classroom "atmosphere" for each student (see hooks, 1994, pp. 145-146). I often find myself hypersensitively replaying my interaction with class members for several hours after each weekly class meeting, wondering, for example, if the students and I interpreted each other's comments as we meant them.

The students. I also want my students to personalize *their* learning. I encourage them to come to class each week with a written list of five things in the readings that they found interesting, confusing, doubtful, or incredible. I begin class by asking a different student each time to share the list, a process which invariably provokes discussion. Sometimes I direct them to "write for ten minutes about number four on your list" as a quiz. They begin with "I," and they explain why they noticed a particular finding or conclusion among the myriad possibilities in each chapter. I ask them to offer evidence of their understanding of the concepts presented. We discuss what various students have noted as their interests and needs for approximately one-third of every class meeting.

We also personalize students' interactions with children, adolescents, and adults during class, which are a fundamental part of the course. For example, during debriefings following these in-class interactions, I insist on an honest assessment of "what worked" and what did not, how they felt, and what they might have been reminded of in themselves.

Students' work on the "self-study" final paper, which is explained later in this chapter, also involves highly personalized learning. In this paper, students apply what they have learned about development to themselves (I say, "To the most interesting person on earth—right?").

Finally, personalized learning occurs when we attend to the "construction" of relationships in class. I wait until I feel confident that relationship changes have occurred and will be recognized before I process the changes. Then we call attention to these evolving relationships, noting not only that this phenomenon parallels the building of trust in the counselor-client relationship, but also that it probably contributes to tolerance for complexity in the learning environment. I laud them for their growing collective tolerance, unabashedly and simultaneously communicating my bias in that direction.

Experiential Learning

Interactive interviews. Almost every week we interact with real people who represent various life phases, bringing in individuals from the community or taking field trips to schools or other institutions. Each week's group represents a particular age range so that we become acquainted with individuals who can teach us about developmental experiences across the lifespan. There are several purposes for this interactive contact:

• students see clients as potential teachers and themselves as learners in the counseling relationship,

• students become acquainted with and comfortable with people at various developmental levels,

• students have the opportunity to corroborate or challenge what is presented in textbook and handouts about development,

• students gain experience in adapting communication to various developmental levels,

• students anticipate client issues.

Each week at least one student expresses anxiety about interacting with a particular age group. Their discomfort may stem simply from moving out of a comfort zone, away from familiarity. It may also reflect a potential loss of control. Students who are not usually risk-takers sometimes comment on their tense anticipation as they face new experiences. I normalize and process this anxiety before the guests arrive, or before we leave campus, often reviewing basic listening skills and sometimes pairing students who are anxious with those who are experienced with a particular age group.

Examples of the groups who visit class or whom we visit are as follows. We begin the second class meeting with an hour-long visit to the neonatal unit at a local hospital, during which time parent concerns are noted as potential counseling issues. A nurse comments on neonatal tasks and development and demonstrates neonate reflexes. During the following weeks, we advance through childhood and adolescence. Students see a demonstration of and then apply play therapy with pre-schoolers at a Head Start facility. They interact with various groups of children either in school classrooms, at the local Boys and Girls Club, or on campus (Children from the Scouts often receive merit badges for their contribution to our class). Students interact with at-risk adolescents at a local alternative school. If our class is held in the evening, many of these groups come to our campus classroom.

The general format for interactions with children and teens. The emphasis in our students' interacting with school-age children and adolescents is on learning about development during the school years. The format for these interactions remains fairly constant across sessions. In order to engage a child or adolescent in comfortable conversation, each graduate student prepares an "instigating" technique for the visitors, such as asking for a drawing (e.g., their family, their classroom, their house), completion of sentence stems (e.g., "If I could live anywhere in the world . . ."; "My friends think I'm . . ."), responses to open-ended questions (e.g., "If you were king, what would you change about the world?"), interactions with toys or games (e.g., Battleship; doll house; action figures), or responses to a thematic activity (e.g., "If you could send each person in your family on a special vacation, where would you send them?" "Tell me about the nicest time you ever had with someone from your family."). The counseling students are told a week ahead what age group they are to prepare for (each successive class period involves an age group somewhat older than the one before), and they choose a technique which is developmentally appropriate. I place two books containing activities (Peterson, 1993, 1995) on reserve in the library for them to use as references for ages nine through eighteen, but I also encourage the students to be creative and independent with their approach. I emphasize that the techniques are meant to generate conversation that includes more than just "favorite things," but they are free to follow the interviewee in any direction. The goal is to engage "efficiently" with the client groups, given time constraints, and to allow clients to "teach us" about themselves, without our imposing meaning based only on the counselor's own experiences. Most students quickly find that some structure is advantageous and nonthreatening for this type of brief interaction.

During the actual interactions, the children or teens are "distributed" among individual or paired counseling students. The counseling students interact with the children or teens using their prepared techniques. After ten or fifteen minutes, the students move to a second interviewee. We also subsequently spend approximately twenty minutes doing a group interview with a "panel" of the guests, who are encouraged to interact with each other as well as with the counseling students. On occasion, when parents have accompanied a group, we ask the adults to serve as an additional brief panel, and we interview them about their own developmental and parenting issues and the development of their children. Sometimes we even invite the children to interview these adults; in this case I usually establish some guidelines in the interest of discretion and comfort for all participants.

Reflection and response. Two responsive paragraphs are due for the following class. One describes the technique the student used to engage their young partner and any adaptations they made in order to make the technique appropriate to capabilities and interests. The other explains how the child or adolescent's behaviors fit into what had previously been learned about development. If we have conducted an interview of a guest group or of part of a school classroom, the students also add comments about what they observed about development in the group as a whole. Reflecting on the interviews provides an opportunity to focus on the constructivist theme: How was each child or teen constructing meaning?

The students also write about their own comfort level, as well as the effectiveness of their techniques in engaging the interviewees. "Effective" is based on their own subjective judgment, reflecting the phenomenological world they are learning to pay attention to. The students might also include how their view of development affected their questioning and interaction. The paragraphs become increasingly process oriented and reflective of interpersonal nuances as the semester progresses.

I do not grade these responsive paragraphs, but I do give a "plus" mark if they represent thoughtful commentary about development. I write responses in the margins to recognize observations or comments about development. Such responses are meant to discourage students from writing only narratives about "what happened" during the interviews. Among many purposes, these assignments give students guidance and practice in writing about human development in preparation for their final paper, which also must be more than just a narrative. If some students are still making few comments about development when half of the responsive papers have been submitted, in spite of my written and oral admonitions, I mark their papers with a "check," a certain number of which may ultimately lower their course grade.

At each class meeting, I set aside time for the students to share their observations, techniques, and comfort level related to the interviews. Their increasingly forthright comments and their vulnerability while sharing uncomfortable moments from the interviews contribute to a growing sense of classroom community, which emerges from an "engaged pedagogy" that values student expression (hooks, 1994, p. 20). Again, I refer to "constructing" by asking, "How were you constructing meaning during the interview? How did that influence your questioning? How are you continuing to construct meaning during this discussion?"

Panels of adults. When we focus our collective attention on adulthood, we use class members or others in their twenties, thirties, forties, fifties, and sixties for in-class panels discussions, again for approximately one hour during each meeting. My participation in an appropriate age panel reminds them that I, too, am a "developing person." Occasionally, representatives from every decade through near-retirement take the class. Normally, however, we have to recruit individuals from the community to supplement the few in class who represent the older age-decades. Eventually we move off campus again, spending time at a retirement center, again interviewing individuals and a panel, but with no requirement for pre-planned "techniques" for the individual interviews. A hospice representative speaks to us at our final meeting.

Panels of four or five people seem to work best, offering enough participants for variety in perspective and experience, and yet giving participants sufficient time to elaborate on their thoughts. Although representing a developmental life stage fully may be impossible, a small panel that discusses concerns more than superficially can generate a great deal of thought-provoking material about a particular stage.

I usually begin the interview of a guest panel myself, asking open-ended, developmental questions about differences from the preceding age-decade, about changing roles and relationships with various members of the family of-origin and the current family, and about new concerns and thoughts relative to direction, career, meaning, goals, and health. I then turn over interviewing responsibility to the students. Late in the semester they take over my now-familiar format almost entirely. On occasion, if a student's question or remark is indiscreet or discomfiting, I might interfere, giving the panelist permission not to respond, for example. At other times I might extend my own questioning because I am aware of the potential for some particularly instructive information from a group of guests. Generally, however, I trust that the students' questions will be thoughtful and appropriate. Their comments and responses seem to become more supportive and facilitative as the semester progresses.

The students do not write responsive paragraphs concerning any of the adult panels because they are occupied with other writing at that point in the course, and because I am confident that they have developed the skills for interaction and an ability to self-monitor and reflect. The in-class discussions which follow the adult panels often reveal that students have been amazed at some information, touched by some comment, reminded of someone, or helped to understand someone in their own lives. In short, the students inductively "gather data" through the interaction both with guests and with each other.

Through that process, they may add their own theories of development to those they have been reading about. For one essay question on the final exam, I ask students to articulate their own inductively drawn theory of adult development, based on what they gained from three of the adult panels. They demonstrate that they have constructed their own knowledge, reflecting what Kolb (1984) calls "deep learning."

Dialectical discourse. Students rarely agree fully when they conceptualize the "clients" or members of the panels they have interviewed. They argue most about the earlier developmental stages; it seems to be more difficult for them to challenge a perception about panelists older than they are. However, the textbook information provokes the most dialectical discourse. Whether it is about parental discipline, relationship issues, gender differences and socialization, young-adult developmental tasks, emotional expressiveness, moral development, or family roles, students engage each other readily in confrontational and sometimes conflictual interaction. I try to use such situations to point out external communication patterns, to draw attention to internal processes, and to affirm the idea of multiple perspectives.

According to Yalom (1997), when there is sufficient safety and support, as well as feedback and honesty of expression, group tensions can emerge and be processed, leading to a therapeutic "corrective emotional experience" (p. 26). When these necessary conditions exist in the human development course, both bonding and intrapersonal awareness are enhanced.

Cognitive development also seems to move forward as students gradually and "correctively" build tolerance for differences between themselves and others and even learn to value such differences (cf. Loevinger, 1976). Giroux (1981) speaks of developing a pedagogy that, through dialogue and supportive interaction, helps students move beyond the "taken-for-grantedness" that shapes their view of the world (p. 124). The students in this course seem to develop a "dialectical language" that enables them "to understand the meaning of frame of reference" (p. 124), a worthy goal in the development of counseling expertise.

We also discuss differences in theories of young adult development, not only to respect and gain from discoveries of various fields, but also to enhance students' awareness of their own evolutionary cognitive development. We refer, for example, to Perry's (1970) scheme regarding how students move from dualistic, truth-versus-falsehood thinking to conceptual relativism and then to self-chosen commitment; to Riegel's (1973) concept of dialectical adult thought; to Labouvie-Vief's (1984) advocacy of exposure to complexity as a way to escape dualistic thinking; and to Kegan's (1982) emphasis on the continued development of systems of meaning. Loevinger (1976) views developmental stages as somewhat related to chronological age, but not necessarily dependent on it, and the age panels across the lifespan underscore that reality during this course. Making sense of theories about nonphasic development (e.g., Kegan, 1982; Kohlberg, 1981; Loevinger, 1976; Piaget, 1965) is not so difficult when real children, adolescents, and adults are regularly interacting with the students and representing wide variations within age groups.

Whatever cognitive conflict occurs for them as they struggle to integrate new information into existing structures, many students in this course qualitatively change by resolving disequilibrium through the process of accommodation (cf. Wadsworth, 1979). Students often report that they know themselves better than before and are more comfortable with the self they have explored, which perhaps reflects movement along a continuum of identity development (cf., e.g., Chickering, 1969; Erikson, 1980; Widick, et al., 1978) and development as an "organization of increasing complexity" (Sanford, 1967, p. 47).

The final paper: Another personalized learning experience. Throughout all of the interactive experiences, the students remain aware of the self-study paper that they will eventually have to write. By midterm they have begun the time-consuming process of organizing it. Their frequent identification with young interviewees has helped them to focus on their own school years. During post-interview class discussions about various developmental stages, they have also been reminded to make notes for later reference. The assignment for the paper is as follows:

Write a paper about four to six developmental phases with your-self as the subject. (If you wish not to use yourself as the subject of your paper, you may write the paper with someone else as the subject. This person must be at least thirty years of age and will be named in the paper only by pseudonym. The content of your paper will be based on in-depth interviews with this person.) The paper should be no more than twenty pages in length and should use the new APA style. You may want to conduct some interviews of family members in order to gain insight about your own development, but that is not a requirement. Choose from the following phases: Infancy and Early Childhood, ages 0–5; Middle Childhood, ages 6-11; Adolescence, ages 12-19; Early Adulthood, ages 20-39; Middle Adulthood, ages 40-59; Beyond?

As you discuss each stage, consider *major influences* (e.g., individ-uals, family/sibling constellation, personal responsibilities and roles in family, institutions, circumstances), *role models* (e.g., at school, home, extended family, neighborhood/community), and *"nodal" life events* (e.g., moves, injuries, trauma, illness, death of someone close, changes/losses, "successes," "failures"). Include *references to develop-mental theorists* (at least four times). Consider these questions (listed only to give you ideas):

1. Keeping in mind that "typical" is a social construction, what aspects of your life represent *typical or atypical development* in each phase?
2. In each phase, what evidence shows that you were moving forward, "on hold," or "stuck" in regard to *developmental tasks?*
3. What were the *easiest phases* for you?
4. What were the *most difficult phases* for you?
5. What were some questions, feelings, or concerns you had during each phase or during the most difficult phases?
6. What were some "problems in living" which were related to devel-opmental issues, and which, if you had had comfortable access to counseling, could have been alleviated or lessened by such services—at least by having an objective, knowledgeable listener?
7. What kinds of counseling interventions might have been helpful?
8. What developmental theoretical perspectives are reflected in these interventions?

9. What prevented (or might have prevented) your receiving some intervention? (Or, if you experienced some sort of intervention, what kind was it?)

10. Where are you now developmentally? (What phase[s]? Are you "stuck"? Where are you *in* the phase[s]?)

11. If you could go back and traverse a particular phase again, which would it be, and what would you do differently?

As you write this paper, remember that you are in charge of the content. As your instructor, I promise confidentiality. No one will see your paper, no copy will be made, it will be returned to you at the end of the semester in person, and there will be absolutely no discussion of the content outside of any potential discussion between you and your instructor—unless you cite something from it in class yourself.

The rationale behind assigning this paper is that it is helpful for counselors-in-training to be aware of their own issues—"trigger areas," vulnerabilities, concerns, and history—as they work with clients, no matter what the clients' ages or phases. The more aware counselors are of themselves, and the more they can actively and accurately monitor their responses during sessions, the more effective they can be, and the more they can allow exploration and growth in clients. To date, all students taking this course have written the final paper with themselves as subject. Their feedback has indicated that the assignment is an invigorating, positive (even though perhaps difficult at times), growth-producing experience, and is quite helpful in their training as counselors. When they have finished the final paper, they have expressed appreciation for the process.

The final paper is a culminating activity, requiring linkages among theory, the earlier experiential dimensions of the course, personal insights gained throughout the course, and courage and discretion in self-presentation.

Routinely, during the weeks just preceding submission of the paper, there are phone calls from students requesting individual meetings to process complex emotions or "stuckness." When the papers are all submitted, we "process the process" as a group, and most describe a long and complex process. When the processing begins, some erupt with pent-up emotions as they share their experiences. Some report that interviews with family members rekindled or precipitated new family connections. The actual writing process seems to be a solitary, pensive, and sometimes lonely activity. The students appear collectively to be proud of their accomplishment, and they often interject references to theorists in their comments. During such end-of-the-semester processing, it becomes clear that developmental theory has been personalized—and sometimes challenged. Whatever theories students used to analyze their own development for the paper are not likely to be forgotten. They have also become a community of learners, as advocated by Belenky, Clinchy, Goldberger, and Tarule (1986), and usually are overtly and warmly supportive of each other during this discussion.

Hearing Student Voices

The second constructivist theme which is integral to this human development course is that of hearing and honoring students' voices. The general focus on development, the open-endedness-within-structure of class activities, and the students' participation in the panels all encourage them to lend their unique voices to the discussions. The almost total absence of traditional teacher lectures and the general deemphasis on fact and "truth" also help to keep the focus on student contribution.

The papers, too, offer an opportunity for students to give voice to themselves and to their experiences. Whether on the reflective paragraphs or on the final paper, I give them feedback through marginal notes, establishing a written dialogue that continues throughout the course. They learn early that personalized comments evoke personal response, even though my part of the dialogue is relatively brief. I believe my validating their thoughts and opinions nurtures the teacher-student relationship and students' personal growth. I am "noticing" them. Evaluations have included statements such as "I appreciated your personal involvement with me," "insightful comments on my paper," "sensitive responses to comments and ideas in my papers," and "particularly nurturing and validating comments on papers."

Encouraging Multiple Perspectives

The third constructivist theme of the course lies in evoking and offering multiple perspectives on ideas and situations. For example, during most of the interviews at least two students (perhaps four, if they worked in pairs) interview a single child or adolescent. This means that opportunities exist to observe multiple reactions to a single experience. The follow-up discussions routinely include divergent assessments of those who were interviewed. The "age-panels" also underscore that even though each panel generally represents remarkable commonality regarding developmental concerns, panelists may articulate widely varying views on the aging process, on relationship issues, on what is "normal," on family-of-origin contributions to developmental concerns, and even on what it is like to be ten (or twenty, forty, or sixty-five) years old. Considerable variation may be evident within each age group regarding development and life experience.

Just one perspective among many. My own perspective, I hope, becomes just one among several. I try not to present myself as an "authority," no matter how much I have studied a particular area. The theorists that we study also add their various perspectives. Based on his clinical experience, the author of our textbook one year (Rice, 1997) often included personal comments in addition to documented information. The students appeared to feel freer to argue with his opinions than with the cited research. Interestingly, even though the text served as an authoritative framework for the course, their willingness to dispute it helped the textbook to become "just another perspective" that semester, one with potential value like all perspectives in class, but one which could be challenged as students constructed meaning.

In order to help students see my perspective or the textbook's perspective as "one among many," I try to laud students for insights and commend them for risk-taking when they express divergent views in response to readings or panelists and when they are creative in their writing. I also emphasize the phenomenological nature of counseling—including that both counselor's and client's perspectives are affected by a multitude of factors, including cultural lenses (cf. Peterson, 1997; 1999).

Process questions. At times I stop the adult-panel discussions and ask process questions of the class: "What was your gut-reaction to what she just said?" "What is going on for you right now (e.g., when "forty-somethings" are reassessing their career choices)?" "What feelings were evoked (e.g., when a panelist reveals he has already had three heart attacks at age forty-three)?" "What is it like to witness this clever bantering (in a panel of individuals over age sixty)?" "Give these folks some feedback about how you are responding to their sharing so much." Even during energetic discussions among class members, I sometimes stop and ask process questions, communicating that their thoughts and experiences are valuable and underscoring the wide variety of intrapersonal experiences in the class. I also mean to enhance their ability to monitor their own thoughts and feelings during future interactions with clients.

Interpersonal connections. Heightened intrapersonal awareness enhances the interpersonal connections in class, especially as students gain confidence in expressing themselves and can validate their own experiences and perspectives. I am interested in these connections at two levels: building community for the sake of comfortable communication and personal growth and parallel learning about group interaction for the sake of professional development. Class discussion, especially during debriefings after hands-on experiences, regularly addresses the interpersonal dynamics of the groups we interact with and even of the graduate class itself. I inject systemic observations of a classroom we visited, a group of at-risk teens, or a group of retirees. I want them to become sensitive observers of group dynamics, of nonverbal behavior, and of communication sequences. I also hope that they can learn "how to listen, how to hear one another" (hooks, 1994, p. 150). Students frequently include comments in their final papers about their interpersonal styles and roles at various developmental stages, and about their struggles with differentiation issues (cf. Bowen, 1978). For this I give credit to their raised awareness of interpersonal dynamics and the social "embeddedness" that Kegan (1982) describes.

Facing incongruity. The experiential dimensions of the course provide many unsettling inconsistencies and incongruities for the students, but incongruity may also suddenly appear among class members themselves. As we become better and better acquainted, and as each student serves as a self-disclosing panel member, we invariably discover complexity in the students themselves. Incongruities also appear when we interact with those we interview. Surprises emerge especially when interacting with those in the later developmental stages—rejuvenation, resilience, activity, and insights, for example. At first glance, a panel may appear to be a relatively homogeneous, middle-class, educated group. However, they invariably present developmental diversity. Usually guests are articulate and quickly warm up to sharing their experiences and insights with counseling students. However, because they present themselves well, revelations concerning childhood poverty, trauma, deprivation, personal loss, or significant health concerns "don't fit" and teach prospective counselors about client surprises.

These interactive experiences, with their paradoxes and incongruities, generate insights that are applied in the final paper. The students have been bombarded with contrasts and contradictions in this complex learning process, and their papers attest to their personal growth and ability to view themselves and others more complexly.

Valuing approximation over precision. It is comparatively easy to be precise and sure when examining abstract concepts, hypothetical clients, and imaginary (or real, but "digested") cases. It is less easy when sitting cross-legged on the floor with an unkempt and needy six-year-old; sitting across a narrow table from an angry, disenfranchised teenage survivor of abuse; interacting with a panel of eleven-year-olds; hearing a middle-aged woman reveal childhood trauma; or interviewing an irascible eighty-year-old military retiree in a wheelchair. Contact with real people challenges any belief that counseling is an exact science, or that counseling programs will provide recipes for responding to clients. In their responsive papers the students discuss directions they might explore in a second session, but they are well aware that their hypotheses are tentative and subject to change. The atmosphere of the class moves and shifts, as do the relationships that develop within the class, and these have impact on the learning that takes place. Class discussion is also a dynamic, recursive process of constructing knowledge. Similarly, when a student wants a prescribed format for the papers, I encourage unique and personal expression to match the unique situations and developing lives that are represented.

For essay questions on tests, hoping to encourage awareness of King and Kitchener's (1994) stages six and seven, I try to de-emphasize the idea of "right answers," giving credit for well-reasoned arguments, even if they disagree with the textbook or other sources. My clinical examples might include references to directions taken without suggesting that they were the only possibilities.

Modeling incompleteness. I chose counseling as a second career because I wanted to immerse myself in a field where one never "arrives" and where I would never be bored. I have accumulated enough experience that I can approach a new client and each counseling session with some degree of confidence that I will be able to respond appropriately and help clients live more effectively. Every client teaches me, and I am fascinated by how I am continually informed about human nature and human development. But I have moments of great doubt as a counselor, and there is not always someone available to ask for assistance. Like my clients, I am human; I am "becoming." I comment on my humanness now and then in order to help alleviate student anxiety. I model error, glaringly at times, as when I ask poor-quality questions of panelists or respond unsmoothly. They see me accept my ineptitude.

My high tolerance for ambiguity is probably apparent in how I set up this course each year. I comment in class about the uncertainty I experience, often reminding students that uncertainty also exists when a counselor anticipates a session with a client. But the complexity, and the fact that the content is always new, help to generate energy in me, which I assume has a positive effect on the experience of the students. I hope I am modeling that not being "sure" can be both all right and energizing.

Near the end of the course, usually after the final papers are submitted, the students seem to feel less burdened by the intensity of the course and begin to comment about its administrative complexity. I seize that opportunity to repeat the explanation of my teaching methodology. Those students with a high need for structure and order, who may never have quit wishing for lectures on the textbook, may be more relieved than the others that the course is nearly done. However, usually they now recognize the value of the experiential, open-ended nature of the course. We process their experience.

Reflections on My Experiences Teaching Human Growth and Development

Not everything I have tried in Human Growth and Development has been effective, and each semester I try new approaches in the interest of improvement. As varied as the format and methodology have been, not all learning styles and developmental levels have been accommodated with adequate balance, and strategies meant to foster accountability regarding textbook reading (quizzes, for instance) have not always been perceived as valuable. I continue to try to devise effective ways to encourage faithful reading, particularly through intrinsic means.

Because many opportunities exist in this course for written expression and personalized learning, and because I want to accommodate students whose learning preferences and cognitive development contribute to their comfort with an exam format, I continue to use multiple-choice and short-answer questions for about half of the midterm and final examination. The other half of the exam consists of fairly open-ended essay questions. Most of the "objective" questions require more than simple recall. Nevertheless, I continue to try to devise more personalized ways of assessing familiarity with established literature in the field.

The responsive writing, according to most, has been "valuable," but is "too much writing" for some students. The guest groups have always received high marks, but the field trips have been uncomfortable and stressful for a few students. No matter how much I present a rationale for the experiential dimension, there are some students, perhaps those representing Perry's (1970) first three positions or the received knowledge of Belenky et al. (1986), who do not agree that the interaction with "developing" people is important. These students' resistance, or their reticence, has not deterred me, however, from approaching human development with this particular format. I do my best to nurture them toward greater tolerance for ambiguity, and I encourage them to process their frustrations both in and out of class.

Only once have I experienced a class that demonstrated, as I perceived it, considerable collective resistance to the field experiences. That year I had an unusually small class (eight students), all age twenty-two or twenty-three except one, who was twenty-six. I still have many questions about what made the experience more difficult and less positive that year, although I suspect that age homogeneity, developmental level, and personality structure of the students all played a part.

The format and methodology of this course demand intense personal involvement from everyone. An atmosphere of sustained interpersonal engagement exists, much like what hooks (1994, p. 164) describes as fluid movement among the various parts of the experience. The substantial involvement, responsibility, and creativity required of teacher and students creates a developmentally powerful system (cf. Astin, 1985). Perhaps as a result of the nature of the learning, student-to-student and student-to-teacher bonding develops more significantly in this course than in other courses I teach. Students become something different from what they once were: they understand themselves, human development, and the counseling relationship better at the end than they did at the outset. They have been exposed to social complexity (cf. Labouvie-Vief, 1984) and have "made sense" of the experience, in Loevinger (1976) terms. They have moved along the continuum of "becoming a counselor." And I feel very much alive myself as a counselor educator, continually prodded into growth.

References

Astin, A. W. (1985). *Achieving educational excellence: A critical assessment of priorities and practices in higher education.* San Francisco: Jossey-Bass.

Belenky, M. F., Clinchy, B. M., Goldberger, N. R., and Tarule, J. M. (1986). *Women's ways of knowing: The development of self, voice, and mind.* New York: Basic Books.

Bowen, M. (1978). *Family therapy in clinical practice.* New York: Jason Aronson.

Chickering, A. W. (1969). *Education and identity.* San Francisco: Jossey-Bass.

Delworth, U., Hanson, G. R., and Associates. (1989). *Student services: A handbook* (2nd ed.). San Francisco: Jossey-Bass.

Erikson, E. H. (1980). *Identity and the life cycle.* New York: Routledge.

Giroux, H. (1981). *Ideology, culture, and the process of schooling.* Philadelphia: Temple University Press.

Helms, J. E. (1995). An update of Helms's white and people of color racial identity models. In J. G. Ponterotto, J. M. Casas, L. A. Suzuki, and C. M. Alexander (Eds.), *Handbook of multicultural counseling* (pp. 181-191). Thousand Oaks, CA: Sage.

hooks, b. (1994). *Teaching to transgress: Education as the practice of freedom.* New York: Routledge.

Kegan, R. (1982). *The evolving self: Problem and process in human development.* Cambridge, MA: Harvard University Press.

_____. (1994). *In over our heads: The mental demands of modern life.* Cambridge, MA: Harvard University Press.

King, P. M., and Kitchener, K. S. (1994). *Developing reflective judgment: Understanding and promoting intellectual growth and critical thinking in adolescents and adults.* San Francisco: Jossey-Bass.

Kirby, J. R. (1988). Style, strategy and skill in reading. In R. R. Schmeck (Ed.) *Learning strategies and learning styles* (pp. 229-274). New York: Plenum Press.

Kohlberg, L. (1981). *The philosophy of moral development.* New York: Harper and Row.

Kolb, D. (1976). *Learning styles inventory technical manual.* Boston: McBer.

_____. (1984). *Experiential learning: Experience as the source of learning and development.* Englewood Cliffs, NJ: Prentice Hall.

Komives, S. R., Woodard, D. B., Jr., and Associates. (1996). *Student services: A handbook for the profession* (3rd ed.). San Francisco: Jossey-Bass.

Labouvie-Vief, G. (1984). Logic and self-regulation from youth to maturity: A model. In M. L. Commons, F. A. Richards, and C. Armon (Eds.), *Beyond formal operations: Late adolescence and adult cognitive development,* (pp. 158-179). New York: Praeger.

Lamborn, S. D., and Fischer, K. W. (1988). Optimal and functional levels in cognitive development: The individual's developmental range. *Newsletter of the International Society for the Study of Behavioral Development* 14 (2): 1-4.

Loevinger, J. (1976). *Ego development: Conceptions and theories.* San Francisco: Jossey-Bass.

McMillan, J. H., and Forsyth, D. R. (1991). What theories of motivation say about why learners learn. In R. J. Menges and M. D. Svinicki (Eds.), *College teaching: From theory to practice* (New Directions for Teaching and Learning No. 45, pp. 39-52). San Francisco: Jossey-Bass.

Perry, W. G. (1970). *Forms of intellectual and ethical development in the college years: A scheme.* New York: Holt, Rinehart and Winston.

_____. (1981). Cognitive and ethical growth: The making of meaning. In A. W. Chickering and Associates (Eds.), *The modern American college: Responding to the new realities of diverse students and a changing society* (pp. 76-116). San Francisco: Jossey-Bass.

Peterson, J. S. (1993). *Talk with Teens About Self and Stress.* Minneapolis: Free Spirit.

_____. (1995). *Talk with Teens About Feelings, Family, Relationships, and the Future.* Minneapolis: Free Spirit.

_____. (1997). Naming gifted children: An example of unintended 'reproduction.' *Journal for the Education of the Gifted* 21 (1): 82-100.

_____. (1999). Gifted—through whose cultural lens? An application of the postpositivistic mode of inquiry. *Journal for the Education of the Gifted* 22: 354-383.

Piaget, J. (1965). *The moral judgment of the child.* (M. Gabain, Trans.). New York: Free Press. (Originally published 1932).

Rice, F. P. (1997). *Human development: A lifespan approach.* Englewood Cliffs, NJ: Prentice Hall.

Riegel, K. (1973). Dialectic operations: The final period of cognitive development. *Human Development* 16: 346-370.

Sanford, N. (1966). *Self and society.* New York: Atherton.

_____. (1967). *Where colleges fail: A study of the student as a person.* San Francisco: Jossey-Bass.

Schon, D. (1987). *Educating the reflective practitioner.* San Francisco: Jossey-Bass.

Wadsworth, B. J. (1979). *Piaget's theory of cognitive development* (2nd ed.). New York: Longman.

Widick, C., Parker, C. A., and Knefelkamp, L. (1978). Erik Erikson and psychosocial development. In L. Knefelkamp, C. Widick, and C. A. Parker (Eds.), *Applying new developmental findings* (New Directions for Student Services No. 4, pp. 1-17). San Francisco: Jossey-Bass.

Witkin, H. A. (1976). Cognitive style in academic performance and in teacher-student relations. In S. Messick and Associates (Eds.), *Individuality in learning* (pp. 38-72). San Francisco: Jossey-Bass.

Yalom, I. D. (1997). *The theory and practice of group psychotherapy.* NY: Basic Books.

Part Four

CONCLUSIONS

Chapter Ten
Implementing Constructivist Counselor Education: Pushing the Zone of Proximal Development
Garrett McAuliffe, Old Dominion University
Karen Eriksen, Radford and Walden Universities

At once it struck me what quality went to form [an individual] of achievement . . . I mean "negative capability," that is, when [she or he] is capable of being in uncertainties, mysteries, doubts, without any irritable reaching after fact and reason.

John Keats, 1817

The growth of any craft depends on honest dialogue among the people who do it. . . .

Parker Palmer, 1998

The preceding chapters might by now have stirred enthusiasm for the constructivist inclination in some readers. You have been urged, ever so gently, to pay attention to both the teacher's and learner's experiences, to honor both instructional process and content, to share and reinvent methods in dialogue with students, to strive for equality between teacher and learner, to favor induction, and to embrace uncertainty and contradiction. These proposals resonate with those who gather together under the constructivist umbrella, who acknowledge that learning occurs in a zone among the teacher, the subject matter, and the learners. But proposals are mere unfulfilled potentials. In order to end a constructivist counselor education, we must stretch ourselves to embrace Keats' appreciation of uncertainty and Palmer's call for dialogue.

Perhaps we now agree that constructivist education is more than any one method. Above all, it is the practice of having teacher and learner become mutual knowledge-creators in a continuing cycle of input and feedback, construction and deconstruction. It includes much of what Dewey (1938) has already said about the necessity of experience, the meeting of student and curriculum, and the value of inductive exploration (cf. Freiberg and Driscoll, 1996). Many of us also embrace the implications of social constructionism—valuing diversity, being multiculturally competent, promoting student development, and helping students to think from a "socially critical" perspective. Thirty years of educational research seem to support many of the programmatic and teaching strategies delineated thus far (Freiberg and Driscoll, 1996).

These seemingly compelling findings bring us to a disturbing question: Why aren't these ideas being implemented more extensively in counselor education, psychology, social work, or psychiatric nursing training programs, let alone in undergraduate education? Why does 80 percent of teaching in most disciplines continue to be of the traditional, lecture-read-and-test style?

We offer below a litany of the possible obstacles to a constructivist counselor education. We hope that naming these obstacles will not be daunting to mental health educators, for we also offer "correctives," or conditions that might enhance constructivist education. These correctives include both internal and external factors that might make a consistent, reflexive educational practice possible. We particularly describe those habits of mind that might serve as a roadmap for faculty training and development.

Some Obstacles and Possible Solutions

The constructivist educational endeavor is not for the faint of heart, nor for the developmentally "overchallenged." My own (McAuliffe) experience of opening up my pedagogy to more constructivist dimensions was accompanied by the following "disconcerting" consequences: It was "epistemologically irritating" to co-create understandings with other learners. It was harder work and it was less predictable. It required interpersonal and intrapersonal intelligence, comfort with dissonance, and vigilance about my own tacit assumptions. I had to be willing to self-disclose and to behave in an egalitarian manner.

These dimensions are, in many ways, "counter-cultural" to the norms of the academy. They challenge the prevailing super-rationality, the pursuit of certainty, the aim for objectivity, the norm of hyper-autonomy, and the established hierarchies. Luckily, counselor educators are perhaps already inclined to question the "normal science" (Kuhn, 1970) of current college teaching practice. Not only are counselor educators grounded in a developmental perspective, but constructivist education has striking parallels to the act of counseling itself.

Internal Obstacles

We have identified seven so-called conditions which might constitute "internal" obstacles to enacting a more constructivist counselor education. They are: epistemological irritation, comfort with the hegemony of intellect and reason in the academy, discomfort with dissonance, disinclination to examine our tacit assumptions, squeamishness about personal disclosure, the threat of egalitarianism, and the necessity to work harder. We will discuss each potential obstacle separately.

Obstacle 1: Epistemological irritation. Constructivist-developmental counselor education aims at creating constructivist, self-authorizing professionals (Kegan, 1994). Such helpers would be reflective, dialogical, socially critical, and humble. Constructivist educators would have the "negative capability," using Keats' phrase from the chapter epigram, to dwell in uncertainty, to consult, to hear, to shift direction, and, ultimately, to recognize that the story they are telling is one among many, contingent on historical, temporal, personal, and cultural contexts.

We would include under such negative capability Parker Palmer's (1998) notion of "holding paradoxes." Palmer proposes that "good" teaching incorporates such paradoxes as keeping boundaries and structure, yet being open to student ideas; being supportive and hospitable, but making the environment "charged" (read "challenging"); valuing individuality, but encouraging group consensus; and honoring both personal ("little") stories, but also abstract ("big") generalizations. Such is the "negative capability" of simultaneously focusing on one method, while leaving room for its seeming opposite. Tensions would be held between action and reflection, intellect and affect, closure and divergence—but each would be entertained.

And there is the rub. A goal of embracing uncertainty may stretch us as mental health educators beyond our current capacities. For constructivist education requires a parallel epistemology, a capacity to recognize that all human beings, including social scientists, tell stories;

they do not "find" ultimate realities about human behavior. How many of us are willing to deconstruct our stories, to recognize the "intertextuality" that is masked when we declare "our" opinion, "our" chosen theory, "our" world view?

Negative capability is a rare achievement, given our current educational modes. Research shows that fewer than 20 percent of our mental health practitioners (Kegan, 1994; Neukrug and McAuliffe, 1993) seem to be consistently able to engage in dialogue, entertain uncertainty, and let experience unfold in a social context. Many practitioners, perhaps up to 50 percent (Kegan, 1994; Neukrug and McAuliffe, 1993), are prone to either an individualistic "hyper-autonomy" or to a convention-embedded dependency. Either of these tendencies can be dangerous for clients, as they may be accompanied by cultural encapsulation, adherence to a single technique, and/or maintenance of the status quo when more inclusive and socially critical interventions are needed.

If so few mental health practitioners achieve an interdependent, reflective state of mind, what can we say about counselor educators? How ready are we, as counselor educators, to face this mental challenge? Many of us are "ready," but not consistently "there," if the current research on post-formal (or nonabsolute/relativistic) thinking in college faculty is to be believed (cf. Yan and Arlin, 1995). We might define post-formal thinking as having a "full constructivist" (Lovell and McAuliffe, 1997) bent; that is, an interest in and ability to think outside of systems, to consistently embrace fluidity and change, and to recognize the socially constructed nature of one's perspectives. Yet Commons (1999) found that only 25 percent of faculty at a regional state university were able to think post-formally. The vast majority of the others tended toward a more convention-reliant, nondialogical orientation.

I (McAuliffe), for instance, regularly find myself declaring allegiance to my favorite, and always limited, stories. Mine often favor practices like encouraging affect in the classroom, promoting use of words over numbers, and preferring cultural explanations for human behavior over individualistic ones. Derrida (1978), as I understand him, indicates that we constantly practice "erasure" when we make declarations. That is, we erase other unsaid but possible declarations each time we speak or think. I should know better, however. I should instead relativize my current story, turn it into a verb, recognize that a phenomenon is more complex than words (and numbers) can ever express, and try to include other, even seemingly contradictory stories in my attempts at understanding the world. Trying this is both humbling and liberating, and perhaps exemplifies a practice of negative capability.

But there is hope. According to the developmental literature (e.g., Kohlberg, 1969), individuals can understand reasoning which is slightly beyond their current capacities (called "one-up" reasoning). Therefore, "nonabsolute/relativistic" thinking is within faculty members' reach, or their "zone of proximal development" (Vygotsky, 1934/1986). With the help of in-service faculty development activities, many of us might be able to periodically enter the fluid constructivist zone.

How might the development of negative capability occur? We must have opportunities to safely "lose composure." Constructivism asks that we recognize that we *are* already composed, by individual others and by culture, as much as we compose. And, in Kegan's usage (1982), we can "lose our composure" when we expose our tacit assumptions as "mere" constructions. The constructivist epistemology asks us to lose composure in favor of an ongoing composing. We would have to incorporate the following assumptions into our composing. We would have to recognize: the pervasiveness of power in all relationships (cf. Foucault, 1972), the ultimacy of dialogue as "reality" creator (Habermas, 1984; Derrida, 1978), and subjectivity as the only certainty (Nietzche, 1974). Can we as counselor educators be ever so humble as to embrace the finality that there is no final, objective truth in human affairs? And can we give up the sinecure of the profess-or who is the arbiter of counseling truths, in favor of a context-sensitive storying? Most of us are ill-prepared for such an amorphous condition. Yet we propose here that this understanding is within our grasp; it is "one-up" epistemologically for most of us; it is in our zone of proximal development.

Obstacle 2: Comfort with the hegemony of intellect and reason in the academy. Another obstacle to constructivist education is many educators' exclusive comfort with reason and intellect and corresponding lack of attunement to the emotional domain. "Above the shoulders" (i.e., intellectual only) education (Belenky, Clinchy, Goldberger, and Tarule, 1986) is the model we have inherited in our one-size-fits-all university culture. For many good reasons, the Enlightenment's emphasis on rational deliberation was seen as a major advance over the traditional dominance of "mere emotion," intuition, and, worst of all, superstition in public discourse. Thus rationalism became the hallmark of the university.

Yet such is the sway of a once-good idea that it can exclude other, complementary, and more inclusive ways of knowing. This is seen in the problematizing of emotion in education. The reigning "knowledge-transfer" model of education allows information and skills to crowd out emotional experience (hooks, 1994). Here's how bell hooks (1994), an English professor, describes the tension: "Few professors talk about the place of emotions in the classroom. . . . [Yet] if we are all emotionally shut down, how can there be any excitement about ideas?. . . The restrictive, repressive classroom ritual insists that emotional responses have no place. . . . [yet] the emotions . . . keep us aware or alert . . . they enhance classrooms" (pp. 154-155). Hooks' views on the value of emotion or arousal in learning is confirmed in the literature (e.g., McNamara, Chapter Three of this volume). In parallel fashion, I (McAuliffe) found (see Chapter Two) that students identified empathic support from faculty as a major condition that contributed to their learning.

Two dimensions of emotion seem important in education: (1) "affective excitement" which enhances memory and (2) personal attention and support. Each has been overlooked as a factor in learning in the academy. We as faculty must rediscover and use our inter- and intrapersonal intelligence in order to increase our comfort and interest in affectively loaded encounters and to be sensitive to students' emotional messages. When we wear our "emotional intelligence hat," we would feel connected with others in spite of seeming differences and showing "attentive caring" for the lives of others. These are constructivist knowing characteristics (Belenky, Clinchy, Goldberger, Tarule, 1986).

Affect extends to the interpersonal domain also. An instructor must have the sensitivity to read student cues—from indifference to discomfort to involvement—whether in the advising moment or during a class discussion. The instructor must then follow up this sensitivity to cues with listening in a manner that encourages students to further disclose and explore. Only then can the instructor intervene with an optimal mix of challenge and support which might be needed for particular students at particular times. This alertness to the interpersonal domain contrasts with the monological singlemindedness that characterizes much traditional college teaching.

We must also practice internal reflexivity if we are to include affect in education. Such reflexivity might, for instance, include the intrapersonal affective attunement which allows the instructor to bracket her or his immediate responses of dislike and discomfort or attraction, and to instead choose the response that is most helpful in meeting student needs. The struggle to know and integrate personal feelings toward a student is captured in these words of Jane Vella (1994): "This relationship [teacher-student] must transcend personal likes and dislikes. If a teacher feels a strong dislike for an adult learner, she knows she must be even more careful about showing respect, affirming, and listening carefully. When the teacher fails to show respect or fails to affirm a learner in a group . . . , the whole group begins to doubt the learning relationship and often manifests anger, fear, and disappointment" (p. 9). Emotional intelligence thus requires both the interpersonal ability to judiciously blend support with challenge (e.g., instructor to student supervised: "Although I think your directness can be very challenging for the client, that tone of voice could make the client feel ashamed. Try this. . . .") and the intrapersonal ability to access personal responses. (e.g., instructor to herself: "I'm feeling defensive," "I'm prejudging this student.").

Obstacle 3: Discomfort with dissonance. A further obstacle to constructivist education is discomfort with dissonance. Most of us, in the traditional autonomous mode of the academy, aim for closure, convergence, and "finishedness." We quake at challenges to our clean-cut arguments. We prepare our lectures so that our logic is unassailable. Belenky et al. (1986) describe the predicament of an English professor whose students sit silently after he has delivered a well-formed, tightly constructed argument for a literary interpretation. He had hoped that they would "rip into it" after he was finished:

He has . . . toiled much of the previous night over his interpretation [of a novel]. They treat his words as sacrosanct. He cannot understand why they will not risk a response. But the teacher himself takes few risks. . . . He invites the students to find holes in his argument, but he has taken pains to make it airtight. He would regard as scandalous a suggestion that he make the argument more permeable. . . . So long as teachers hide the imperfect processes of their thinking, allowing students to glimpse only the polished products, students will remain convinced that only . . . a professor . . . could think up a theory.

Belenky et al. (1986) remind us that "the problem is especially acute with respect to science." However, we would also include the social science and counseling fields as problematic. For instance, adherents of behaviorism, psychodynamic thinking, reality therapy, and humanism present their theories as final and as available for wholesale adoption by students, rather than as one way to story their experiences of clients or students.

In contrast, constructivist educators must be willing to tolerate the dissonance that arises from "co-constructing" both the class content and the teaching process with their students and colleagues. The constructivist instructor must be able to entertain and manage her or his own irritation in the face of contradiction and uncertainty.

Dialogue and attention to the process of the class might mean that we do not achieve the satisfaction of "proving" a point at times and that we are not fully in control of the classroom process. Dialogue inevitably invites difference and newness. I (McAuliffe) think of a recent student whose rabid opposition to Affirmative Action was initially daunting to me. When I was able to entertain her perspective and ask her to consider multiple dimensions of the issue, we both learned and she felt both heard and challenged. When members of the class ask me to rethink an assignment or to emphasize a particular topic, I inevitably experience an initial annoyance and discomfort, for I have been "knocked off" of my pedagogical track. And while some educators might pray for patience, I repeat the mantra of dialectical thinking (learned from Michael Basseches, 1991), "Contradiction is my friend." Similarly, I remind myself of Paolo Friere's position that education might be viewed as an event in which "a teacher-learner is among learner-teachers" (Friere, 1994) and that knowledge is created by the community (Rorty, in Olson, 1989).

Obstacle 4: Ignorance about our tacit assumptions and standpoints. Still another obstacle to constructivist education is many educators' ignorance about their tacit assumptions and standpoints. Stepping back from and evaluating one's constructions requires constant vigilance and courage. We often hold unquestioned loyalties to counseling theories, teaching methods, and moral positions. We also may "be subject to" (Kegan, 1982) our inherited cultural norms, religious allegiances, and gender-based values. These tacit allegiances may drive much of our sense-making. When we don't "take responsibility for the sense we make," we are likely to impose culturally derived personal constructions on others, in the name of "objectivity," "reality," or "truth" (Kegan, 1994).

To counter the potential obstacle to constructivist education of educators imposing such an "objectivist" (Palmer, 1998) world view on students, constructivist education asks instructors to develop "standpoint awareness," which in the feminist literature refers largely to the ability to step back from gender-, race-, and class-based assumptions, and to evaluate the impact these assumptions might have on our current perspectives. We must have faith that what is tacitly constructed can also be "deconstructed," that is, examined for the implicit stories embedded in all human discourse (Derrida, 1978). Constructivist educators are asked to relativize all of their stories by remembering that, but for the (mis)fortune of being "thrown" into a particular cultural context, they might be different. The poet Walt Whitman asks for such deconstruction in the line, "Question everything you have been taught in church, at home, or in school."

An example of a "story" that we might deconstruct comes from my experience: I (McAuliffe) had a male colleague who was certain that a competitive debate-style class discussion format was the "only" way to get students to challenge ideas and analyze evidence. And yet that type of academic discourse, which depends upon point-counterpoint competition, fails to extend others' ideas in favor of single-mindedly looking for deficits in their arguments. It also precludes the expression of emotion (cf. Belenky et al., 1986; hooks, 1994) in favor of an argumentative logic. The debate style of academic discourse is founded on the possibility of there being a Kantian "pure reason" which will emerge from tightly argued analyses.

Our objectivist colleague might instead have asked himself a variation on Richard Rorty's questions: "Have I been "fooled" into thinking that the predominantly male, European-based academic traditions are somehow a final, objective way to teach and learn?" and "Perhaps I have been inducted into a 'tribe' which has socialized me to favor this perspective." By exercising "standpoint awareness" or "critical consciousness" (Friere, 1994) about the origins and effects of our historically and culturally based constructions, we can take responsibility for the sense we make, and thus, we are more likely to make choices from among options. We are also more disposed, in turn, to allow others to make such choices. Open-minded inquiry, or "leaning into" (McGoldrick, 1994) challenges to our comfortable assumptions, would replace the insular privileging of theorics, disciplines, and cultures. We might instead be heard to say, "How might my understanding of the optimal counseling training program be limited by my current standpoints, and how might I inquire about alternative approaches on admissions, curricula, and field work?"

Obstacle 5: Discomfort with personal disclosure. Instructors' squeamishness about sharing personal stories can be another barrier to constructivist education. Traditional education often expunges personal stories from the classroom. The only "way of knowing" that is considered valid is the supposedly depersonalized, scientific method. Further, some educators—hopefully not counselors—may echo the cliche that "familiarity breeds contempt;" that is, they fear that sharing aspects of their personal lives makes them less respectable to students, and thus makes what they teach less credible or authoritative. However, students might instead be empowered by our personal stories. They might identify themselves as part of the same universe as we. They might see themselves in us.

Personalizing need not be privileged over the impersonal dimensions of knowing constructivist education can be a "big tent." Bell hooks (1994), for instance, suggests that the general and the personal, and the intellectual and the emotional can share the stage in education. In parallel fashion, Palmer (1998) asks us to welcome the tension between the "big" stories (e.g., theories) and "small" stories (e.g, concrete individual experiences).

How might the personal be brought into education? Instructors might share their doubts and their enthusiasms, and relate anecdotes. We might include our struggles for intimacy, gratification, and success. Remembering the humanness and wisdom of the supposed "fools" in Shakespeare's plays, we could risk looking "foolish" in some eyes. We could demonstrate that we too are "unfinished" learners-in-process. Through this self-disclosure, we as educators will be known in our act of making sense, and others will be heartened to see knowledge creation in action. Knowledge creation will then no longer be the province of, in one student's words, "experts who are different from us." Students may in fact join the "club of knowledge creators," which would now have an open admissions policy.

Obstacle 6: The threat of egalitarianism. Many educators are uncomfortable with the notion of egalitarianism in the classroom. This automatic allegiance to hierarchy might further hinder the movement toward constructivist education. Constructivist and postmodern thinkers have proposed that the role of power needs to be factored into all human relationships (Burbules and Rice, 1991), from teacher-to-student encounters to colleague-to-colleague relationships. Misuse of power or allegiance to hierarchy might reveal itself in considering the automatic valuing of titles, age, height, strength, gender, rank, and ability, to name just a few reference points in the social environment.

How might we counter such misuse? Perhaps by recognizing it's role and defusing its strength, when it seems appropriate. Constructivist educators would recognize the fundamental equality in all relationships while noticing and distinguishing their use of both official authority and informal influence that is due to their power. Authority might then intentionally be used in context, as in the case of the instructor who declares, "Yes, this paper is required, and I do want you to work in groups." However, even when such authority is exercised, instructors can still maintain an open ear to student input on possible modifications of course topics, instructional formats, and grading methods.

Educators might also encourage themselves to become more comfortable with the instability that egalitarianism brings. If we encourage emergent ideas to grow in conversation with colleagues and students (and ourselves!) as equals, through "exploration, talking and listening, speculation, sharing, and questions" (Belenky et al., 1986, p. 144), we will experience discomfort. The alternative, however, is to hide behind the illusory sinecure of authority.

Obstacle 7: The necessity for harder work. Constructing education in the ways described in this book is more labor intensive than traditional, teacher-centered education. In preparing a class, it is easier to merely read material, line out a lecture, and deliver it verbatim, perhaps leaving room for a few questions. Constructivism, as does counseling, demands instead that we explicitly seek out the experience of the other. Attention to the learner requires the willingness and ability to match and mismatch instruction to her or his learning needs. We must attend to both *content* and *process.*

The constructivist/developmental teacher in me typically follows this progression in class preparation: Read the material (after assigning it in a sequence that might work), and jot down notes on the content (So far, all responsible college teachers are with me!). Then— and now the added dimension is revealed—I begin to plan the teaching process. I must ponder ways to instigate mental activity on the part of the learners. And that way lies the labyrinth. If I "go inductive," I will set up a problem to begin the session, perhaps an illustrative role play or anecdote. Or I might trigger student reflections on their own experiences in order to "pull out" generalizations. The results of such induction are somewhat unpredictable; I cannot fully control the direction of the discoveries. So I live with ongoing concerns about focusing the direction of the learning, and I worry about whether I have "covered" the objectives sufficiently. And thus I labor—wheeling through the Kolbian (1984) learning cycle, from experience to reflection to abstraction and back again to new experience.

The hard work of education also does not begin and end at the classroom door, of course. Constructivist teaching might also be understood more broadly to include attending to the learner's experience during advising, graduate assistant mentoring, admissions interviewing, and cohort group facilitation. In each case, I need to pay attention to the process—the intersection among teacher, learner, and curriculum. That is hard work.

External Constraints

Constructivist education, then, clearly places demands on the person of the educator. However, educators also function as members of the larger educational system, and this system exerts pressures which may also work against the practice of constructivist education. These constraints include the traditional reward system in academia, the related subordination of teaching to scholarship, the absence of pedagogical training for college faculty, and possible student opposition to an inclusive pedagogy.

Teaching has not historically been given the highest priority by tenure and promotion committees at most universities. In turn, faculty members, in order to survive professionally, "cut" the time and energy spent in preparing for teaching. A faculty member might justifiably fear that time taken to think about changing course structures, assessing student development, and engaging in dialogue with colleagues about creative ideas for stimulating critical thinking will take away from investing in the scholarly activities that are a priority for tenure and promotion. Some would say that the tenure and promotion process values success in promoting a profession through research and scholarly writing over educating students. Those of us who are interested in constructivist education might thus feel threatened by the diminishment in reward if we "steal" the time necessary for constructivist teaching from time that might be invested in writing and research.

Worries about achieving tenure in such university systems may drive junior faculty to over-control the classroom environment. Students will question and challenge us, and yet, especially if constructivist developmental education aims at helping students to think critically, to challenge the status quo, to reflect on the "ways things have always been done," to become self-authoring systemic thinkers, to become activists, and to develop a "voice." Faculty will have to prepare themselves to hear divergent views on methods and procedures that they may have invested a great deal of time in developing.

Some university systems and tenured professors may not want to have their content-driven, directive ways examined during such student challenges. Some constructivism-inclined junior faculty may not want to encourage students to question the system that is "owned" by the tenured faculty, for fear that their own prospective tenure might be threatened. Some personal anecdotes may illuminate faculty and program inability or unwillingness to deal with empowered students. I (Eriksen) remember one dean telling me that this university's students rarely complained. I wondered if that was really the indicator of success that she seemed to think it was. In yet another situation, I remember my own anxious experience of wondering whether I should really teach my students about advocacy, because if they were unhappy with my teaching, I might be giving them the tools to advocate for my removal. I have also felt quite intimidated by being handed a prior instructor's syllabus for a course and discovering that for the last five years the course I was to teach has not included assessment by project-based or experiential learning, but has utilized only multiple choice exams. I remember pondering whether I should continue that tradition in the interests of fitting in, even though I was pretty sure that the students would learn skills and information more relevant to their future work from a more participatory method.

The emphasis on scholarship over teaching also results in universities hiring faculty members who have only a secondary interest in teaching. I (Eriksen) personally made a mid-career shift to counselor education precisely because I wanted to teach. However, I have observed that not all educators share such enthusiasm. For example, it is a known fact that most university professors teach without themselves having received prior pedagogical training. In contrast, kindergarten through twelfth grade teachers are required to take methods courses in which they learn to design curricula and promote students' intellectual development. In such courses, they encounter research on teaching strategies and ideas about creative ways to help students to learn. University professors are hired largely on the basis of scholarly potential.

We might expect our students to complain about our teaching limitations. They often do not protest, however, for, fortunately or unfortunately, many have themselves received sixteen years or more of traditional, passive education, and may not know the alternative.

A final external threat to constructivist innovation lies in the negative or uncertain reaction of students themselves to a more participatory education. In one new teaching situation, this author wondered how her students would handle the obvious disparities between the way her class was taught and the way the rest of their instruction was delivered. I worried that students, particularly those whom developmentalists might describe as operating out of a "received" knowing framework (Belenky, et al., 1986), might be unwilling to participate so fully in creating their own learning experiences, might be uncomfortable with the ambiguity of co-constructed learning, and might complain about inductive and experiential teaching strategies.

And such has been the case, in my experience. I found students in a recent Community Agencies course to express many fears as they faced experiential learning assignments. In that course, they were required to visit an agency, interview a counselor, and then demonstrate, in class, some form of human service work in a staged simulation. When I inquired further about why they had so many questions, I discovered that in all of their university education, they had never encountered a teacher who hadn't largely lectured. Needless to say, I wondered whether, given such a contrast, I would survive to teach there again. As Perry (1970) has noted, our own teaching evaluations may reflect the developmental variations among students' own as much as our pedagogical proficiency or lack thereof.

Possible Responses to Obstacles

Happily, colleges and universities have increased their focus on teaching and learning in recent years. We can encourage or actively advocate for our institutions to continue to implement such measures. This section suggests changes in organizational culture, in the academy in general, and in professional association practices that might serve to support a shift toward constructivist education.

Constructivist organizational culture. Our efforts to rethink teaching and learning will be enhanced if our organizations themselves move toward a more "constructivist culture" (Cunningham, 1993;

Torbert, 1987). Such a culture would honor the twin themes of egalitarianism and multiple perspective-taking. It would provide a "counter-cultural" challenge to the hierarchy and autonomy that is traditional in the academy (hooks, 1994; Kegan, 1994; Palmer, 1998).

The inclusive egalitarianism which is implicit in constructivism favors "co"-construction in organizational decision-making, an inclination toward dialogue among equals over "auto"-construction (Lovell and McAuliffe, 1997), manipulation, and so-called political uses of power in the organization. In the social constructionist paradigm, it is recognized that the community creates knowledge. The social constructionist recognizes the illusion of complete autonomy, for any seemingly autonomous act is inextricably influenced by the historical, social, and political environments which swirl around the decision-maker. And that organizational decision-maker can ultimately benefit, in the form of new perspectives, from recognizing those influences.

In contrast, "auto-naming" ("autonomy") or auto-governing ("auto-cratic") impulses rely on the "wisdom" of the individual, "rational" decision-maker. An autonomy-oriented organization can suffer from an absence of diverse perspectives. A constructivist egalitarianism does not discount the use of selective autonomy or hierarchy, but instead relativizes their use. For instance, an instructor might use her authority to choose a text after she has filtered the voices of others.

An organizational emphasis on egalitarianism also implies a fundamental equality between student and teacher and among faculty members. Such equality replaces the privileges of title, rank, age, gender, and expertise with more open, "authentic" encounters. Equality might manifest itself in such practices as student participation in position searches and program meetings, and full inclusion of new, nontenured faculty in deliberations. Instructors would exhibit inclusion by regularly checking in on the student learning process, asking "How am I doing?" and "How are you doing?" An air of openness and humility would permeate the halls of the counselor education program, perhaps symbolized by the at-least-occasional use of first names and circular seating arrangements in the classroom.

Such an inclusive egalitarianism links easily with the constructivist theme of *valuing multiple perspectives*. The domain of ethnic culture provides a ready example. A constructivist organization would be characterized by affirmative, proactive attempts to ensure that more cultural standpoints are not tacitly assumed and represented. The "multicultural organization" is one that zealously seeks out potentially "hidden" or underrepresented perspectives. It embraces "otherness," making the other part of its (multi)culture. It consistently and vigilantly opposes the deadening, hegemonic dominance of any one perspective, whether in classroom décor, or admissions and hiring policies. In the multiperspectival organization, staff would consistently "look under every rock" for new life in the form of additional gender, ethnic, religious, and class perspectives. And where there is life, there is movement—for better and worse, as for instance in a family, when the quiet of a coupleship is forever interrupted with the arrival of a new child. Similarly, the noise of multiple perspectives in an organization vitalizes any moribund patterns. That is the price and the gain of having a diverse "learning community."

An anecdote might illustrate: I (McAuliffe) noticed at one point a few years ago that very few African-American students were attending graduate student social gatherings in our counseling program. When I made inquiries, I discovered that student gatherings were being held in predominantly White neighborhoods and in settings to which African-Americans rarely went. When we varied the location to a place more oriented to African-Americans, attendance was more diverse. Black students attended in greater numbers. My lesson was that we had to actively challenge hegemonic assumptions, even about the location and style of a restaurant, if we weren't to commit the "sin of omission," or "erasure" (Derrida, 1978)—that is, taking our perspective as universal.

Multiple perspective-taking is not, however, limited to the ethnic cultural domain. Inductive teaching and qualitative research, with their focus on discovery, also invite multiple narratives. Within and without the classroom, we can invite alternate views. For example, I recently commented on my own liberal political bias in teaching of social and cultural issues in counseling (McAuliffe, 1999). I then invited and nurtured, I hope, the expression of alternative, perhaps more conservative, views on culture. Thus, an ethic of equality breeds a welcoming organization, one in which many voices are heeded. In the service of such an ethic, our stories must be constructed, deconstructed, and reconstructed constantly.

Changes in the academy. Many practices of the academy have endured scrutiny in recent years. Among them, a tenure system which values research over teaching, and the failure to produce educational outcomes that are clearly relevant to social problems and practice expectations, have increasingly been criticized. Perhaps such scrutiny foreshadows changes in the academy along the lines that we have been suggesting.

There has, in fact, been a slow movement over the past ten years to recognize good teaching in the academy. Some universities already require teaching experience and demonstrations of teaching competence in their new faculty. We might go further and require prospective professors to take a course on teaching prior to graduation from their doctoral programs. In such a course, students might learn about adult and student development, and might have their own epistemologies challenged. We could require demonstrations of teaching during faculty hiring interviews (rather than the more typical presentation, which often ends up being a formal presentation of the candidate's doctoral research).

Some universities have also instituted teaching projects—offering incentives for participating—in which faculty discuss how to teach, observe one another's teaching, receive feedback on their teaching strategies, and attempt to incorporate strategies more in line with the principles in this book. Perhaps teaching project personnel, who are educated in such strategies and may be outside of our own departments, could be recruited to evaluate faculty so that student evaluations alone would not be the measure of a faculty member's successful performance. In this way, creative teachers could be rewarded, rather than being punished for failing to conform to long-standing and habitual departmental teaching methods. An additional incentive might include making merit pay for tenured faculty contingent on improvements in their teaching. Such an approach might motivate them to seek and accept feedback on their teaching. Such faculty evaluation strategies offer an alternative to the common current system that is almost exclusively reliant on the "customer's" feedback. And customer- (in this case student-) driven practices may be partially responsible for the "dumbing down" of education, as students may not know what they need to know or be willing to become active creators of knowledge.

Other options that would require collegial departmental environments include the following. Faculty might agree to observe each other's teaching, to team teach, and to collaborate in creating more active teaching styles and strategies. They could be encouraged to pursue such collaborations by the dissemination of research that supports active, experiential teaching. They might engage in new research in which experiential methods are compared with traditional lecture in terms of long-term retention of knowledge and skills.

Multiple tracks for faculty have been considered, but are not yet common. Institutions would recognize "gifts differing" in setting up teaching and research tracks. In the counseling field, we are already familiar with the benefits of matching people and environments (e.g., Holland, 1985). Organizations have found that, for example, in promoting researchers into management, that they often mismatch "investigative" personality types with "enterprising" tasks. It seemed that the skills necessary to be a strong researcher were not the skills necessary to be an effective manager. Consequently, some organizations have changed the system. They created two tracks—a manager track and a researcher track—and rewarded them with equal status and pay. Employees were then promoted within their track, and not required to perform in a track for which their skills were not well-matched.

Some colleges and universities might follow this example by creating research and teaching tracks. Teachers could focus on instruction and training. Researchers could focus on knowledge creation. Researchers could then serve as resources to teachers, and vice versa, to ensure that both remained current.

Professional association shifts. Finally, professional associations might highlight the training dimension as well. For example, the Association for Counselor Education and Supervision (ACES) might dedicate a section of their journal to innovative and constructivist teaching methods. ACES might also develop a special interest group on teaching. The American Psychological Association already has a division on the teaching of psychology. Further, significant portions of the ACES national and regional conferences might be dedicated to forums on creative teaching ideas.

Conclusion

The work of reconstructing counselor education will require us to challenge finality and autonomy as final resting places. In their place would be a commitment to fluidity, reflexivity, and inclusion. Constructivist counselor education would be marked by thoughtful choices, rather than assumed and tacit allegiances to any metanarratives—for instance, rationalism, humanism, or traditionalism. Such counselor education would particularly require that we pass thorough the Scylla and Charybdis of tradition and fear. No longer would college pedagogy be content-driven, teacher-centered, and predominantly directive. Two of our education colleagues have reported such a confrontation with tradition and fear when they tried to introduce inclusive, experiential methods to a training setting. We relate their anecdotes here.

In the first case, Jane Vella (1994) reported the resistance she encountered when she was training Bangladeshi physician-educators to teach. Preventable deaths of patients had created a crisis, and this crisis had led the physicians to recruit her expertise. She asked the medical educators to be open to being critiqued and proposed that they try more inclusive, experiential teaching methods. In doing so, she met much shock and resistance, for she had challenged "ancient hierarchical relationships." The physicians were not used to receiving personal feedback. Vella's experience bespeaks both the difficulty and urgency of opening up the conversation. Like the patients who were dying as a result of faulty medical training, are our students mismanaging their work with clients because they have not achieved a constructivist consciousness, one that seeks alternate assessments and methods and identifies social structures that maintain disabling conditions for their clients?

Jean Peterson (1999, personal communication), the author of a chapter in this volume, had a similar experience when teaching principals-in-training about school counseling. She wanted them to tune in to the affective concerns of teachers, parents, students, and other staff. Soon after she introduced inductive and participatory learning methods she faced a class rebellion. Many of the administrator-students cried, "This isn't relevant!," "It isn't clear.," and "I don't like gray areas." They had lost their epistemological and pedagogical bearings. They wanted "content" and to be given clear solutions. They themselves used exclusively directive methods in dealing with student discipline and faculty performance. They were used to being in charge. They expected a parallel method from Peterson. As Peterson described it,

By the middle of the second week I might have feared mutiny, except that I have faith in my approach, and I could see that some of the most assertively negative students were beginning to become more receptive . . . I used my own counseling skills as I listened to their frustrations and anxiety. I carefully self-monitored my internal responses and outward reactions in order to model counselor behaviors and not take their challenges personally. I taught them about "processing." I de-emphasized "product" . . . I made sure we continually came back to basic counseling tenets, ethical standards, and principled decision-making.

Peterson persisted in her experiential method, which included leading dilemma discussions and requiring students to interview practicing counselors. By the three-quarter mark of the course, as she reports, "There was a palpable difference in atmosphere." Students were able to consider multiple factors when confronting student problem behaviors. They honored ethical principles. They had energy and enthusiasm for group work and in-process thinking. Peterson's students swam through the fear, buoyed by her supportive manner and her empathic hearing of their concerns, until they reached a different shore. They had begun to explore the territory of social construction.

What made the difference for Vella, Peterson, and their students? Petersen's response is instructive for both adult learners and adult teachers: "the opportunity to process the experiences and to promote parallel processing [of the course itself by the students], recognition and affirmation of varying learning styles, individual and group nurturance, patience, and application of my own counseling skills in response to their . . . distress. I think these factors were key." Peterson personified the characteristics of the constructivist knower herself in her willingness to stay with the dialogical process, to pay attention to others' experiences, and to dedicate herself to a larger moral vision of the work. In any faculty development program, these factors need to be accounted for, in order that "fear and tradition" might not overwhelm dialogue and risk-taking.

So, we must tread gently, but with faith in our colleagues' and students' capacities to let go of the fixities of over-structure, hyper-autonomy, super-rationality, and ultimate hierarchy. In their place, while we might honor fear and recognize tradition, we would ultimately, in Parker Palmer's words, "teach from curiosity or hope or empathy or honesty . . . [and] have fear but not be fear." We might then participate with the whole community of designer-builders who would construct a more inclusive, cosmopolitan, and therefore more humane, counselor education.

References

Basseches, M. (1991, June). *Dialectical thinking.* Paper presented at the Clinical-Developmental Institute, Harvard University, Cambridge, MA.

Belenky, M. F., Clinchy, B. M., Goldberger, N. R., and Tarule, J. M. (1986). *Women's ways of knowing.* New York: Basic Books.

Burbules, N. C., and Rice, S. (1991). Dialogue across differences. *Harvard Educational Review* 61: 393-416.

Cunningham, W. G., and Gresso, D. W. (1993). *Cultural leadership: The culture of excellence in education.* Boston: Allyn and Bacon.

Derrida, J. (1978). *Writing and difference.* Trans. by Alan Bass. Chicago: University of Chicago Press.

Dewey, J. (1938). *Logic: The theory of inquiry.* New York: Holt.

Foucault, M. (1972). Truth and power (C. Gordon, Trans.). In Colin Gordon (Ed.), *Power/knowledge: Selected interviews and other writings, 1972-1977* (pp. 131-133). New York: Pantheon.

Freiberg, H. J., and Driscoll, A. (1996). *Universal teaching strategies.* Boston: Allyn and Bacon.

Friere, P. (1994). *Pedagogy of the oppressed.* New York: Continuum.

Habermas, J. (1984). *Theory of communicative action.* (T. McCarthy, Trans.). Boston: Beacon.

Holland, J. L. (1985). *Making vocational choices.* Englewood Cliffs, NJ: Prentice-Hall.

hooks, b. (1994). *Teaching to transgress.* New York: Routledge.

Kegan, R. (1982). *The evolving self.* Cambridge, MA: Harvard University Press.

_____. (1994). *In over our heads: The mental demands of modern life.* Cambridge, MA: Harvard University Press.

Kohlberg, L. (1969). Stage and sequence: The cognitive-developmental approach to socialization. In D. Goslin (Ed.), *Handbook of socialization theory and research* (pp. 347-480). Chicago: Rand McNally.

Kolb, D. (1984). *Experiential learning.* Englewood Cliffs, NJ: Prentice-Hall.

Kuhn, T. S. (1970). *The structure of scientific revolutions.* Chicago: University of Chicago Press.

Lovell, C. W., and McAuliffe, G. J. (1997). Principles of constructivist training and education. In T. L. Sexton and B. L. Griffin (Eds.), *Constructivist thinking in counseling practice, research, and training* (pp. 211-227). New York: Teacher's College.

McAuliffe, G. J. (1999). Is There a Liberal Bias in Multicultural Counselor Education? Becoming a "Multicultural Liberal." *ACES Spectrum* (Summer 1999): 9-12.

McGoldrick, M. (1994). The ache for home. *Family Therapy Networker* 18: 38-45.

Neukrug, E. S., and McAuliffe, G. J. (1993). Cognitive development and human service education. *Human Service Education* 13: 13-26.

Nietzche, F. (1974). *The gay science.* (W. Kaufmann, Trans.). New York: Random House.

Olson, G. A. (1989). Social construction and composition theory: A conversation with Richard Rorty. *Journal of Advanced Composition* 9: 1-9.

Palmer, P. J. (1998). *The courage to teach.* San Francisco: Jossey-Bass.

Perry, W. (1970). *Forms of intellectual and ethical development in the college years.* New York: Holt, Rinehart, and Winston.

Torbert, W. (1987). *Managing the corporate dream.* Homewood, IL: Dow-Jones Irwin.

Vella, J. (1994). *Learning to listen, learning to teach.* San Francisco, Jossey-Bass.

Vygotsky, L. S. (1934/1986). *Thought and language.* (A. Kozulin, Trans.). Cambridge, MA: MIT Press.

Yan, B., and Arlin, P. K. (1995). Nonabsolute/relativistic thinking: A common factor underlying models of postformal reasoning? *Journal of Adult Development* 2: 223-240.

INDEX

D

E

F

About the authors:

Garrett J. McAuliffe has been a counselor educator and practitioner for over twenty-five years. He experienced his own life-changing professional training at the University of Massachusetts and at the University at Albany in New York. He currently leads the nationally accredited counselor education program at Old Dominion University in Virginia. He has written over forty articles, monographs, and book chapters on such topics as multicultural issues, college teaching, counselor development, career indecision, and clinical supervision.

Karen P. Eriksen is a national leader in advocacy for the counseling profession and a counselor educator at Radford and Walden Universities. Her book *Making an Impact: A Handbook for Counselor Advocacy* marks out a direction for promoting the helping professions and the welfare of clients. Her own training was experienced at California State University at Fullerton and at George Mason University. She has held leadership positions in the fields of marriage and family therapy and clinical counseling. She has had eighteen years of experience as a licensed professional counselor.